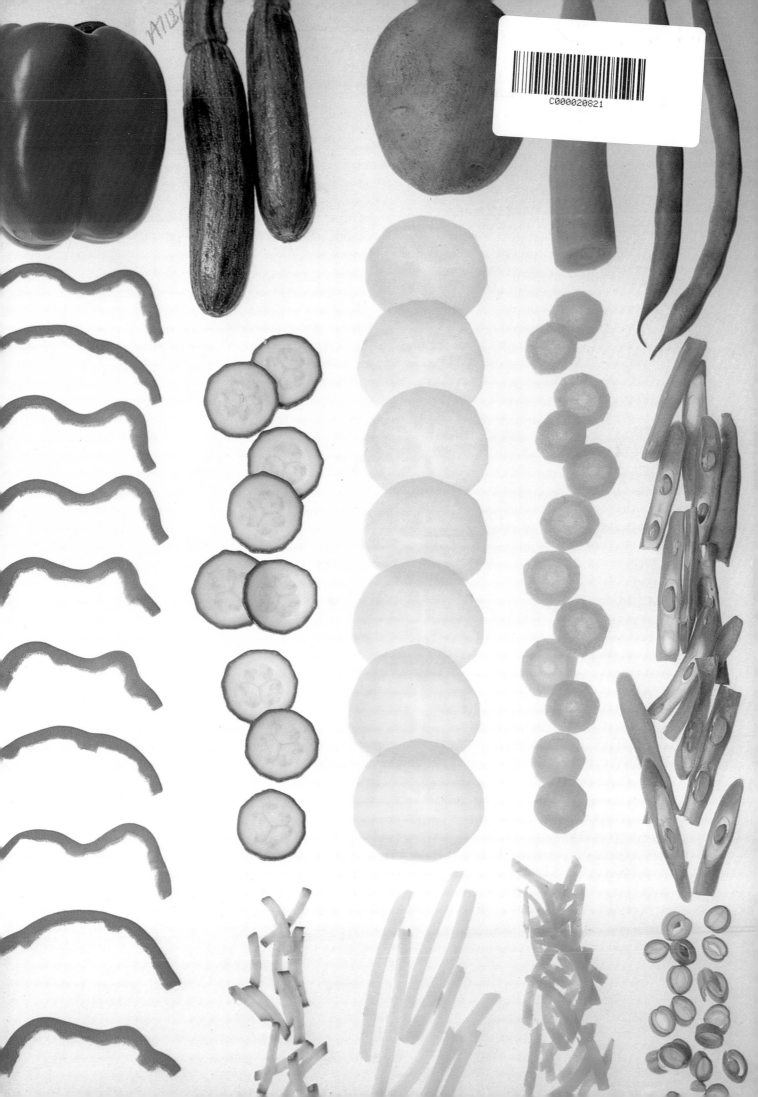

Hamlyn
Food Processor
Cookbook

Shirley Guy
Marty Klinzman

HAMLYN

Contents

Introduction

We feel entertaining should be fun. You as the hostess should enjoy the party as much as your guests. Entertaining invariably means more work for the hostess and this is one of the reasons why the food processor has become so popular. However, we have found through our teaching, writing articles and speaking to the public that people who own processors do not make the most of them.

Firstly you have to 'think' food processor: the more you use it, the more you will discover what it can do. Regard it as another pair of hands in the kitchen. It saves time and it saves trouble; many favourite sauces and dishes you once hesitated to make because they were so time-consuming and fiddly, can now become part of your repertoire – sauce tartare, hollandaise, pâtés, stir-fried dishes, carrots julienne and a host more.

Entertaining should be a pleasure for you as well as for your guests. Take time to plan ahead: organize extra crockery, cutlery and glassware. Make up your mind about the menu and, where possible, prepare dishes in advance. Let your food processor keep drudgery to a minimum and you will find entertaining more fun.

With this in mind we have selected the best of our food processor recipes for parties and entertaining. Although a few traditional favourites have been included, most of the recipes have a new and exciting quality which will make you want to start experimenting right away.

Acknowledgements

Special thanks to Heather Carstensen and Fiona Sadman for their long hours of work on the manuscript, to Peter Brooks for his patience with 'the cooks' during the photographic sessions, and to Graham Beadle for his encouragement, and for his confidence in us.

Thanks also to Style magazine for the photograph of savoury quiches, page 67, and to THORN EMI Domestic Electrical Appliances (International) Ltd, for use of the photograph of the Kenwood Gourmet food processor, page 21.

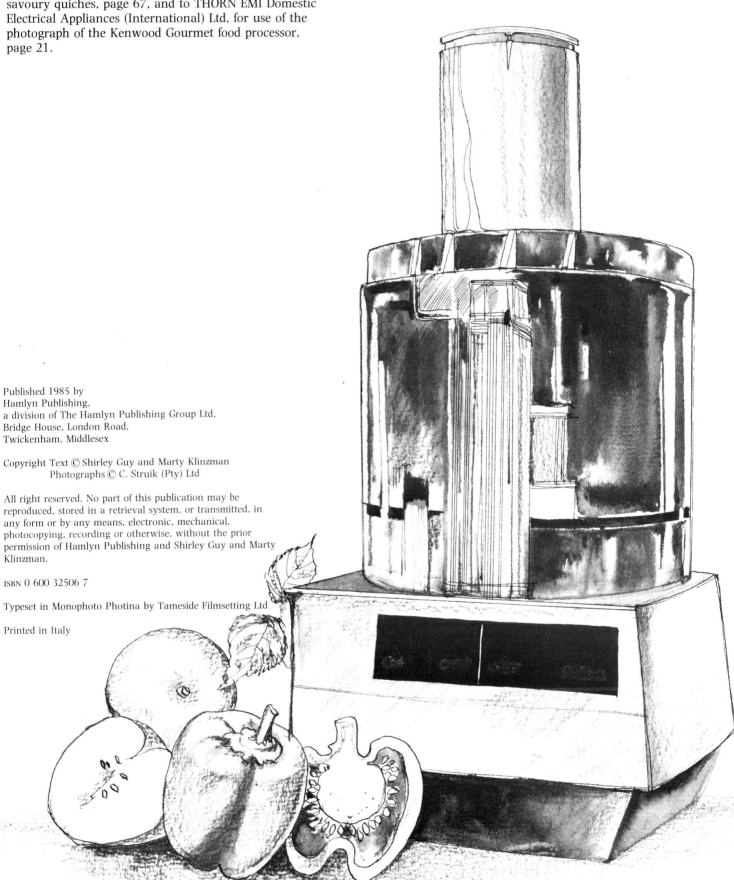

Published 1985 by
Hamlyn Publishing,
a division of The Hamlyn Publishing Group Ltd,
Bridge House, London Road,
Twickenham, Middlesex

ISBN 0 600 32506 7

Typeset in Monophoto Photina by Tameside Filmsetting Ltd

Printed in Italy

Processor Basics

How to Chop

The metal blade is the master tool when it comes to chopping but in order to chop evenly, the food first needs to be cut into small pieces. Generally, the smaller you cut the food, the quicker and more even the results from the processor will be. For example, an onion cut in half will take longer to process, and the results will not be as uniform, as an onion cut in quarters. Any foods to be chopped or minced, such as carrot, onions, green peppers, raw or cooked meat, will need to be cut into uniform pieces. It is also important to distribute the pieces of food evenly in the work bowl. Do not pile all the onion pieces on one side and expect to have them uniformly chopped. When chopping large amounts of food, it is better to process several batches, rather than overload the machine.

The pulse button gives greater control over the texture of the food. Each time the machine is turned off, food drops to the bottom of the bowl and will be in the path of the blades when the machine is turned on again. Check the texture of the food often and scrape down the sides of the bowl when necessary.

Different foods with different textures should be processed separately. For example, if a recipe calls for chopped carrot, which is hard, and chopped onion, which is watery, the best results are obtained by chopping the ingredients separately. Ingredients with similar textures such as green pepper and onion may be cut into uniform pieces and chopped together.

A dry bowl is needed for many chopping tasks. Foods such as parsley, nuts, bread and biscuits need to be processed in a dry bowl or the ingredients may cling together and become mushy.

How to Slice

The secret of making neat, perfectly even slices is to pack the feed tube snugly. When slicing long foods such as celery, carrots, green beans or bananas, cut the pieces into equal lengths about 1 cm/½ in shorter than the feed tube. Fill the feed tube, wedging in the last pieces. This method of filling the feed tube holds the food upright, thus producing uniform slices. Food can also be arranged horizontally in the feed tube. Leave just enough room at the top to rest the food pusher. Some fruits and vegetables may need to be trimmed before they will fit the feed tube but remember that the feed tube is slightly larger at the bottom, so before trimming foods, try inserting from the bottom instead of the top. Larger foods such as onions, cucumbers and apples may have to be cut in half vertically before being placed in the feed tube. When slicing fruits or vegetables with a heavy peel or skin such as lemon or halved green pepper, place the skin side towards the centre of the work bowl. The blade then cuts into the peel first, giving a clean slice.

When the feed tube is filled, turn the processor on and exert an even pressure on the food pusher to work the food through the rotating slicing plate. The thickness of the slices will depend on the amount of pressure used. For thin slices, apply a light pressure and for thicker slices, apply a heavier hand. Some foods, such as mushrooms, olives, water chestnuts or strawberries, may give slightly angled slices which are quite acceptable for sauces, stews, casseroles, salads or mixed desserts. However, when perfect slices are required, as for garnishing, it is easier to slice the food by hand. Lastly, do not let the work bowl overfill when slicing ingredients. Check the level often and empty the bowl when necessary.

How to Shred

The technique for shredding foods is very similar to the method used for slicing. Fill the feed tube in the same way and remember that it is the amount of pressure that determines the coarseness or fineness of the shred. Apply light pressure for a fine shred and heavy pressure for a coarse shred. The way in which food is placed in the feed tube will determine the length of the shred. Stack food upright for short shreds or horizontally for longer shreds. Take the opportunity to shred large amounts of food for later use. For example, a large quantity of cheese may be shredded very quickly and frozen in convenient amounts.

The processor easily shreds both soft foods such as cucumber or courgette, and hard foods such as carrot or chocolate. Do not let the work bowl overfill. Check the level often and empty the ingredients when necessary.

How to Mix

The processor is not an electric mixer, but it can perform some of the same actions. Although the nylon blade may be used for mixing light batters or doughs, it is the metal blade which is generally used for all mixing purposes. It combines the ingredients for a variety of foods such as crêpe and pancake batters, dips, biscuit dough, pastries, some cake batters, icings and salad dressings. It also handles with ease small quantities of quick breads and yeast doughs. In addition, is a real whiz at making sauces such as hollandaise and mayonnaise.

In some cases, the ingredients are added all at once to the work bowl, then mixed together. In other recipes, such as those for cakes, the sugar and butter are creamed before adding the flour. Butter or margarine for creaming or rubbing in does not necessarily have to be at room temperature as the processor easily handles cold butter: just cut it into cubes and add to the work bowl.

When mixing liquids or thin batters, always check the capacity of the bowl. As a general rule, the work bowl can hold up to 600 ml/1 pint thin batter or up to 1 litre/2 lb thick cake mixture. Hold the metal blade firmly in place while removing the work bowl so that none of the liquid or batter will leak through the centre opening. When mixing yeast doughs, remember that most processors will handle up to 350 g/12 oz flour in a mixture at one time. To avoid a tough texture, do not over process; yeast doughs take just 60 seconds to be mixed and kneaded.

Symbols used in recipes

Each recipe title is followed by one to four symbols to show at a glance which blades and plates will be required. The symbol for freezing indicates that the recipe freezes well.

Metal blade   Nylon blade   Shredding plate   Slicing plate   Chipper plate   Freezes well

Step-by-step processor techniques

Metal blade ☯

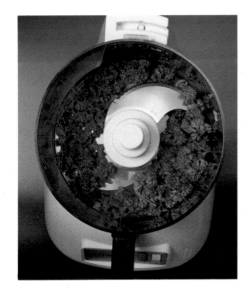

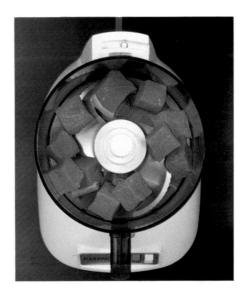

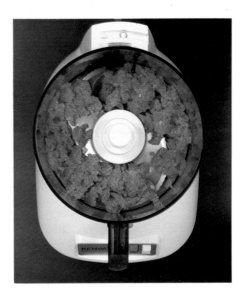

Chopping parsley. Wash the parsley, dry thoroughly and remove the stems. With the metal blade in position, distribute the parsley leaves evenly in the work bowl. Using the pulse button, process until the parsley is chopped as finely as desired. Store it in a plastic bag or sealed container in the refrigerator or freezer. Use this method for chopping other herbs and leafy vegetables.

Parmesan cheese. Parmesan is a very hard cheese and must be at room temperature before it can be processed. Trim away any crusts or hard ends and cut the cheese into 1 cm/1½ in cubes. Drop the cheese, a few cubes at a time, onto the moving blades and process as finely as desired. Store it in a sealed container in the refrigerator or freezer. Use this method for other very hard cheeses.

Mincing meat. Trim away the bone, gristle and excess fat and cut the meat into 2–3 cm/1–1½ in cubes. Do not remove all the fat as a small amount is needed for juiciness and flavour. With the metal blade in position, distribute up to 225 g/8 oz meat cubes evenly around the work bowl. Using the pulse button and watching carefully, process the meat as finely as desired. Coarsely chopped or minced meat takes only 4–6 seconds. This method may also be used for cooked meat.

Note: Always consult your processor instruction book for maximum quantities.

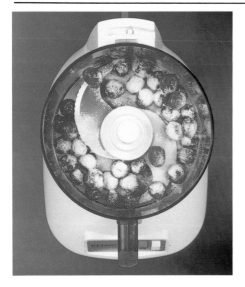

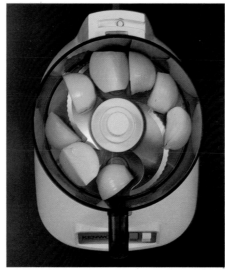

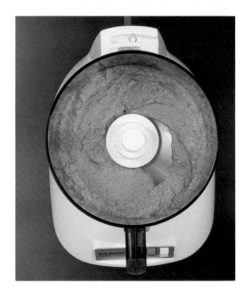

Chopping glacé cherries, glacé fruit and dried fruit. With the metal blade in position, add up to 225 g/8 oz glacé cherries, glacé fruit, dates or dried fruit to the work bowl. Take approximately 50 g/2 oz flour or sugar from the quantity in the recipe and sprinkle it over the fruit in the work bowl. Pulse until the desired texture is obtained. The flour or sugar allows the fruit to be evenly chopped, without the pieces sticking together. Watch this process carefully.

Chopping onion. Peel the onion, trim the ends and cut into quarters. With the metal blade in position, distribute the onion quarters evenly in the work bowl. Process with the pulse button until as fine as desired. Process 2 large or 3 small onions at one time. Use this method for chopping green pepper, carrots, nuts, biscuits and mushrooms.

Making purées. With the metal blade in position, add up to 450 ml/$\frac{3}{4}$ pint cooked vegetables such as peas together with about 150 ml/$\frac{1}{4}$ pint liquid: process until the food is smooth. Add more liquid if required and scrape down the sides of the work bowl when necessary. Use this method for puréeing cooked fruits, soups and for making pâtés.

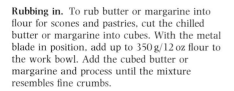

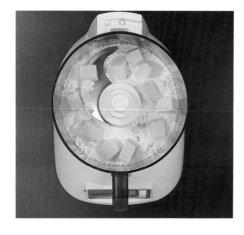

Rubbing in. To rub butter or margarine into flour for scones and pastries, cut the chilled butter or margarine into cubes. With the metal blade in position, add up to 350 g/12 oz flour to the work bowl. Add the cubed butter or margarine and process until the mixture resembles fine crumbs.

Shredding plate

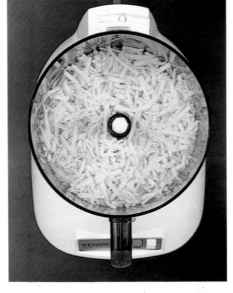

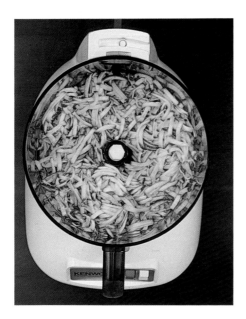

Shredding courgettes. Wash and dry the courgettes. Slice off the ends and cut the courgettes 1 cm/1½ in shorter than the feed tube. With the shredding plate in position, pack the food into the feed tube, wedging in the last courgettes. To process the optimum number at one time, place some courgettes large-end up, others large-end down. Applying steady pressure on the food pusher, push the courgettes through the rotating shredding plate. Use the same method for carrots, potatoes and apples.

Shredding cheese. Place the shredding plate in position. Trim the chilled cheese, such as Cheddar, to fit the feed tube. Applying steady pressure on the food pusher, push the cheese through the rotating shredding plate. Steady, firm pressure yields coarsely shredded cheese and steady, light pressure gives a finer result.

Shredding chocolate. Have the chocolate at room temperature. Fit the shredding plate in position and place the chocolate in the feed tube. With a steady pressure on the food pusher, push the chocolate through the rotating shredding plate. (Chocolate may also be chopped with the metal blade or with the chipper plate.) Use this method to shred nuts and fresh coconut evenly.

Slicing plate

Slicing vegetables such as green beans, celery and carrots. For best results cut long, narrow foods 1 cm/½ in shorter than the feed tube. Pack the feed tube full, wedging in the last piece. This will ensure evenly shaped slices, as the food cannot slide about. With the slicing plate in position and applying steady pressure on the food pusher, push the vegetables through the rotating slicing plate. Use a firm pressure for thick slices and a light pressure for thin.

Slicing foods with peel or skin, such as apples, lemons and green peppers. Quarter and core the apples. Halve the peppers and remove the stems, seeds and inner membranes. Halve the lemons and trim the ends. For green peppers and lemons, place the halves in the feed tube and position them so that the skin side faces the centre of the work bowl. For apples, stack the quarters horizontally in the feed tube. With the slicing plate in position and applying steady pressure on the food pusher, push the food through the rotating slicing plate. Use the same method for oranges and large firm tomatoes.

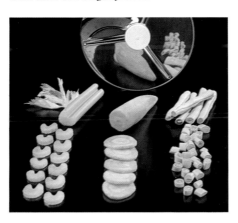

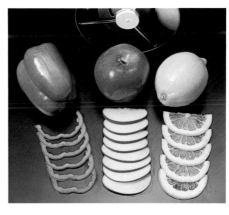

Slicing bulky foods such as salami, potatoes and onions. To prepare the salami, remove the casing and trim the length to fit the feed tube. To prepare potatoes, peel if desired and trim to fit the feed tube. For onions, peel and trim the ends. With the slicing plate in position and applying steady pressure on the food pusher, push the food through the rotating slicing plate. Use the same method for firm tomatoes and cucumbers.

Slicing lettuce, cabbage and mushrooms. To prepare lettuce, wash and dry the leaves thoroughly. Place several leaves together and fold to fit the feed tube. To prepare cabbage, cut into wedges to fit the feed tube. To prepare mushrooms, wipe clean and stack in the feed tube. With the slicing plate in position and applying steady pressure on the food pusher, push the food through the rotating slicing plate.

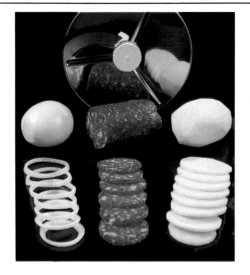

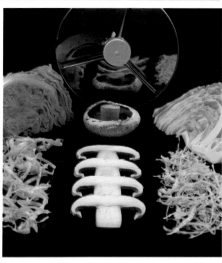

How to cut julienne strips using the slicing plate ◗   Chipper plate ◖

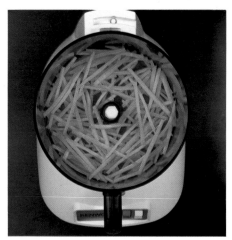

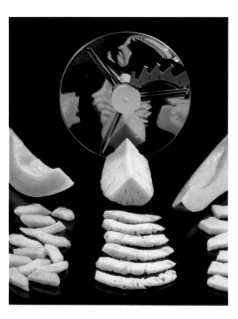

1. Cut the carrots so that they fit the feed tube horizontally. Pack the carrots in the feed tube and slice.

2. Stack the carrot slices together. Hold the work bowl cover sideways and insert the food pusher part of the way through the feed tube to form a shallow cup. With the cut sides at right angles to the cover, stack the carrot slices in the bottom of the feed tube. Wedge the slices in tightly and replace the cover.

3. Slice again. This time the cross-cut produces the julienne strips. The same method may be used to make julienne potatoes, courgettes and turnips.

Dicing fruit for fruit salad. Cut the apple, pineapple, pawpaw or melon to fit the feed tube. Fit the chipper plate and lock the cover in place. Place the fruit in the feed tube and, applying steady pressure, push the food through the rotating chipper plate. Use the same method for coarsely chopped nuts and chocolate, French fried potatoes, diced tomatoes and aubergines.

Know your Processor

Before using your food processor you should familiarise yourself with the different parts and know how to utilise them efficiently.

Parts of the machine

Food pusher: The food pusher fits snuggly inside the feed tube of the work bowl cover and is used to guide food onto the swiftly rotating chipper, slicing or shredding plates. By varying the degree of pressure when slicing or shredding, either thick or thin slices, or fine or coarse shreds are produced. The food pusher also prevents splashing when the metal or nylon blades are in use. In some cases it is hollow and clearly graduated, allowing liquids to be measured easily.

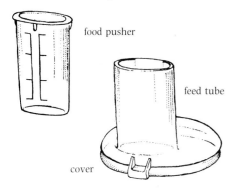

food pusher

feed tube

cover

Work bowl cover with feed tube: Most work bowls and covers are made of transparent, strong acrylic or plastic; an interlock system ensures that the processor is correctly assembled before the machine will start. The work bowl cover has a tall, chimney-like feed tube protruding from the top through which ingredients are fed into the processor. The feed tube is used to hold food when the slicing, shredding or chipper plates are in place. Flexible foods such as green pepper, raw beef and lettuce leaves may be folded and fed into the feed tube for slicing. Larger foods such as potatoes and whole green peppers may be fitted into the bottom of the feed tube, as that opening is slightly larger than the top one. To do this remove the work bowl cover, invert and pack the feed tube with the ingredients. Replace the

cover and slice or shred. The feed tube is also used for adding ingredients to the work bowl while the metal or nylon blade is in motion.

Work bowl: The capacity of the work bowl varies with the make of food processor. Check your instruction booklet for the maximum quantities that can be processed without straining the motor. The work bowl locks onto the base of the food processor by means of a locking system and the machine will not operate until both the bowl and cover are correctly positioned. The work bowl has a central opening to fit over the drive shaft on the processor base so it is important not to overfill it with liquid as some leaking may occur.

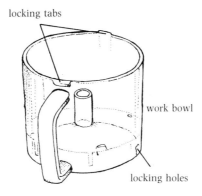

locking tabs

work bowl

locking holes

Processor base: The machine pictured is a direct drive processor. This means that the work bowl sits on top of the motor base and the power to rotate the blades and plates comes directly from the motor. For this reason, the direct drive machine is considered more powerful than a belt-driven one. With a belt-driven processor, the motor base is located either behind or beside the work bowl. Power to rotate the blades and plates comes indirectly from the motor by means of a belt. One advantage of this is that it is possible to have variable speeds so that some mixing or beating tasks can be performed at lower speeds. Some

belt-driven machines have an instant mechanical stop for blades and plates when the motor is turned off.

Power controls: An on/off switch is used for slicing, shredding, chip-making or other processes where a steady power is needed. Use it when making mayonnaise, kneading yeast dough and adding liquids while the motor is running. It may also be used if your machine does not have a pulse button.

The pulse button gives short bursts of power and permits the cutting blade to operate with a start-stop action, thus controlling the texture of the food being processed. Food can be pulsed, checked for texture and pulsed again if a slightly finer result is required. When you begin working with your food processor, it is advisable to make use of the pulse button to prevent overprocessing.

Some processors have high, medium and low speed settings for various processing procedures. If you have a variable speed processor, consult your instruction manual for recommended settings.

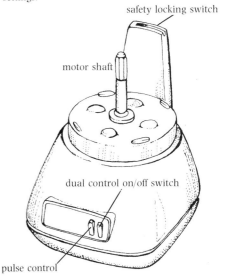

safety locking switch

motor shaft

dual control on/off switch

pulse control

Blades and Plates

Metal blade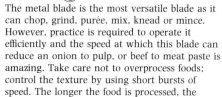
The metal blade is the most versatile blade as it can chop, grind, purée, mix, knead or mince. However, practice is required to operate it efficiently and the speed at which this blade can reduce an onion to pulp, or beef to meat paste is amazing. Take care not to overprocess foods; control the texture by using short bursts of speed. The longer the food is processed, the smoother will be the texture.

To use the metal blade, lock the work bowl into position and place the blade over the motor shaft. Ensure the blade is correctly fitted before adding the food.

Metal blade

Nylon blade
The nylon blade is a standard part for many processors although its function is limited to either mixing or blending ingredients that do not need to be chopped. It has no cutting edge, but can mix dips, sauces, cake batters, egg whites, salad dressings and quick desserts. The metal blade works equally well for most of these functions.

To use the nylon blade, lock the work bowl into position and place the blade over the motor shaft. Ensure the blade is correctly fitted before adding the food.

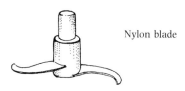

Nylon blade

Slicing plate
The slicing plate will slice a wide variety of foods, from fruit as soft as bananas to vegetables as hard as carrots. The blade will also slice firm cheeses such as Cheddar, and processed meats such as salami (with the casing removed). Oranges, lemons, apples, potatoes, courgettes, pickles and mushrooms can all be sliced efficiently. The slicing plate can also be used to cut vegetables julienne (see page 8) or to slice evenly for stir-frying. A heavy pressure exerted via the food pusher on the food will result in thick slices, while a light pressure will give thinner ones.

To use the slicing plate, lock the work bowl into position and place the slicing plate over the motor shaft. Ensure the plate is correctly fitted before locking the cover into place and filling the feed tube.

Slicing plate

Shredding plate
The shredding plate is used to shred cheeses, hard fruits and vegetables as well as most foods you have been shredding or grating by hand. It is easy and quick to use and will keep your fingers and fingernails safe from nicks and scrapes. Just fill the feed tube with the food to be shredded and push through, using the food pusher. Heavy pressure will yield a coarse shred, while light pressure produces a finer result.

To use the shredding plate, lock the work bowl into position and place the plate over the motor shaft. Ensure the plate is correctly fitted before locking on the cover and filling the feed tube.

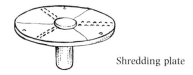

Shredding plate

Chipper plate
The chipper plate is a standard plate for some food processors and an optional extra for others. It was developed mainly for making potato chips or French fries, but it has many other uses, including dicing tomatoes and other vegetables, and dicing fruits such as pineapple, apples, pears and melons for fruit salad. It can also be used to coarsely grate chocolate and nuts, as well as chilled butter or margarine for certain pastries.

To use the chipper plate, lock the work bowl into position and place the plate on the motor shaft. Make sure the plate is correctly fitted before locking on the cover and filling the feed tube.

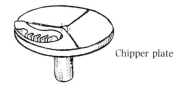

Chipper plate

Additional accessories

Whisk: The whisk fits onto the drive or motor shaft and consists of two beaters which will whip cream and beat egg whites.

Julienne plate: This plate cuts firm fruits and vegetables into slightly curved julienne strips.

Expanded feed tube: A larger feed tube to hold whole tomatoes, onions, oranges and potatoes for slicing.

Slicing plate for thin slices: The slicing space on this plate is reduced, making finer slices.

Fine shredding plate: A plate with smaller holes, producing finer shreds.

Split food pusher: The food pusher is in two parts to assist in slicing and shredding small quantities. Place one half in the feed tube and place one carrot, a few sticks of celery or a few green beans in the other half. Use the second part of the food pusher to guide the food onto the blades.

Continuous feed cover: This special kit allows food to be sliced or shredded into an outside bowl. It is useful when processing large quantities of food because you do not have to keep emptying the work bowl.

Funnel: A wide-mouthed funnel attachment that fits over the feed tube. It is useful for adding dry ingredients to the work bowl when the machine is running.

Juice extractor: This attachment fits directly over the motor shaft and is used for squeezing juice from citrus fruits.

Slicing guide: An attachment that resembles a set of metal fingers and is used in the feed tube to hold one carrot or stick of celery in an upright position for slicing or shredding.

Cleaning tools: Special spatulas or cleaning tools make emptying the work bowl easier.

Attachment holders: Some makes of food processor have special holders for the blades and plates for easy storage. Stored in this way, they retain their sharpness.

Cover: Various fabric and plastic covers for keeping the machine clean when not in use.

Bowl liners: These fit the inside of the work bowl when the slicing and shredding plates are in use.

Dome covers: A domed work bowl is useful for additional volume when making pastries, quick breads and yeast doughs.

Parmesan plate: A plate for shredding Parmesan cheese.

Dough blade: A nylon blade with short blades designed for kneading dough in larger batches than the metal blade can handle.

Special Processing Techniques

Cleaning the blade: To clean the metal blade when making sticky batters, cake batters or soft pâtés, remove the work bowl and hold the bowl and the blade, making sure the blade is correctly positioned. Pulse three or four times to clean the blade, then lift it out and scrape the remaining mixture out of the work bowl.

Emptying the work bowl: With chopped foods such as carrot, onion, meat or breadcrumbs, it is easier to remove the blade before emptying the bowl. You can then hold the work bowl with one hand and use a spatula to scrape out the ingredients with the other. When it comes to pouring out liquids, however, it is important to hold the blade in place with a spatula or finger as this prevents the liquids from spilling through the central opening of the work bowl.

Folding in: One or two beaten egg whites can be folded into a mixture in the work bowl by pulsing two or three times to incorporate them. Do not overprocess as this will tend to deflate the egg whites.

Rubbing in: For pastry or scones, cut the cold butter or margarine into cubes and add to the flour in the work bowl. Pulse to rub in and process to the desired fineness, checking the texture often.

Yeast doughs: Before making yeast doughs check on the capacity of the work bowl. In general, dough can be mixed and kneaded with the metal blade in about 1 minute.

Soft cheese: Soft cheeses such as mozzarella need to be partly frozen, but not solid. Slice or shred applying medium pressure.

Hard cheese: Hard cheeses such as Parmesan need to be at room temperature before being processed. Trim away the hard crust or ends and cut the cheese into 1 cm/$\frac{1}{2}$ in cubes. With the machine running, drop a few cubes at a time onto the metal blade and process.

Dried or glacé fruit: If flour or sugar is called for in the recipe, add a small amount to the work bowl when chopping dried or glacé fruits. Another way is to soak the dried fruit in part of the liquid required. This softens the fruit and allows the metal blade to chop it with ease.

Herbs: Chopping large amounts of parsley, fresh basil, oregano and other leafy herbs is easy in the processor. For best results, wash the herbs and pat very dry. Remove all stems and process the leaves until the desired texture is reached. To chop small quantities of fresh herbs and garlic, drop them through the feed tube onto the moving metal blade. For very small quantities it is easier to chop them by hand.

Processing hot foods: Hot foods can be processed in most machines but consult your instruction book first and do not process more than the amount suggested. Hot foods such as puréed vegetables, soups and sauces may be served immediately after processing. The processing is so quick that ingredients do not have the time to cool.

Processing chocolate: Chocolate should be at room temperature and broken into pieces before chopping with the metal blade. Use a pulse action and watch the texture carefully as heat formed by friction may melt some of the chocolate. To shred chocolate, fit the shredding plate in position and place the chocolate pieces in the feed tube. Apply even pressure to work the chocolate through the rotating plate. Use the chipper plate to chop chocolate coarsely.

Crushing ice: Either drop a few cubes directly onto the rotating metal blade or, with the metal blade stationary, place a few cubes at a time in the work bowl and process until crushed. Consult the instruction book as not all processors can be used to crush ice.

Homemade peel (for thickly cut marmalade or candied peel): Wash, dry and quarter oranges, lemons or grapefruit. Remove the flesh and some of the pith. Fit the slicing plate and pack the peel, cut side down, from the bottom of the feed tube, curving the peel slightly to fit the tube. Slice, applying light pressure.

Processing home-dried peel: Drop small pieces of dried peel onto the moving metal blade. Process until finely chopped.

Factors Affecting the Results of Food Processing

Size of the food: To chop foods such as potatoes, onions and green peppers, first quarter them or cut them into 2 or 3 cm/1 or 1$\frac{1}{2}$ in cubes. For slicing and shredding, trim the fruit or vegetables to fit the feed tube. When shopping for foods for food processor recipes, select cucumbers, onions, potatoes and so on that will fit the feed tube.

Quality of the food: Fresh, crisp fruits and vegetables process easily and give the best results when slicing or shredding. For purées, use ripe, soft fruits or vegetables. For casseroles and stews, more mature vegetables may be used.

Quantity of food: When chopping foods, a medium-sized load chops more evenly than a large one, so chop food in batches rather than overload the machine. It is easier to chop or slice very small quantities by hand.

Temperature of the food: Medium hard cheeses such as Cheddar can be processed at refrigerator temperature. Hard cheeses such as Parmesan need to be at room temperature, while soft cheeses such as mozzarella need to be almost frozen for best results. Fruits and vegetables can be processed while chilled or at room temperature. Butter for creaming and rubbing-in may be used cold.

Pressure: The amounts of pressure applied on the food pusher varies the texture of sliced and shredded foods. For most foods a steady, even pressure is best. For thick slices or coarse shreds, apply a heavy pressure and for fine slices or shreds, apply a light pressure.

Time: It is time taken to process foods with the metal blade that determines the texture of those foods. It stands to reason that the longer the machine runs, the finer the texture of the food will be. To prevent overprocessing, use the pulse button or turn the machine on and off momentarily and check the texture of the food often.

Arrangement of food: For the besT results when the slicing, shredding or chipper plates are used, it is important to pack the feed tube full of ingredients. With the metal blade, food should be evenly distributed in the work bowl. See the step-by-step section for the arrangement of food processing (pages 9–12).

Converting Recipes for Processor Use

Many of your favourite recipes can be prepared in the food processor. Take a good look at the recipes in your file. Can the processor slice, chop, grind or mince any of the ingredients? Ingredients should be rearranged in the correct order for processing. Look for dry ingredients first. For example, make breadcrumbs before chopping moist vegetables, as this saves cleaning the bowl between steps. If any ingredients need to be minced, use the metal blade and pulse to control the texture.

For yeast mixtures and quick breads, you may have to divide your recipe and prepare two batches. For quick breads, look for ingredients such as nuts that can be processed in a dry bowl. Chop them first and set aside. Next process the sugar, butter, eggs and liquid until smooth. Add the dry ingredients and spices and process until no flour is visible, before stirring in the nuts and fruit.

Biscuit and cookie making is easy with the processor. Check quantities and reduce recipes if necessary. Look for nuts and fruit to process first, then follow the recipe as you would when using a mixer or by hand. Start with the sugar, lemon rind, butter and eggs. Add the flour and any liquid, then finally the nuts, fruits or chocolate and pulse to mix in. If the mixture is very stiff these last ingredients may have to be mixed in by hand.

When making pastry, use the metal blade for rubbing the butter into the flour. Add the liquid and pulse to mix to a dough. Do not overporcess or the pastry will be tough.

With practice you will be able to adapt recipes easily for food processor preparation. Here are two recipes to get you started.

Sweet and Sour Meatballs

450 g/1 lb pork
1 clove garlic
1 tablespoon soy sauce
1 tablespoon dry sherry
salt and black pepper
plain flour to coat
oil

— Cube pork. Place all these ingredients in work bowl with metal blade. Pulse to mince.

SAUCE
½ small onion
1 green pepper
2 carrots
3 gherkins

— Place in work bowl with metal blade and chop. Slice with slicing blade.

1 (227-g/8-oz) can pineapple chunks
7 tablespoons pineapple juice
7 tablespoons water
1 tablespoon brown sugar
1 tablespoon tomato sauce
3 tablespoons white vinegar
1 tablespoon cornflour

Mince the pork and place in a mixing bowl. Crush the garlic and add to the meat. Add the soy sauce, sherry and seasonings. Form into small balls, toss lightly in flour and fry in a little oil. (See page 57 for complete processor instructions.)

For the sauce, chop the onion finely and set aside. Chop the green pepper finely. Slice the carrot and the gherkin thinly. Add all the ingredients except the vinegar and cornflour. Bring to the boil and simmer for 5 minutes. Mix the vinegar and cornflour and add a little boiling liquid to the mixture before pouring it into the sauce. Stir until boiling and thickened. Pour over the meat balls and serve with rice.

SERVES 4

Banana Orange Loaf

100 g/4 oz butter, softened
200 g/7 oz sugar
2 eggs
1 tablespoon orange rind
1 tablespoon vanilla essence
6 drops of almond essence
225 g/8 oz plain flour
1 teaspoon bicarbonate of soda
½ teaspoon salt
3 medium bananas ——————— 2. Purée
50 g/2 oz pecan nuts ——————— 1. Chop
75 g/3 oz desiccated coconut
2 tablespoons orange juice
3 tablespoons milk

3. Combine all remaining ingredients, except bananas, pecan nuts and coconut.

Cream the butter well, add the sugar and cream again. Lightly beat the eggs, add to the sugar a little at a time and beat well after each addition. Add the orange rind, vanilla and almond essence and beat well. Sift the flour, bicarbonate of soda and salt and set aside. Mash the bananas and chop the pecan nuts finely. Combine the bananas, pecan nuts, coconut, orange juice and milk. Add a little flour to the egg mixture. Beat well. Add some of the banana mixture. Continue in this way until all the ingredients are combined. Turn into a greased 23 × 13-cm/9 × 5-in loaf tin and bake in a moderate oven (180 c, 350 F, gas 4) for about 60 minutes, or until a skewer inserted in the centre comes out clean. Turn out of the tin onto a wire rack and cool thoroughly before slicing. (See page 127 for complete processor instructions.)

Processor Problems

Problem: Ingredients are unevenly chopped.
Solution: The bowl may be overloaded. Remove some of the food and chop in smaller batches. The combined items may be of different textures. Only foods of similar texture should be chopped together. The food may have been cut into uneven pieces before processing.

Problem: Liquid leaks out of the cover or from the centre of the bowl.
Solution: The bowl has been overfilled. Limit liquids or semi-liquids to the amount suggested in the instruction book. Process large amounts in batches and do not fill the bowl to a point higher than the central opening.

Problem: Slices of food vary in thickness.
Solution: Uneven pressure has been applied to the food in the feed tube. Some vegetables such as cucumbers or potatoes will feed themselves through the feed tube, but the thickness of slices or shreds will vary.

Problem: Some foods such as lemons or green peppers give torn slices.
Solution: Foods with a heavy peel or skin should be placed with the skin side toward the centre of the work bowl.

Problem: Some of the food remains on top of the plate or drops over the side of the plate after slicing or shredding.
Solution: This is normal. There will be some wastage with cheese, carrots and vegetables after slicing or shredding. Remove larger pieces of food and, if desired, slice or shred by hand.

Problem: Shredded or sliced food builds up on one side of the bowl.
Solution: This is normal. When food reaches the full level on one side of the bowl, stop the machine and empty the bowl before continuing. Never operate the processor with a full bowl.

Problem: The machine stops when making bread or processing a heavy mixture.
Solution: Most machines have an automatic 'cut out' that comes into operation when the machine is overloaded. If this happens, remove the work bowl from the machine and wait a few minutes before continuing. You may have to process the mixture in batches. Follow the instructions for your machine and endeavour to keep the amount of various mixtures below the maximum. With some stiff doughs, you may have to remove the dough from the work bowl, break it into pieces and drop it through the feed tube onto the moving blades.

Additional Problems

Egg whites: The metal blade is not an aerator and cannot whisk up egg whites to perfection. For best results use an egg beater, balloon whisk or mixer.

Beating cream: The processor will beat cream to spooning and piping consistency. However, most machines do not give a fluffy, light texture to the cream. If that is the texture you require, beat the cream with a mixer. The difference between stiffly beaten cream and butter is only 1 or 2 seconds, so take care when beating cream in the processor.

Coffee beans, grains, peppercorns and whole spices: Most processors do not grind these items with any success.

Potatoes: Most processors make a sticky, gluey mess of mashing potatoes. Some machines claim to mash potatoes if they are shredded after cooking. Consult your instruction book for specific instructions for mashing potatoes.

Soft foods: Most processors do not do a satisfactory job of slicing soft foods, such as hard-boiled eggs, or very soft fruits and vegetables. It is better to slice these foods by hand.

Frozen foods: It is recommended by food processor manufacturers that solidly frozen food should not be sliced or shredded as it may damage the plates or break the machine.

Overprocessing: When you are first learning the techniques of using a food processor, you may find that the chopped onions are mushy and the cream is buttery. You may produce peanut butter rather than finely chopped peanuts and pastry that resembles shortbread. All of these faults are due to overprocessing. Until you know just how long to process each item with the metal blade, rely on the pulse button to give you better control over the texture of the food.

Helpful Hints for Optimum Use

- Leave your food processor assembled and out on a counter so that it is always at the ready to handle food preparation chores.
- When preparing a dish with a wide variety of ingredients, process the hard, dry ingredients first, then prepare the moist ingredients. This saves on washing up.
- To attain a uniform texture, ensure that the ingredients to be processed are cut into pieces of approximately the same size.
- Consult your instruction book for maximum quantities. Processing larger loads may overwork the machine.
- Do not overload the machine or bowl when slicing or shredding ingredients. Excess ingredients in the bowl may force the plates up against the lid.
- When mixing or chopping moist ingredients with the metal blade, you may find that some of the food collects around the sides of the bowl. If this happens, stop the machine and scrape down the sides with a spatula.
- Take care not to overprocess foods. The food processor is a speedy machine, so when chopping or mixing use the pulse button until you become more familiar with the processing technique. Check the texture of the food often.

- To avoid excess splashing, add the liquid ingredients last while the motor is still running.
- Be careful not to add liquids to a point higher than the central opening of the work bowl. Overfilling will cause overflowing.
- When the work bowl contains liquid ingredients, always remove the bowl before removing the blade. Hold the blade in place with one finger while pouring out the liquid to prevent spillage from the central opening of the bowl.
- When adding hard or solid ingredients through the feed tube while the machine is running, make sure the ingredients are cut into small pieces so they will feed easily onto the moving blades.
- When blending a variety of different ingredients, start with the harder items as they will need more time to process than the softer ones.
- Meat can be sliced neatly with the slicing blade if it is partially frozen.
- Always use the food pusher when feeding ingredients onto the slicing or shredding plate.
- When slicing round foods, firmly fill the feed tube to give uniform slices.
- Be creative and whip up a quick spread from leftovers. Mince turkey or chicken and add mayonnaise, raisins, nuts and a dash of Tabasco sauce.

- Start saving leftovers. Turn extra bread into crumbs and dry or freeze. Grate cheese ends and freeze.
- If the recipe calls for 1 chopped onion and 1 chopped clove of garlic, chop them together. This also applies to small amounts of parsley or herbs in a recipe calling for breadcrumbs. Look for ways to combine chopping.
- Experiment with your food processor. Chop fresh herbs and add salt to make your own savoury mix. Make up savoury butters for meats or vegetables and sweet butters for tea breads.
- Making perfect slices requires practice. To slice one carrot or cucumber, check the slicing plate's direction of rotation. If your processor blade rotates anti-clockwise, place the food on the left side of the feed tube. If it rotates clockwise, place the food on the right side of the feed tube. The movement of the blade will tend to keep the food upright.
- The handle of a spatula or wooden spoon makes a handy tool to help fill the feed tube. Use the handle to hold the food upright while adding more to the tube. Remove the spatula or wooden spoon before running the machine.
- To save time, assemble all the ingredients and utensils near your food preparation centre before starting to process.

Safety

- Read all the instructions before using the food processor.
- Handle the cutting attachments carefully, as they are very sharp.
- Store blades and plates on a special rack or in a safe place.
- Keep spatulas and other utensils away from the moving blades or plates during operation.
- Always use the food pusher when slicing or shredding. It is designed so as not to come into contact with the moving plates.

- Never immerse the base of the machine in water.
- Do not operate the machine with a damaged cord or plug.
- Let the processor blades or plates stop completely before removing the lid or disassembling the machine.
- Keep the machine and blades out of the reach of young children.
- Do not leave the metal blade to soak in soapy water as you may forget it and be unable to see it. A nasty cut could result.

Care of the Food Processor

- Wash the lid, work bowl and food pusher in hot, soapy water as soon as possible after using. Rinse well and dry thoroughly. Check the instruction book to establish whether these parts are dishwasher-proof.
- Take care when washing sharp cutting plates and blades. It is best to use hot, soapy water and a long-handled brush. Rinse

under the tap and leave to drip-dry or preferably slot into a special rack.
- Wipe the base clean with a wet cloth or sponge. For stubborn dirt use a mild, non-abrasive detergent.
- Store loosely assembled to allow a free circulation of air.

Useful Facts and Figures

Notes on Metrication

In this book quantities are given in metric and Imperial measures. Exact conversion from Imperial to metric measures does not usually give very convenient working quantities and so the metric measures have been rounded off into units of 25 grams. The table below shows the recommended equivalents.

Ounces	Approx g to nearest whole figure	Recommended conversion to nearest unit of 25
1	28	25
2	57	50
3	85	75
4	113	100
5	142	150
6	170	175
7	198	200
8	227	225
9	255	250
10	283	275
11	312	300
12	340	350
13	368	375
14	396	400
15	425	425
16 (1 lb)	454	450
17	482	475
18	510	500
19	539	550
20 ($1\frac{1}{4}$ lb)	567	575

Note: When converting quantities over 20 oz first add the appropriate figures in the centre column, then adjust to the nearest unit of 25. As a general guide, 1 kg (1000 g) equals 2.2 lb or about 2 lb 3 oz. This method of conversion gives good results in nearly all cases, although in certain pastry and cake recipes a more accurate conversion is necessary to produce a balanced recipe.

Liquid measures The millilitre has been used in this book and the following table gives a few examples.

Imperial	Approx ml to nearest whole figure	Recommended ml
$\frac{1}{4}$ pint	142	150 ml
$\frac{1}{2}$ pint	283	300 ml
$\frac{3}{4}$ pint	425	450 ml
1 pint	567	600 ml
$1\frac{1}{2}$ pints	851 ml	900 ml
$1\frac{3}{4}$ pints	992	1000 ml (1 litre)

Spoon measures All spoon measures given in this book are level unless otherwise stated.

Can sizes At present, cans are marked with the exact (usually to the nearest whole number) metric equivalent of the Imperial weight of the contents, so we have followed this practice when giving can sizes.

Notes for American and Australian users

In America the 8-oz measuring cup is used. In Australia metric measures are now used in conjunction with the standard 250-ml measuring cup. The Imperial pint, used in Britain and Australia, is 20 fl oz, while the American pint is 16 fl oz. It is important to remember that the Australian tablespoon differs from both the British and American tablespoons; the table below gives a comparison. The British standard tablespoon, which has been used throughout this book, holds 17.7 ml, the American 14.2 ml, and the Australian 20 ml. A teaspoon holds approximately 5 ml in all three countries.

British	American	Australian
1 teaspoon	1 teaspoon	1 teaspoon
1 tablespoon	1 tablespoon	1 tablespoon
2 tablespoons	3 tablespoons	2 tablespoons
$3\frac{1}{2}$ tablespoons	4 tablespoons	3 tablespoons
4 tablespoons	5 tablespoons	$3\frac{1}{2}$ tablespoons

An Imperial/American guide to solid and liquid measures

Imperial	American
Solid measures	
1 lb butter or margarine	2 cups
1 lb flour	4 cups
1 lb granulated or caster sugar	2 cups
1 lb icing sugar	3 cups
8 oz rice	1 cup
Liquid measures	
$\frac{1}{4}$ pint liquid	$\frac{2}{3}$ cup liquid
$\frac{1}{2}$ pint	$1\frac{1}{4}$ cups
$\frac{3}{4}$ pint	2 cups
1 pint	$2\frac{1}{2}$ cups
$1\frac{1}{2}$ pints	$3\frac{3}{4}$ cups
2 pints	5 cups ($2\frac{1}{2}$ pints)

Note: when making any of the recipes in this book, only follow one set of measures as they are not interchangeable.

Menus for All Occasions

Menu planning should be fun, but for the inexperienced it can sometimes prove to be a nightmare as even the most delicious dishes, when served together, could turn into a catastrophe. You have to take into consideration not only the colour, texture and flavours when selecting dishes but also the amount of time and help you have on hand. The choice of menus which follow will give you a head start when planning for a wide variety of occasions.

Dinner

Whether the dinner is formal or informal, you will be able to entertain with confidence if you use your best culinary talents as well as your food processor. Most of the recipes are included in this book and these are marked with *.

Formal dinner 1	Formal dinner 2	Casual patio dinner	Dinner party which may be completed in advance
Spinach salad starter*	Mussel bake*	Pina Colado de luxe*	Shrimp pâté*
Fillet combo*	Lamb with mustard crust*	Instant gazpacho*	Surprise pork fillets*
Potato crowns*	Soured cream scallop potatoes*	Curried chicken*	Risotto Milanese*
French peas*	Baked stuffed artichokes*	Potato crisps*	Green beans in sherry sauce*
Dilled cauliflower*	Spicy peas*	Green salad	Ratatouille*
Crêpes Suzette*	Frozen silk cream*	Kiwi cheesecake*	Strawberry pig's ears*
Coffee	Café brûlot* or coffee	Coffee	Coffee
Chocolate truffles*	Bittersweet grapefruit bites*		

Buffet

When a large selection of foods is displayed on the serving table at one time, your guest can see at a glance just what and how much you are serving and pace themselves accordingly. The buffet main course recipes in this book average twenty servings.

Special occasion buffet dinner	Buffet dinner	Cold buffet	Informal buffet dinner
Egg and ham mousse*	Artichoke pâte´*	Salmon mousse de luxe*	Broccoli and white wine soup*
Glazed duck terrine*	Pâté maison*	Aubergine terrine*	Smoked salmon quiche*
Nasi goreng*	Wholewheat yogurt loaf*	Chicken galantine*	Cheese and leek quiche*
Sambals*	Melba toast	Rare roast beef	Spinach quiche*
Chocolate nut pie*	Chicken à l'orange* and rice	Glazed ham	Mixed salad
Old fashioned ice cream*	Tuna Mediterranean*	Pressed tongue	Beans mimosa*
	Tossed salad	Leeks with sauce verte*	Frozen plum cassis mousse*
	Apple streudel*	Chick pea salad*	Layered coffee gâteau*
	Rum peachy sherbet*	Pawpaw and avocado salad*	
		Spicy cabbage slaw*	
		Green salad	
		Peachy rice salad*	
		Luscious lemon cheesecake*	
		Choux puffs with praline filling*	

Lunch

Maybe it's Sunday lunch or lunch for a few friends. Make it light, make it ahead and make it in the food processor.

Sit-down lunch

Asparagus mayonnaise*
Spanikopita*
Layered vegetable salad*
Melon dessert soup*

Informal lunch

Tropical fruit cooler*
Courgette pâté*
Country pâté en croûte*
Chicken à la Klinzman*
Fish lasagne*
Cooked rice
Mixed salad
Garlic bread (garlic butter*)
Fresh fruit ice*

Light lunch

Apple and liver spread*
Haddock roulade*
Finger rolls*
Chive and courgette salad*
Sherbet lemon cups*

Brunch

Surprise your guests with a beautiful, bountiful mid-day menu. Go for make-ahead casseroles, spreads and pâtés that let the processor do the work and keep your time in the kitchen to a minimum.

Brunch 1

Grapefruit stinger*
Minty fruit salad*
Chicken liver and onions
Cheesey chicken lasagne*
Crispy seafood pie*
Reuben casserole*
Tossed salad
Strawberry banana freeze*

Brunch 2

Grenadine stinger*
Ham and pineapple quiche*
Mushroom quiche*
Grilled bacon and sausages
Scrambled eggs
Herbed scones* with caviar butter* and green butter*
Honey yogurt freeze*
Selection of rolls and toast
Preserves

Tea-time

Within the baking section, you will find a large selection of delicious tea-time treats. Many can be made ahead and frozen, to be kept on hand for entertaining those friends who just happen to drop by for a cup of tea. For a more formal tea, include one or two savoury dishes.

Tea-time 1

Butterscotch sherry cake*
Greek cookies*
Carrot cake*
Bacon fingers*

Tea-time 2

Lemon oil cake*
Chocolate chip cookies*
Apricot bars*
Banana orange loaf*
Cheese and wine spread*

Tea-time 3

Chocolate oil cake*
Golden cherry loaf*
Bachelor buttons*
Mushroom quiche*

Cocktails

The recipe sections for starters and for snacks give you party foods with minimum effort. The beverage section has some splendid ideas with which to bedazzle your guests.

Cocktails 1

Iced kir*
Chequer board*
Variety of stuffed eggs*
Ham and chicken puffs*
Aloha spareribs*
Olive cheese bites*
Sardine crescents*

Cocktails 2

Spicy cucumber cocktail*
Smoky cheese ball*
Smoked salmon pâté*
Chicken liver and mushroom pâté*
Stuffed eggs*
Prawn and cheese puffs*
Anchovy crisps*

Supper

This has become an easy, cosy way to entertain informally. Prepare soups, casseroles and puddings ahead of time or, for impromptu entertaining, look for almost instant recipes in each section.

Supper 1

Mushroom and cheese bake*
French salad
Fudge walnut pie*

Supper 2

Chilled herb soup*
Moussaka*
Cauliflower, mushroom and courgette salad*
Apple tart with cinnamon crumble*

Supper 3

Old fashioned vegetable soup*
Country garden casserole bread*
Crêpes Romanoff*

Appetisers and Starters

Appetisers should be imaginative and set the stage for the meal that follows. As a general rule, serve light appetisers or starters before a heavy meal, and more substantial ones when your main dish is not very filling. When planning your menu take into consideration the weather. In summer, cold appetisers may be more appealing, while hot ones make a great start to a winter meal.

For a large gathering or cocktail party, serve an array of snack foods on medium sized platters. These should be replenished frequently as no one likes to be confronted with one appetiser left on a large tray. Bite-size finger foods should be small enough to eat in two mouthfuls. Hot appetisers are easily prepared in advance and heated as required. Remember too, dips are for dipping, so make them thick enough to cling to crisps, biscuits or vegetable crudités. Spreads should be spreadable, not thick and heavy.

The following pages will show you how to prepare a delectable selection of starters and appetisers ranging from popular dips and spreads to elegant dinner party hors d'oeuvres and terrines. Some recipes may be made in an instant, while others require a little more time and culinary skill.

Spinach Starter Salad

1 large bunch fresh spinach leaves	1 onion
4–6 rashers bacon	1 tomato
50 g/2 oz feta cheese	a little lemon juice
40 g/1½ oz blue cheese	150 ml/¼ pint French
4 slices of bread	Dressing (page 97)

Wash and pat dry the spinach. Break the leaves into small pieces discarding stalks and place in a salad bowl. Fry the bacon rashers until crisp, then drain reserving the fat. Chop finely in the processor and sprinkle over the spinach. Place the cheeses in the work bowl, pulse twice to crumble and add to the bacon and spinach. Cube the bread and fry in the bacon fat until golden brown, adding a little oil if necessary. Drain, cool and add to the ingredients in the salad bowl. Fit the slicing blade to the processor, slice the onion and tomato thinly, then sprinkle with lemon juice. Just before serving, pour the French dressing over the salad and toss. Garnish with onion and tomato slices.

SERVES 4

Smoked Salmon and Watercress Pâté

This baked pâté is delicious served either hot or cold.

1 large bunch watercress, stems removed	2 teaspoons dill
	2 teaspoons lemon juice
1 onion, quartered	½ teaspoon white pepper
350 g/12 oz fresh salmon, skinned, boned and cut into pieces	250 ml/8 fl oz single cream
	2 eggs
	watercress leaves to garnish
100 g/4 oz smoked salmon	

First grease a 23 × 12-cm/9 × 5-in loaf tin, line with non-stick baking parchment or greaseproof paper and grease once again. Using a few watercress leaves, create a design on the paper lining.

Blanch the remaining watercress leaves in boiling water for 10 to 15 seconds, then drain and plunge into cold water. Drain once more and pat dry between absorbent kitchen paper.

Using the metal blade, coarsely chop the onion. Add the fresh and smoked salmon, dill, lemon juice, white pepper and process until well combined. With the machine running, pour the cream slowly through the feed tube and process until well mixed. Now add the eggs and process for a further 25 seconds. Transfer all but about 5 tablespoons of the mixture to another bowl. Add the blanched watercress leaves to the remaining mixture in the work bowl and process until smooth. Use a spatula to scrape the sides of the bowl when necessary.

Turn half the salmon mixture into the prepared loaf tin. Cover with the watercress mixture, then add the remaining salmon mixture. Smooth the top, cover the loaf tin with greased greaseproof paper and secure tightly with aluminium foil. Bake in a cool oven (150c, 300f, gas 2) for 25 minutes,

then reduce the heat to very cool (120c, 250f, gas ½) and bake for a further 25 minutes. The pâté should be firm, but not hard. Remove from the oven and allow to stand for 5 to 10 minutes to allow the juices to be absorbed and the pâté to set. To serve, invert onto a serving platter, remove paper and garnish with watercress leaves, then slice. To serve cold, chill the pâté before slicing.

SERVES 10

Shrimp Pâté de Luxe

A really delicious pâté for special occasions.

5 tablespoons white wine	dash of Tabasco sauce
250 ml/8 fl oz water	1 teaspoon French mustard
½ teaspoon salt	100 g/4 oz butter, softened
450 g/1 lb peeled shrimps or prawns	salt and freshly ground black pepper to taste
3 tablespoons Pernod	GARNISH
2 tablespoon lemon juice	fresh dill or parsley sprigs
½ teaspoon ground mace	lemon slices
1 teaspoon fresh dill or ½ teaspoon dried dill	

Combine the wine and water, add the salt and bring to the boil. Now add the shrimps, lower the heat and simmer until just tender, about 3 to 4 minutes. Drain the shrimps well. Using the metal blade, coarsely chop the shrimps, then add the Pernod, lemon juice, mace, dill, Tabasco and mustard. Add half the butter and process until well blended. Lastly, add the remaining butter, process until smooth and season with salt and pepper. Spoon into a serving dish and chill thoroughly. Before serving, garnish with dill or parsley and lemon slices. Serve with brown bread or Melba toast.

MAKES ABOUT 450 ML/¾ PINT

Salmon Pâté

1 (225-g/8-oz) can pink salmon	1 tablespoon lemon juice
	salt and black pepper
225 g/8 oz creamed cottage cheese	50 g/2 oz smoked salmon
	lettuce leaves to serve
4 tablespoons butter, softened	GARNISH
	parsley
1 tablespoon chopped onion	gherkins or capers

Drain the fish and remove the bones and skin. Fit the metal blade to the processor and place the canned salmon, cottage cheese, butter, onion, lemon juice and seasonings in the work bowl. Pulse until smooth, then stir in the smoked salmon pieces. Turn into a bowl, cover and chill. To serve, arrange a crisp lettuce leaf on each plate, add a scoop of pâté and decorate with parsley and gherkins. Serve with savoury biscuits or Melba toast.

SERVES 4

Freezes for up to one month.

Country Pâté en Croûte

2 slices white bread
3 sprigs parsley, stems removed
4 spring onions, cut into pieces
½ small onion, cut up
2 cloves garlic
40 g/1½ oz butter or margarine
225 g/8 oz veal, cut into cubes
450 g/1 lb uncooked sausage meat
7 tablespoons beer
½ teaspoon fennel seeds
1 teaspoon dried sage
½ teaspoon dried mixed herbs
2 eggs
salt and freshly ground black pepper to taste
double quantity Shortcrust Pastry (page 131)
225 g/8 oz chicken livers
10 rashers bacon, rinds removed
4 tablespoons pistachio nuts
1 beaten egg to glaze
1 teaspoon powdered gelatine
250 ml/8 fl oz beef stock
lettuce to serve
pickle to garnish

Using the metal blade, process the bread into fine crumbs and set aside. Place the parsley, spring onion and onion in the work bowl and with the machine running, drop in the garlic. Process for about 8 seconds or until the mixture is finely chopped. Melt 25 g/1 oz butter in a heavy frying pan and sauté the parsley-onion mixture for about 2 minutes. Remove from the pan and set aside.

Use the metal blade to finely mince the veal in batches, it takes about 6 seconds per batch. Set aside. Crumble the sausage meat into the frying pan, add half the beer and cook, stirring, until the sausage begins to lose its pink colour. Stir in the fennel. Remove from the heat and add to the parsley-onion mixture. Melt the remaining 15 g/½ oz butter, add the veal and sauté until partially cooked. Pour in the remaining beer and cook for a further minute. Remove from the heat, add to the bowl with the sausage meat. Now add the breadcrumbs, sage, herbs, beaten eggs, salt and pepper. Mix well.

Roll out the pastry and cut strips to fit the sides of a 23-cm/9-in loaf tin or pie mould. Press into place, leaving 1 cm/½ in extra pastry at the top. Cut a piece of pastry slightly larger than the bottom of the tin and press into place, sealing the edges well. Finally cut a piece of pastry a little larger than the top of the tin and reserve.

Wash and trim the chicken livers and pat dry. Place the bacon rashers on a wooden board and stretch each one with the back of a knife. Use the bacon to line the pastry crust. Turn half the meat mixture into the pastry case and press down firmly. Arrange the chicken livers down the centre of the mould and sprinkle nuts over and around them. Carefully pack the remaining meat into the pastry case and press down well. Fold the bacon ends over the meat. Fit the pastry top on the mould. Wet, then seal and crimp the edges. Cut a small hole in the top crust and place a small, round metal cutter or cardboard tube wrapped in aluminium foil in the hole. If desired, decorate the top crust with pastry leaves. Brush the pastry with beaten egg and bake the pâté in a moderate oven (160 c, 325 f, gas 3) for 90 minutes. Remove from the oven and allow to cool.

Meanwhile dissolve the gelatine in 3 tablespoons hot water then add to the stock. Put on one side until on the point of setting. When the pâté has nearly cooled, spoon the jellied stock through the hole in the pastry crust. Chill the pâté before slicing. Serve on lettuce leaves and garnish with sliced pickle.

SERVES 10 TO 12

Chicken Liver and Mushroom Pâté

225 g/8 oz mushrooms
2 cloves garlic
4 spring onions, cut into pieces
150 g/5 oz butter
225 g/8 oz chicken livers
5 tablespoons dry white wine
2 tablespoons tarragon vinegar
½ teaspoon dried tarragon
6 tablespoons canned tomato, chopped and drained
salt and pepper to taste
2 tablespoons brandy
6 tablespoons double cream

Using the metal blade, finely chop the mushrooms, garlic and onions. In a frying pan, melt 25 g/1 oz butter and fry the livers until golden brown and still tender. Remove the livers and set aside. Now add the mushrooms, garlic and onion to the pan and sauté for 1 minute before pouring in the wine, vinegar and tarragon. Cook, stirring until the liquid is reduced by half (5 minutes). Add the tomato and heat through. Return the livers to the pan and season with salt and pepper.

Melt the remaining butter. Using the metal blade, purée the liver mixture in batches, adding a portion of melted butter, brandy and cream to each batch. Spoon the pâté into a serving dish and chill for several hours or overnight. Serve with brown bread or toast.

MAKES ABOUT 450 ML/¾ PINT

Freezes well for up to 2 weeks.

Courgette Pâté

8–10 courgettes, washed and ends trimmed
300 ml/½ pint tomato juice
2 teaspoons Worcestershire sauce
½ teaspoon soy sauce
dash of Tabasco sauce
2 tablespoons chopped onion
½ teaspoon dried basil
450 g/1 lb cottage cheese
generous pinch of cayenne pepper
salt to taste

Use the shredding plate to shred the courgettes. Place the shredded courgette in a large saucepan and add the tomato juice, Worcestershire sauce, soy sauce, Tabasco, onion and basil. Bring to the boil and simmer, uncovered for about 20 minutes. Remove from the heat and cool. Fit the metal blade to the processor and process in batches, adding a portion of cottage cheese and a little cayenne pepper to each batch. Season with salt and chill until required. Serve with savoury biscuits or crudités.

MAKES ABOUT 600 ML/1 PINT

Pâté Maison

225 g/8 oz streaky bacon, rind removed	40 g/1½ oz butter
275 g/10 oz fatty pork	1 tablespoon single cream
50 g/2 oz veal	1 tablespoon brandy
50 g/2 oz ham	1 teaspoon plain flour
150 g/5 oz ox liver	1 egg
2 spring onions	pinch of allspice
1 clove garlic	salt and black pepper
	bay leaf

Use bacon to line the sides and base of a small, 25 × 12-cm/ 10 × 5-in loaf tin. Reserve a few slices of bacon for the top. Cube the pork, finely chop in the processor with the metal blade and set aside. Repeat with the veal, ham and liver and add to the pork. Chop the spring onions and garlic and sauté in butter for a few minutes. Add to the meats, together with all the remaining ingredients except the bay leaf. Combine well, then press the mixture into the loaf tin. Cover with the reserved slices of bacon and arrange the bay leaf on top. Lastly, cover with foil, place in a roasting tin filled with 2.5 cm/1 in water and cook in a moderate oven (160 c, 325 f, gas 3) for about 1 hour or until the fat, which rises to the top, is clear and yellow. Remove from the oven and cool. Place weights on top and chill overnight. To serve, turn out onto a bed of lettuce and slice thickly. Accompany with wholewheat bread or Melba toast.

SERVES 6

This dish will freeze for one to two months.

Brioche with Mushroom Pâté

BRIOCHE DOUGH	225 g/8 oz chicken livers
15 g/½ oz dried yeast	1 clove garlic, crushed
2 teaspoons sugar	½ teaspoon dried thyme
5 tablespoons warm milk	salt and freshly ground
350 g/12 oz strong plain flour	black pepper
½ teaspoon salt	225 g/8 oz mushrooms, wiped clean
75 g/3 oz margarine	1½ tablespoons port
2 eggs	4 tablespoons double cream
1 beaten egg for glazing	2 teaspoons lemon juice
MUSHROOM PÂTÉ	pinch of ground cloves
100 g/4 oz butter	

To make the brioche, dissolve the yeast and sugar in the milk and sprinkle 50 g/2 oz of the flour over the liquid. Cover with plastic wrap and stand in a warm place for about 15 minutes. Fit the metal blade to the processor, place the flour and salt in the work bowl and pulse twice to aerate. Now add the margarine and pulse again about three times to combine the ingredients. Lightly beat the eggs, then pour into the yeast mixture. With the processor running, pour the liquid through the feed tube and process the dough until smooth (about 60 seconds). Place the dough inside a greased plastic bag and set aside in a warm place for about an hour or until the dough has doubled in size.

Meanwhile, make the pâté. Heat the butter, add the cleaned livers, garlic, thyme and seasonings. Sauté for 10 minutes. Use the metal blade to chop the mushrooms, then set aside in a bowl. Remove the livers from the heat and add the port, cream,

lemon juice and cloves. Place this mixture in the processor bowl, pulse until smooth, then add to the mushrooms. Allow the mixture to cool slightly.

Now with the metal blade in place, distribute the brioche dough around the base of the clean work bowl and process for 45 seconds. Grease a brioche mould. Roll the dough out until it is large enough to line the mould. Add the mushroom pâté, cover with excess dough and place a small ball of dough on top. Stand in a warm place for 15 minutes before brushing with beaten egg. Bake in a hot oven (220 c, 425 f, gas 7) until golden brown, about 20 minutes. Serve warm or cold.

SERVES 6

Freeze the mushroom pâté on its own for up to one month.

Artichoke Pâté

2 (396-g/14-oz) cans artichoke hearts	salt and black pepper
	a little lemon juice
100 g/4 oz cream cheese	shredded lettuce to serve (optional)
150 ml/¼ pint double cream	
1–2 cloves garlic	GARNISH (optional)
100 g/4 oz butter	chopped parsley
5 tablespoons olive oil	stuffed olives, sliced

Fit the metal blade to the processor. Drain the artichokes, place in the work bowl and add all the remaining ingredients. Process for 30 seconds, adjust seasonings and pour into a serving dish or mould lined with foil. Chill in the refrigerator overnight. If the pâté has been moulded, turn out onto a bed of shredded lettuce, decorate with chopped parsley and slices of stuffed olives.

SERVES 8 TO 10

This pâté will freeze for one month.

From left to right: Glazed Duck Terrine, Country Pâté en Croûte (page 26), Shrimp Pâté de Luxe (page 25)

Glazed Duck Terrine

1 duck, about 1 kg/2 lb, boned	2 teaspoons Cointreau
225 g/8 oz streaky bacon, rind removed	1 onion, finely chopped
	1 teaspoon rosemary
225 g/8 oz belly of pork	pinch of allspice
225 g/8 oz chicken livers	salt and black pepper
1 onion	GLAZE
1 clove garlic	4 orange segments
50 g/2 oz fresh breadcrumbs	1 bay leaf
MARINADE	15 g/½ oz powdered gelatine
Juice of one orange	3 tablespoons hot water
2 tablespoons brandy	300 ml/½ pint chicken stock
	2 tablespoons orange juice

Cut the breast meat from the duck and slice thinly. Combine all the ingredients for the marinade, add the duck breast and allow to stand overnight. Line a 600-ml/1-pint terrine or ovenproof dish with the bacon; use the back of a knife to stretch the bacon before using. Place the remaining duck (without the bones) in the processor, and process until fine. Repeat with the pork, chicken livers, onion and garlic. Combine all these ingredients as well as the breadcrumbs. Add a little marinade and season well. Turn half this mixture into the terrine and carefully arrange the marinated breast meat on top. Pack in the remaining mixture and cover with heavy foil. Place in a roasting pan filled with warm water to a depth of 2.5 cm/1 in and bake in a moderate oven (160 c, 325 f, gas 3) for 2¼ hours. Cool, pour off any liquid, then place weights on top and chill.

Finally, decorate with orange segments and a bay leaf. To make the glaze, dissolve the gelatine in the hot water over a basin of boiling water. Add the stock and orange juice, strain and pour over the top of the pâté. Allow to set firmly. Serve with home-made brown bread or toast.

SERVES 6

If you wish to freeze this dish, freeze without the glaze for up to three months.

Aubergine Terrine

4 small aubergines
2 onions, quartered
2 cloves garlic
2 green peppers, deseeded
4 tablespoons oil
3 courgettes
salt and pepper
bouquet garni (sprig
  parsley, bay leaf, thyme,
  peppercorns, mace, tied
  in muslin)

450 g/1 lb tomatoes, peeled
4 tablespoons natural yogurt
1 egg
1 slice bread, cubed
GARNISH
1 green pepper, deseeded
1 hard-boiled egg
French bread to serve

Cut the aubergines in half lengthwise and score the cut sides with a knife. Place on an oiled baking tray and bake in a hot oven (220 c, 425 f, gas 7) until tender. Remove the pulp carefully and reserve the skins. Using the metal blade and pulse button, chop the onion, garlic and green pepper. Heat the oil, add the chopped vegetables and sauté lightly. Fit the slicing plate and slice the courgettes. Add the sliced courgettes and the aubergine pulp to the sautéed vegetables. Season well and add the bouquet garni. Simmer for 15 minutes, then cool slightly. Meanwhile, use the chipper plate to chop the tomatoes. Place in a separate pan and carefully simmer the tomatoes until thick. Add the cooked tomatoes, yogurt and egg to the vegetables. Fit the metal blade to the processor, place the bread in the work bowl and pulse until fine. Add the breadcrumbs to the vegetable mixture. This should now be thick in texture.

Line a 25 × 12-cm/10 × 5-in loaf tin with aluminium foil and oil well. Arrange the aubergine skins, purple side down, along the base of the loaf tin. Remove the bouquet garni from the vegetables and pour into the tin. Cover with foil and place in a roasting tin of warm water. Bake in a cool oven (140 c, 275 f, gas 1) for 45 minutes. Cool, then chill before turning out. Garnish with rings of green pepper and slices of hard-boiled egg. Serve with chunks of French bread.

SERVES 6

Spinach and Onion Dip

225 g/8 oz cottage cheese
150 ml/$\frac{3}{4}$ pint soured cream
6 tablespoons mayonnaise
  (page 95)
$\frac{1}{2}$ packet powdered onion
  soup mix
$\frac{1}{2}$ teaspoon dill

pinch of ground nutmeg
275 g/10 oz frozen spinach,
  thawed
TO SERVE
carrot sticks, celery sticks,
  cauliflower chunks,
  cucumber slices

Using the metal blade, combine the cottage cheese, soured cream, mayonnaise, onion soup, dill and nutmeg. Drain the spinach well, add to the cheese and blend until thoroughly mixed. Turn into a serving bowl and chill. Serve with crisp vegetable pieces. For a softer consistency, add a little more soured cream and mayonnaise.

MAKES ABOUT 600 ML/1 PINT

Shrimp Dip

1 (198-g/7-oz) can shrimps,
  drained
1 hard-boiled egg, quartered
300 ml/$\frac{1}{2}$ pint soured cream
4 tablespoons mayonnaise
  (page 95)
3 spring onions, cut into
  pieces

1 tablespoon lemon juice
1 teaspoon horseradish sauce
  or cream
$\frac{1}{2}$ teaspoon Worcestershire
  sauce
2 teaspoons chopped parsley

Using the metal blade, combine all the ingredients in the work bowl and process until thoroughly mixed. Transfer to a suitable serving dish and chill. Serve with an array of crisp vegetable crudités.

MAKES ABOUT 600 ML/1 PINT

Greek Tuna Dip

This dip will keep for up to a week in the refrigerator. Its strong flavour goes well with crisp crudités such as green pepper chunks, courgette slices and mushrooms.

1 (198-g/7-oz) can tuna,
  drained
5 tablespoons lemon juice
1 (50-g/1$\frac{3}{4}$-oz) can anchovy
  fillets
4 tablespoons capers, drained

20 black olives
2 tablespoons brandy
$\frac{1}{4}$ small onion, cut up
4 tablespoons oil
pepper to taste

Fit the metal blade to the processor and place the tuna, lemon juice, anchovies, capers, olives, brandy and onion in the work bowl. Process until smooth. With the motor running, slowly add the oil in a steady stream. The mixture should be thick and creamy. Season to taste and chill. To Serve, transfer to a serving dish and surround with vegetable crudités.

MAKES ABOUT 300 ML/$\frac{1}{2}$ PINT

Apple Cheese Spread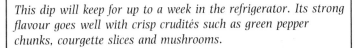

Use as a filling for fruit bread sandwiches, or spread thickly on savoury biscuits.

50 g/2 oz pecan nuts or
  walnuts
1 apple, peeled and cored
100 g/4 oz Gruyère cheese
225 g/8 oz cottage cheese

2 tablespoons dry white wine
2 teaspoons mild prepared
  mustard
5 chives, chopped
salt and pepper to taste

Using the metal blade, chop the nuts and set aside. Fit the shredding plate to the processor, shred the apple and add to the nuts. Shred the Gruyère cheese. Replace the metal blade and cream the Gruyère cheese, cottage cheese, wine, mustard and chives. Add the chopped nuts and shredded apple. Process until well mixed, then season to taste with salt and pepper. Turn into a serving dish, cover and chill.

MAKES ABOUT 600 ML/1 PINT

Caviar Spread

1 piece French bread, about 10 cm/4 in long	3 tablespoons lemon juice
150 g/5 oz red lumpfish caviar	2 teaspoons finely chopped onion
5 tablespoons oil (preferably olive oil)	1 clove garlic, finely sliced
	pepper to taste

Trim the crusts off the bread, then soak it in water until soft. Press out the excess water. Fit the metal blade to the processor, place the bread in the work bowl and add the caviar, oil, lemon juice, onion and garlic. Process until smooth, then season to taste with pepper. Chill until 30 minutes before serving. Take the spread out of the refrigerator and allow to stand at room temperature. Serve with toast or warm, crusty bread rolls and black olives.

MAKES ABOUT 300 ML/$\frac{1}{2}$ PINT

Note: If a thinner mixture is desired, beat in a little cold water.

Cheese and Wine Spread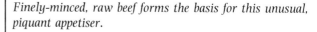

A sharp cheese spread that goes well with rye or pumpernickel bread.

450 g/1 lb mature Cheddar cheese	$\frac{1}{2}$ teaspoon prepared mustard
225 g/8 oz cottage cheese	$\frac{1}{4}$ small onion, cut up
150 ml/$\frac{1}{4}$ pint dry red wine	3 chives, chopped
	2 tablespoons brandy

Fit the shredder plate to the processor and shred the Cheddar cheese. Change to the metal blade and combine the Cheddar cheese, cottage cheese, wine, mustard, onion, chives and brandy. Blend well. Turn into a serving dish, cover and chill until required. This spread will keep, refrigerated, for about three weeks.

MAKES ABOUT 900 ML/1$\frac{1}{2}$ PINTS

Tomatoes Mimosa

6 small tomatoes	2 teaspoons anchovy essence
15 g/$\frac{1}{2}$ oz butter	4 tablespoons double cream
salt and black pepper	100 g/4 oz cream cheese, seasoned
$\frac{1}{2}$ teaspoon sugar	
2 hard-boiled eggs	spring onion tops to garnish
25 g/1 oz Cheddar cheese, shredded	lettuce or endive to serve

Wipe the tomatoes, slice off the tops and carefully scoop out the pulp. Place the pulp in a saucepan and add the butter, salt, pepper and sugar. Cook until thick, stirring occasionally as this mixture will burn if neglected. Remove from the heat and allow to cool. Meanwhile, separate one of the hard-boiled eggs and set aside a small quantity of yolk for garnishing. Fit the metal blade to the processor, add the hard-boiled eggs and pulse until chopped. Add the cooled tomato pulp and the

Cheddar cheese, pulse again twice. Lastly, add the anchovy essence and cream, pulse once. Use this mixture to fill the tomato shells. Pipe or spoon the seasoned cream cheese on top of the filling. Sieve the reserved egg yolk and sprinkle on top of the cream cheese. With a sharp knife, cut the spring onion tops at an angle, making each piece 1.5 cm/$\frac{3}{4}$ in long. This will give a leaf shape. Place three pieces on top of each tomato. Arrange the stuffed tomatoes on a platter with lettuce or endive.

SERVES 6

Steak Tartare with Capers

Finely-minced, raw beef forms the basis for this unusual, piquant appetiser.

450 g/1 lb lean beef such as rump or fillet, cut into chunks	2 teaspoons capers
	3-cm/8-in piece dill pickle
1 onion, quartered	2 teaspoons lemon juice
sprig of parsley, stems removed	1 teaspoon Worcestershire sauce
1 teaspoon freshly ground black pepper	2 egg yolks
	lettuce leaves and lemon wedges to garnish
1 teaspoon salt	

Process the mixture in two batches. Using the metal blade, finely chop half the beef, onion, parsley, pepper, salt, capers, pickle, lemon juice, Worcestershire sauce and 1 egg yolk. Turn into a large bowl. Repeat using the remaining half of the ingredients. Serve at once on lettuce leaves and garnish with lemon wedges.

Alternatively, press the mixture into a foil-lined loaf tin, cover tightly and refrigerate for several hours. Turn out onto a serving dish and garnish with lettuce and lemon. Surround with toast or savoury biscuits and serve as a spread.

SERVES 8

Artichokes and Mushrooms Béarnaise

A great start to a special meal. Each mouthful has a different taste and texture, and the sauce is smooth, rich and tangy.

1 quantity of Béarnaise sauce (page 100)	2 (396-g/14-oz) cans artichoke hearts
1 tablespoon chopped parsley	450 g/1 lb large flat mushrooms
2 teaspoons chopped fresh tarragon or 1 teaspoon dried tarragon	little chicken stock
	parsley to garnish
1 tablespoon lemon juice	

To the completed Béarnaise sauce, add the parsley, tarragon and lemon juice. Cover and set aside until required. Drain the artichokes and cut in halves or quarters, depending on size. Wipe the mushrooms and cut in halves or quarters. Place the mushrooms in a little chicken stock, cover and simmer for a few minutes. The mushrooms should still be firm. Allow to cool in the liquid. Take eight individual ovenproof serving dishes and divide the mushrooms and artichokes between them. Add

1 tablespoon of the mushroom cooking liquid to each dish and mask the vegetables with Béarnaise sauce. Place in a moderately hot oven (200 c, 400 f, gas 6) for about 10 minutes. Garnish with parsley and serve immediately.

This dish may be prepared a few hours in advance. Once the vegetables have been masked with sauce, cover the dishes with cling film and set aside in a cool place, then heat just before serving.

SERVES 8

Crab Stuffed Mushrooms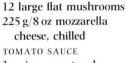

1 small bunch parsley, stems removed	1 teaspoon French mustard
1 slice white bread, trimmed and broken into pieces	1 teaspoon salt
2 spring onions, cut into pieces	1 tablespoon lemon juice
4 tablespoons grated Parmesan cheese	1 (169-g/6-oz) can crab meat, drained
225 g/8 oz cottage cheese	12 large flat mushrooms
2 tablespoons oil	GARNISH
2 teaspoons brandy	garlic butter (page 103)
	lemon wedges
	chopped parsley

Using the metal blade, finely chop the parsley and set aside. Combine the bread, spring onion and 4 tablespoons chopped parsley and process until fine. Add 2 tablespoons Parmesan cheese, the cream cheese, oil, brandy, mustard, salt and lemon juice. Pulse until well mixed. Remove the metal blade and fold in the crab meat.

Wipe the mushrooms and remove the stems. Fill the mushroom cups with the crab mixture and arrange on a baking tray. Bake for 10 minutes in a moderately hot oven (200 c, 400 f, gas 6). Remove from the oven, sprinkle the remaining Parmesan cheese on top and return to the oven for a further 2 to 3 minutes. Garnish with garlic butter, lemon wedges and a sprinkling of chopped parsley.

SERVES 6

Mushrooms Pizzaiola

12 large flat mushrooms	a little oil
225 g/8 oz mozzarella cheese, chilled	2 (397-g/14-oz) cans tomatoes
TOMATO SAUCE	½ teaspoon oregano
1 onion, quartered	1 bay leaf
2 cloves garlic	salt and black pepper
2 tablespoons concentrated tomato purée	little sugar

First make the sauce. Using the metal blade, finely chop the onion and garlic. Sauté in a little heated oil. Chop the canned tomatoes, and add to the pan. Add to the tomato purée, oregano, bay leaf, salt, pepper and a little sugar. Simmer until thick, then remove the bay leaf. Brush the mushrooms and six individual ovenproof serving dishes with oil. Place two mushrooms in each dish and spoon the tomato mixture on top. Fit the slicing plate to the processor and slice the cheese.

Arrange a few cheese slices on top of each portion and bake in a moderate oven (180 c, 350 f, gas 4) for about 15 minutes or until the mushrooms are tender. Serve immediately.

This dish may be prepared some hours in advance. After adding the cheese, cover and set aside in a cool place.

SERVES 6

Salmon Mousse de Luxe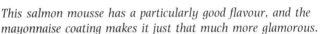

This salmon mousse has a particularly good flavour, and the mayonnaise coating makes it just that much more glamorous.

1 slice onion	6 tablespoons cream
2 teaspoons parsley, stems removed	COATING
15 g/½ oz margarine	4 teaspoons powdered gelatine
15 g/½ oz plain flour	2 tablespoons hot water
6 tablespoons milk	5 tablespoons mayonnaise (page 95)
2 eggs, separated	3 tablespoons chicken stock
1 (225-g/8-oz) can salmon	GARNISH
salt and cayenne pepper	lettuce or endive
a little lemon juice	crimped cucumber
2 teaspoons powdered gelatine	stuffed olives
3 tablespoons hot water	

Fit the metal blade to the processor and chop the onion and parsley. Now make a thick white sauce. Melt the margarine, add the flour and cook for a minute or two before adding the milk. Stirring continuously, cook until the sauce thickens. Remove from the heat, then stir in the egg yolks. Add the white sauce to the onion and parsley in the processor bowl. Skin and bone the salmon and add to the ingredients in the processor bowl. Process until smooth. Season with salt, cayenne pepper and a squeeze of lemon juice. Dissolve the gelatine in the hot water over a basin of boiling water. Whisk the egg whites until stiff and, in a separate bowl, lightly whip the cream. Pour the gelatine into the fish mixture and process for 5 seconds. Fold into the cream, and lastly fold in the egg whites. Pour into a rinsed mould and allow it to set. Cut a piece of heavy foil the same shape as the opening of the mould and place on a wire rack. Turn the mousse out onto the foil.

To mask the mould, dissolve the gelatine in the hot water. Thin the mayonnaise down with a little chicken stock. Stir in the gelatine and stand over ice until the mixture begins to thicken. Spoon quickly over the mould. If the mixture becomes too thick, thin down with a little more stock or stand over hot water. Coat again if necessary, then chill. To serve, carefully lift the mould onto endive or flat lettuce leaves arranged on a platter. Garnish with crimped cucumber and slices of stuffed olives.

SERVES 4 TO 6

Note: A smoother, more even coating is obtained if the mousse is coated three times with a thin layer of sauce rather than once with a single thick layer of sauce.

Smoky Cheese Ball

Smoky Cheese Ball

Three cheeses combine to make this spread really special.

100 g/4 oz smoky-flavoured cheese	3 tablespoons dry onion soup mix
450 g/1 lb cottage cheese	5 tablespoons milk
100 g/4 blue cheese, crumbled	dash of Tabasco sauce
100 g/4 oz butter or margarine	small bunch parsley

Fit the shredding plate and shred the smoky cheese. Change to the metal blade and combine the smoky cheese, cottage cheese, blue cheese and butter or margarine. Soak the onion soup mix in the milk for 5 minutes. Add to the cheese, together with a dash of Tabasco. Blend well. Turn the mixture onto oiled aluminium foil and shape into a ball. Chill thoroughly. Before serving, remove the stems from the parsley and chop finely, using the metal blade. Roll the cheese ball in the chopped parsley and arrange on a platter. Surround with French bread, brown bread and biscuits.

MAKES ABOUT 800 G/1¾ LB

Avocado and Smoked Mackerel au Gratin

50 g/2 oz Parmesan cheese, cubed	3 tablespoons chives, chopped
350 g/12 oz smoked mackerel	1 tablespoon lemon juice
½ quantity of béchamel sauce (page 101)	black pepper to taste
	2 medium avocado pears
5 tablespoons soured cream	1 egg white
3 tablespoons brandy	paprika to dust

Fit the metal blade to the processor and with the machine running, drop the cheese onto the blades. Process until fine, then set aside. Skin and bone the mackerel. Place in the work bowl and pulse a few times to flake. Add the béchamel sauce, soured cream, brandy, chives, lemon juice and a quarter of the Parmesan cheese. Season with black pepper and pulse to combine.

Spray or grease six small flat ovenproof containers or scallop shells. Peel and slice the avocado pears. Lay two or three slices on the base of each container.

Whisk the egg white until stiff and fold into the fish mixture. Divide the fish mixture between the six plates and sprinkle with the remaining Parmesan cheese. Place in a moderate oven (180 c, 350 f, gas 4) for 10 to 15 minutes, then brown under the grill for 3 to 4 minutes. Dust with paprika and serve immediately.

The fish mixture may be prepared a few hours in advance. Cover and keep in the refrigerator. Half an hour before serving, slice the avocado pear, fold the beaten egg white into the fish mixture and complete the dish.

SERVES 6

Mussel Bake

Bacon, tomato and garlic combine to give this mussel dish a tasty, robust flavour.

4 rashers bacon, rinds removed	5 tablespoons white wine
1 onion, quartered	1 teaspoon dried thyme
3 tablespoons parsley, stems removed	salt and black pepper
2 cloves garlic	little chicken stock if necessary
2 slices white bread	4 (250-g/8.8-oz) cans mussels, without shells
3 tomatoes, peeled	triangles of brown bread and butter to serve
100 g/4 oz butter	

Fit the metal blade to the processor, add the bacon and pulse until chopped. Set aside. Place the onion, parsley and garlic in the work bowl and pulse until finely chopped. Add to the bacon. Now process the bread until finely crumbed. Set aside separately. Fit the chipper plate and dice the tomatoes. In a saucepan, melt half the butter and sauté the chopped bacon, onion, garlic and parsley. Add the diced tomatoes, wine, thyme and seasonings. Simmer for about 10 minutes. Add a little stock if the mixture becomes too dry. Drain the mussels, add to the pan and simmer for a further 10 minutes. Turn the

mixture into an ovenproof serving dish or spoon onto individual scallop shells. Melt the remaining butter. Toss the breadcrumbs in the butter and sprinkle over the mussel mixture. Bake in a hot oven (220 c, 425 f, gas 7) for 10 minutes. Serve immediately with triangles of brown bread and butter.

This dish may be made in advance, refrigerated and baked as required.

SERVES 6

Chilled Leek Hors d'Oeuvre

12–16 leeks	2 teaspoons Dijon mustard
a little chicken stock	salt and black pepper
4 rashers bacon	1 tablespoon lemon juice
SAUCE VERTE	lettuce leaves to serve
1 bunch watercress or a few spinach leaves	parsley or watercress to garnish
300 ml/½ pint mayonnaise (page 95)	

Top and tail the leeks, wash well. Bring a little chicken stock to the boil, drop in the leeks and simmer until tender. Cool the leeks in the stock, cover with aluminium foil and chill. Fry the bacon until crisp, then drain. Chop finely in the processor and set aside. To make the sauce, first rinse the watercress or spinach in plenty of cold water and simmer until tender. Drain well and cool. Chop finely in the processor, then add the mayonnaise, mustard, salt, pepper and lemon juice. Pulse to combine. To serve, drain the leeks and arrange on a lettuce leaf. Coat with the sauce, sprinkle with bacon and garnish with a sprig of parsley or watercress.

SERVES 4 TO 6

Chilled Leek Hors d'Oeuvre served with Wholemeal Yogurt Loaf (page 129)

Soups

Soup can play a variety of roles on the menu, from whetting the appetite at a formal dinner to providing a hearty meal-in-one dish. Satisfying hot soup takes the bite out of a cold winter's day, while a chilled soup makes a refreshing start to a summer luncheon or dinner.

Soup made the old-fashioned way, from a good basic stock with plenty of vegetables, is not a lost art. It is still the foundation for a great deal of creative cooking. Furthermore your food processor will do in an instant all the time-consuming tasks of chopping, slicing and puréeing.

Within this section you will find a range of tasty soups, from hot and hearty to cool and smooth. Most can be prepared well in advance and be served as starters, main courses or light meals.

Iced Lettuce and Cucumber Soup

1 onion
1 teaspoon dried tarragon or
   2 teaspoons fresh tarragon
100 g/4 oz margarine
1 medium lettuce
1 cucumber
15 g/1 oz plain flour
1.15 litres/2 pints chicken
   stock
3 egg yolks
300 ml/½ pint soured cream
salt and black pepper
pinch of nutmeg
GARNISH
3 tablespoons chopped chives
a little shredded lettuce

Using the metal blade, chop the onion and tarragon. In a large saucepan, heat the margarine and gently sauté the onion and tarragon until the onion is soft. Meanwhile, fit the slicing plate to the processor and slice the lettuce and cucumber. Add to the pan and cook for 5 minutes. Stir in the flour, then the stock. Cover and simmer for 20 minutes. Replace the metal blade and process the soup in batches. Strain and return to the heat. Bring to the boil, remove from the stove and add the egg yolks, cream, seasonings and nutmeg. Stir well, then chill or freeze. Serve well chilled and garnished with a sprinkling of chives and lettuce.

SERVES 4 TO 6

Chilled Parsley Soup

1 large bunch parsley, stems
   removed
4 leeks, including 5 cm/2 in
   of the greens
3 potatoes
40 g/1½ oz butter
1.5 litres/2¾ pints
   chicken stock
salt and pepper to taste
300 ml/½ pint single cream
chopped parsley to garnish

Using the metal blade, finely chop the parsley and set aside. Fit the slicing plate and slice the leeks and potatoes. Melt the butter, add the leeks and potatoes and sauté for 5 minutes. Add the stock and bring to the boil. Reduce heat and simmer, covered, until the potatoes and leeks are tender. Now add the chopped parsley and simmer for a further 8 to 10 minutes. Season to taste with salt and pepper before setting aside to cool. Stir in the cream and chill until required. Serve garnished with chopped parsley.

SERVES 8

Note: This soup may be served hot, in which case stir in the cream just before serving.

Instant Gazpacho

1 hard-boiled egg, separated	salt and black pepper
3 tablespoons oil	dash of Tabasco sauce
1 (425-g/15-oz) can tomato	1 tablespoon lemon juice
soup	300 ml/½ pint soured cream
1 (397-g/14-oz) can tomato	1 cucumber
juice	3 spring onions
1½ teaspoons Worcestershire	2 cloves garlic
sauce	¼ teaspoon dill

Fit the metal blade to the processor, add the egg yolk and oil to the bowl and process until smooth. Now add the tomato soup and pulse to combine. Pour into a large bowl and stir in the tomato juice, Worcestershire sauce, salt and black pepper, Tabasco, lemon juice and soured cream. Using the metal blade and pulse button, chop the unpeeled cucumber and add to the soup. Chop the onions and the garlic and add to the bowl. Finally, add the dill. Cover and chill thoroughly. Before serving chop the egg white and sprinkle on top of the soup.

SERVES 4

Broccoli and White Wine Soup

4 leeks, cleaned and trimmed	1 teaspoon rosemary
3 potatoes	1 teaspoon basil
50 g/2 oz butter	3 tablespoons lemon juice
450 g/1 lb frozen broccoli	450 ml/¾ pint natural
1.15 litres/2 pints chicken	yogurt
stock	salt and freshly ground
200 ml/7 fl oz dry white	black pepper
wine	450 ml/¾ pint cream
1 teaspoon tarragon	parsley or mint to garnish

Fit the slicing plate to the processor and slice the leeks and potatoes and sauté for 5 minutes. Add the broccoli, stock, wine, tarragon, rosemary and basil. Simmer, covered, for about 15 minutes or until the vegetables are tender. Using the metal blade, purée the mixture in batches adding some of the lemon juice and yogurt to each batch. Season with salt and pepper and chill for several hours or overnight. Just before serving, stir in the cream and garnish with parsley or mint.

SERVES 6 TO 8

Chilled Herb Soup

175 ml/6 fl oz sprigs	2 teaspoons fresh thyme
parsley stems removed	leaves
100 ml/4 fl oz fresh basil	750 ml/1¼ pints chicken
leaves	stock
75 ml/3 fl oz fresh chives,	3 egg yolks
cut into 1 cm/½ in lengths	350 ml/12 fl oz single cream
2 tablespoons fresh mint	salt and pepper to taste
leaves	mint leaves to garnish

Using the metal blade, finely chop the parsley, basil, chives, mint and thyme. Bring the chicken stock to the boil and add the chopped herbs. Reduce heat and simmer gently for 25 minutes.

Process the egg yolks and the cream for about 10 seconds. With the machine running, slowly add half the herbed stock. Return this mixture to the remaining stock in the saucepan and simmer, stirring, for about 5 minutes or until the soup has slightly thickened. Do not boil or the egg will curdle. Season with salt and pepper to taste. Allow the soup to cool before refrigerating. Serve well chilled and garnished with mint leaves.

SERVES 4 TO 6

Large quantities of herbs can be measured by the ml/fl oz by pressing them down gently in a measuring jug.

Old-Fashioned Vegetable Soup

6 carrots	50 g/2 oz butter
3 large leeks, cleaned	2 litres/3½ pints chicken
2 large onions, cut in half	stock
lengthwise	1 tablespoons chopped parsley
2 large turnips	½ teaspoon dried mixed herbs
6 potatoes	salt and pepper to taste

Fit the slicing plate to the processor and slice all the vegetables. In a large saucepan, melt the butter, add the vegetables and sauté gently until soft. Add the stock, parsley and herbs. Season with salt and pepper. Bring to the boil, reduce heat and simmer for 20 to 25 minutes or until all the vegetables are tender.

SERVES 6 TO 8

Variation:

Creamy Vegetable Soup: Mix 2 tablespoons buttermilk with 300 ml/½ pint double cream and stand at room temperature for several hours until thickened. (Buttermilk can be obtained from health food shops.) Refrigerate until required. Make the vegetable soup in the usual way, then purée in batches, using the metal blade. At this stage the vegetable purée can be refrigerated until required. To serve, stir the soured cream into the vegetable purée and reheat gently, but do not boil.

Beer and Gruyère Soup

Beer and Gruyère Soup

150 g/5 oz Gruyère cheese
1 large onion, quartered
1 clove garlic
150 ml/¼ pint sprigs parsley, stems removed
3 tablespoons oil
2 slices white bread, crusts trimmed, cut into cubes

300 ml/½ pint beer
750 ml/1¼ pints chicken stock
freshly ground pepper to taste
1 teaspoon paprika

Using the shredding plate, shred the cheese and set aside. Fit the metal blade and place the onion in the work bowl. With the machine running, drop the garlic through the feed tube and process for 7 to 8 seconds, until both the onion and garlic are finely chopped. Set aside. Now finely chop the parsley and set aside.

In a large saucepan, heat the oil and sauté the chopped onion and garlic until the onion is lightly browned. Meanwhile, toast the bread cubes until golden and stir into the sautéed onion. Add the beer and stock to the pan. Bring to the boil, reduce heat and simmer until the onion is tender, for about 10 minutes. Add the pepper and half the chopped parsley. Mix well, then ladle the soup into ovenproof serving dishes. Sprinkle with cheese and paprika and place under the grill until the cheese melts and turns golden. Serve at once, garnished with the remaining chopped parsley.

SERVES 4 TO 6

Salmon and Asparagus Soup

A soup which can be prepared at a moment's notice. Serve it as a starter or on its own as a tasty light meal.

1 small onion
3 sprigs parsley, stems removed
15 g/1 oz margarine
1 (225-g/8-oz) can salmon, drained
1 (340-g/12-oz) can green asparagus

2 cooked potatoes
250 ml/8 fl oz milk
2 tablespoons sherry
1 tablespoon cornflour
6 tablespoons single cream
salt and black pepper
cayenne to taste
croûtons to serve

Using the metal blade, chop the onion and parsley. Sauté in the margarine until the onion is transparent. Add the flaked salmon and undrained asparagus cuts. Fit the chipper plate to the processor and dice the potatoes. Add to the pan, then pour in the milk and sherry and bring to the boil. Mix the cornflour with a little cream, add a little hot liquid to this mixture, then pour it into the soup. Add the remaining cream and bring to the boil, stirring all the time. Remove from the heat, season well and serve with crisp croûtons.

SERVES 4 TO 6

Blue Cheese Soup

1 head cabbage, cut into wedges	1 teaspoon sugar
1 head cauliflower, broken into pieces	250 ml/8 fl oz cream
100 g/4 oz butter or margarine	75 g/3 oz blue cheese, crumbled
1.4 litres/2½ pints chicken stock	salt and pepper to taste
	a few caraway seeds

Fit the slicing plate to the processor and slice the cabbage. Set aside. Now slice the cauliflower. In a large saucepan, heat the butter. Add the sliced cabbage and sauté gently until soft. Add the cauliflower, stock and sugar and bring to the boil. Reduce heat and simmer, covered, for 35 to 40 minutes. Cool the mixture slightly. Using the metal blade, purée in batches, adding a portion of cream and cheese to each batch. Season to taste. Reheat gently just before serving. Garnish with a swirl of cream and a few caraway seeds.

SERVES 8

Pea and Lemon Soup

1 carrot	salt and black pepper
1 onion, quartered	5 sprigs fresh mint
40 g/1½ oz butter	6 tablespoons dry sherry
225 g/8 oz frozen peas	15 g/1 oz plain flour
8 pea pods (if available)	GARNISH
1 lemon	50 g/2 oz cooked peas
1.15 litres/2 pints chicken stock	5 tablespoons single cream
1 tablespoon castor sugar	croûtons to serve

Using the metal blade, roughly chop the carrot and onion. In a large saucepan, heat the butter and sauté the chopped vegetables. Add the peas and fresh pea pods. Roughly cut the lemon into pieces and add to the peas. Lastly, add the stock, sugar and seasonings. Simmer for 30 minutes. Add the mint and sherry and cook for a further 10 minutes. Blend in batches until smooth. Mix the flour to a smooth paste with a little water, blend in with the final batch. Strain the soup, return to the saucepan and bring to the boil. When ready to serve, stir in the cooked peas and the cream. Serve with crispy croûtons.

SERVES 4 TO 6

This soup freezes for up to three months.
Note: Croûtons will keep for some time if kept warm in an open container lined with absorbent kitchen paper.

Instant Potato Soup

Make this soup in seconds and serve immediately or keep warm until required.

75 g/3 oz instant potato powder	1.15 litres/2 pints boiling chicken stock
1 carrot, cut into pieces	25 g/1 oz butter
1 stick celery with leaves, cut into pieces	5 tablespoons cream or dry white wine
2 leeks, white part only, sliced	salt and pepper to taste

With the metal blade in position, pour the instant potato powder into the processor bowl and add the carrot, celery and leeks. With the machine running, pour in the boiling stock and blend until smooth. Add the butter and continue to process until well combined. For a creamy soup, add the cream and process for 5 seconds. For a tangy soup, add the dry white wine and process for 5 seconds. Season to taste with salt and pepper.

SERVES 4

Pea and Lemon Soup

Fish and Seafood

Fish and seafoods are wonderfully versatile and suitable for all occasions, whether you are cooking for the family or entertaining on a grand scale. Besides the main course, fish makes tempting appetisers, delicious soups and flavourful salads. Furthermore, most fish dishes tend to be light, allowing you to add an appetiser and a luscious desert to the menu without making the meal too heavy.

Fish and seafood lend themselves to easy menu planning, as the delicate flavour blends well with most foods and the tender texture is complemented by crisp salads or vegetables. Not only is fish relatively easy to prepare, but it cooks quickly, thus making an ideal main course when time is short. However, be sure not to mask the delicate flavour nor destroy the texture through overcooking.

Your food processor will not only help you create new ways of serving fish and seafood but will help make traditional recipes easier to prepare. Use the processor to slice, shred and mince ingredients for sauces and stuffings. to blend fish pâtés or to make pastries for fish quiches.

Prawn Bisque

450 g/1 lb cooked
   Mediterranean prawns
   with shells on
1.15 litres/2 pints boiling
   water
generous pinch of salt
40 g/1½ oz margarine
1 onion, quartered
1 clove garlic
1 carrot, cut into chunks
2 tomatoes, quartered

6 tablespoons white wine
salt and black pepper
1 bay leaf
sprig of parsley
1 teaspoon paprika
½ teaspoon dried thyme
2 tablespoons sherry
15 g/½ oz toasted plain
   flour (see note)
croûtons to serve

Shell the prawns and place the heads and shells in boiling, salted water and cook gently for 10 minutes. Strain and reserve the liquid. Chop the prawns coarsely and set aside. Melt the margarine in a large saucepan. Using the metal blade, chop the onion and garlic and add to the pan. Chop the carrot and add to the pan. Leaving the skins on, chop the t matoes and add to the pan. Stir in the white wine and add salt and pepper, the bay leaf, parsley, paprika and thyme. Pour in half the prawn liquid and simmer slowly for at least 30 minutes. Process in batches and strain, using additional prawn liquid to help force as much as possible through the sieve.

Combine the sherry and toasted flour, add a little hot liquid to this mixture and return to the pan with all the strained liquid. Bring to the boil, stirring constantly. To serve, add the chopped prawns and plenty of small crispy croûtons.

SERVES 6 TO 8

Note. To toast flour, sprinkle a thin layer on a baking sheet and place in a moderate oven (160 c, 325 f, gas 3) until golden brown. Store in an airtight container and use to thicken soups, etc. Toasted flour gives foods a slightly nutty flavour.

Shrimp Quiche

1 (23-cm/9-in) unbaked
   shortcrust pastry shell
   (page 131)
FILLING
100 g/4 oz Cheddar cheese
4 eggs
300 ml/½ pint single cream
1 tablespoon chopped parsley

1 tablespoon fresh dill or
  1 teaspoon dried dill
1 tablespoon lemon juice
salt and pepper to taste
pinch of cayenne
pinch of grated nutmeg
450 g/1 lb peeled shrimps·or
  small prawns

Fit the shredding plate to the processor and shred the cheese. Mix all the remaining ingredients together, adding the shrimps and cheese. Spoon into the pastry shell and bake in a moderately hot oven (190 c, 375 f, gas 5) for about 30 minutes or until set.

SERVES 6

Smoked Salmon Quiche

Top each wedge with soured cream and a little red caviar for an elegant starter or main supper dish.

1 (23-cm/9-in) unbaked
   shortcrust pastry shell
   (page 131)
1 lightly beaten egg white
FILLING
225 g/8 oz smoked salmon
100 g/4 oz Gruyère cheese
5 eggs
300 ml/½ pint single cream

1 teaspoon dried dill or
  1 tablespoon chopped
  fresh dill
salt and pepper to taste
2 teaspoons lemon juice
red lumpfish caviar and
  soured cream to garnish

Brush the pastry shell with egg white and bake blind in a moderately hot oven (200 c, 400 f, gas 6) for 5 minutes. Set aside to cool. Using the metal blade and pulse button, finely flake the salmon and spread over the base of the pastry shell. Fit the shredding plate, shred the cheese and spread over the salmon. Replace the metal blade and process the eggs, cream, dill, salt, pepper and lemon juice until well mixed. Pour over the cheese. Bake in a moderately hot oven (200 c, 400 f, gas 6) for 10 minutes, then reduce the heat to moderate (180 c, 350 f, gas 4). Continue to bake for a further 30 minutes until the quiche has set and is golden brown. Serve with red caviar and soured cream.

SERVES 6 TO 8

Prawns Creole in a Rice Ring

1 large onion, quartered
1 clove garlic
4 sticks celery
2 tablespoons oil
100 g/4 oz mushrooms
675 g/1½ lb cooked tomatoes
salt and pepper to taste
2 bay leaves
sprig of thyme

dash of Tabasco sauce
1 kg/2 lb peeled prawns
RICE RING
225 g/8 oz uncooked rice
1.15 litres/2 pints water
salt to taste
100 g/4 oz butter, melted
parsley to garnish

Using the metal blade chop the onion and the garlic. Fit the slicing plate and slice the celery. In a large frying pan, heat the oil and sauté the onion, garlic and celery for 5 minutes. Slice the mushrooms in the processor and add to the pan along with the tomatoes. Season with salt and pepper. Lastly, add the bay leaves, thyme and Tabasco. Cover and simmer for about 40 minutes, stirring occasionally. Add the prawns and cook for a further 10 minutes stirring frequently.

Meanwhile, cook the rice in the boiling, salted water until tender and all the liquid has evaporated. Stir in the butter and pack firmly into a greased ring mould. Cover with foil and place in a moderate oven (160 c, 325 f, gas 3) for about 20 minutes. Unmould onto a heated serving platter. Fill the centre with the prawn mixture and garnish with parsley.

SERVES 8

Crab Soufflé

Crab Soufflé

40 g/1½ oz margarine	6 spring onions
1 slice white bread, cubed	15 g/½ oz plain flour
300 ml/½ pint milk	4 tablespoons single cream
1 small carrot	4 eggs, separated
1 slice onion	1 (169-g/6-oz) can crab meat
2 cloves	salt and black pepper
6 peppercorns	cayenne to taste
1 bay leaf	½ teaspoon paprika
blade of mace	2 tablespoons sherry
25 g/1 oz Parmesan cheese	2 extra egg whites

Use part of the measured margarine to grease a soufflé dish. Fit the metal blade to the processor and pulse to process the bread until finely crumbled. Line the soufflé dish with breadcrumbs. Pour the milk into a small saucepan and add the carrot, onion spiked with cloves, peppercorns, bay leaf and mace. Heat, then allow to stand for 20 minutes to draw out the flavour before straining. Using the shredding plate, shred the Parmesan cheese and set aside. Chop the spring onions and sauté in heated margarine. Add the flour, cook for 2 minutes then stir in the milk infusion. Bring to the boil, stirring constantly, and cook for about 3 minutes. Remove from the heat and add the cream, egg yolks, cheese, crab seasonings and sherry. Cool. With a whisk or electric mixer, whisk the 6 egg whites until stiff. Carefully fold into the prepared soufflé dish. Bake in a hot oven (220c, 425f, gas 7) for 12 to 15 minutes and serve immediately.

SERVES 4

Hake en Papillote

800 g/1¾ lb hake or 4 portions	225 g/8 oz mushrooms
300 ml/½ pint white wine	40 g/1½ oz butter
salt and black pepper	25 g/1 oz plain flour
1 tablespoon lemon juice	7 tablespoons single cream
1 medium onion, quartered	cayenne to taste
2 teaspoons fresh dill or 1 teaspoon dried dill	watercress or parsley to garnish

Place the hake in a saucepan and add the white wine, seasonings and lemon juice. Cover and poach until almost cooked, about 5 to 7 minutes depending on the thickness. Drain the fish and set aside.

Using the metal blade, finely chop the onion and dill. Fit the slicing plate and slice the mushrooms. In a saucepan, melt the butter and sauté the onion and dill. Add the mushrooms and sauté for a few minutes more. Sprinkle with flour and add all the poaching liquid. Boil rapidly until reduced to approximately half. Now add half the cream and continue to boil until well reduced. Add the remaining cream and reduce a little more, stirring constantly. Lastly season with cayenne.

Cut four sheets of non-stick baking parchment into large heart shapes and fold down the centre line. Brush with melted butter. Place a portion of fish on one side of each heart. Spoon a quarter of the sauce over each portion. Fold the paper over the fish and seal the edges by folding over and over, starting at the curve and working towards the point. Place the papillotes on a well-greased baking tray, brush with melted butter and bake for 15 minutes. Serve at once garnished with watercress or parsley.

This dish may be prepared some hours in advance. Refrigerate until required, then complete the cooking.

SERVES 4

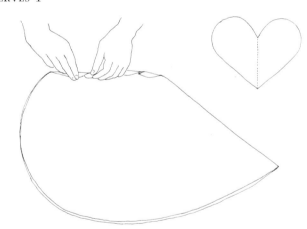

1. Cut 4 heart shapes out of Bakewell paper. Fill and seal as directed above.

2. The completed papillote ready for baking.

Haddock Roulade

25 g/1 oz Cheddar cheese
225 g/8 oz cooked haddock
3 eggs, separated
salt and black pepper
paprika and parsley to garnish
FILLING
25 g/1 oz margarine

25 g/1 oz plain flour
300 ml/½ pint milk
salt and black pepper
1 bunch fresh spinach
paprika and parsley to
   decorate

Fit the shredding plate to the processor and shred the cheese. Place in a large bowl, reserving some for garnishing. Using the metal blade and the pulse button, flake the haddock and add to the cheese, along with the egg yolks and seasonings.

For the filling, melt the margarine and add the flour. Cook for a minute, then stir in the milk. Continue to cook, stirring all the time, to make a thick white sauce. Season to taste. Add 3 tablespoons of the white sauce to the fish mixture. Now wash the spinach and cook until tender. Drain well, then finely chop in the processor. Add the spinach to the white sauce, cover and set aside.

Using a whisk or food mixer, beat the egg whites until stiff. Fold into the fish mixture, then turn into a Swiss roll tin lined with non-stick baking parchment paper. Spread evenly and bake in a moderately hot oven (220 c, 400 f, gas 6) for 10 to 15 minutes. Take another piece of non-stick baking parchment and sprinkle with the reserved cheese. Turn the cooked fish onto the cheese and peel away the top paper. Spread with hot spinach filling, trim the edges and roll up like a Swiss roll. Decorate with paprika and parsley.

SERVES 4

Savoury Salmon Puffs

2 (225-g/8-oz) cans salmon
1 large onion, quartered
15 g/½ oz butter
1 (298-g/10½-oz) can
   condensed cream of
   mushroom soup
1 teaspoon salt

pepper to taste
½ teaspoon paprika
30 stuffed olives
225 g/8 oz Cheddar cheese
a little cream
16 choux pastry puffs
   (page 135)

Drain and flake the salmon. Using the metal blade, finely chop the onion for about 8 seconds. Sauté in melted butter until soft, then stir in the soup and seasonings. Coarsely chop the olives in the processor. Fit the shredding plate and shred the cheese. Now add the chopped olives and shredded cheese to the onion mixture, stir in the salmon and heat through. This filling can be made ahead of time and refrigerated overnight. If the mixture is too thick, thin with a little cream. To serve, spoon the mixture into the choux puffs (or hollowed-out dinner rolls) and place in a moderately hot oven (200 c, 400 f, gas 6) for about 10 to 12 minutes, or until heated through.

SERVES 8 for a light lunch or Sunday supper or SERVES 16 as an appetiser.

Haddock Roulade served with Tomatoes Mimosa (page 30)

Seafood Supreme

A quick and easy dish, ideal for a buffet or large supper party.

1 green pepper, deseeded and quartered	250 ml/8 fl oz mayonnaise (page 95)
1 small onion, quartered	½ teaspoon Worcestershire sauce
3 sticks celery	
450 g/1 lb crab meat, cut into bite-sized pieces	225 g/8 oz crushed potato crisps
450 g/1 lb peeled prawns	paprika

Using the metal blade, chop the green pepper and onion. Place in a large bowl. Fit the slicing plate and slice the celery. Add to the onion, together with the crab, prawns, mayonnaise and Worcestershire sauce. Toss to mix well and turn into a buttered baking dish or casserole. At this point the dish can be refrigerated for several hours. To bake, cover with crushed potato crisps and sprinkle with paprika. Bake in a moderately hot oven (200 c, 400 f, gas 6) for about 25 minutes. Serve as an appetiser or with rice and a tossed green salad for a complete supper.

SERVES 10 as an appetiser or SERVES 6 as a main dish

Crispy Seafood Pie

1 quantity Soured Cream Pastry (page 135)	50 g/2 oz Cheddar cheese
1 beaten egg to glaze	1 hard-boiled egg
FILLING	1 (169-g/6-oz) can crab meat
450 g/1 lb fish (monkfish, hake, and peeled prawns combined), cut into pieces	1 tablespoon chopped chives
	25 g/1 oz margarine
few black peppercorns	25 g/1 oz flour
1 clove garlic	150 ml/¼ pint milk
squeeze of lemon juice	3 tablespoons soured cream
1 onion, quartered	salt and black pepper
3 tablespoons chopped parsley	pinch of cayenne
	½ teaspoon mustard powder
	1 tablespoon grated Parmesan cheese

Make the pastry and chill for at least one hour before using. To make the filling, place the fish in a saucepan with a little water and add the peppercorns, clove of garlic and a squeeze of lemon juice. Cook for a few minutes until just tender. Drain, cut into bite-sized pieces and place in a large bowl. Using the metal blade, finely chop the onion and parsley and set aside. Fit the shredding plate and shred the Cheddar cheese, followed by the hard-boiled egg. Add to the fish, together with the crab meat and chives. In a saucepan, melt the margarine and sauté the onion and parsley. Add the flour, cook for a minute, then stir in the milk. Cook, stirring, until thick and bubbling. Remove from the heat and add the soured cream and seasonings. Add to the fish. Mix well, adjust seasoning if necessary and cool.

Divide the pastry in half, roll both pieces into 28 × 18-cm/11 × 7-in rectangles. Place one of the rectangles on a greased baking sheet and pile the cooled filling on top, leaving 1 cm/½ in of pastry free around the edge. Sprinkle with Parmesan cheese. Brush the edge of the pastry with water. With a rolling pin, lift the second layer of pastry and place on top of the filling. Using a fork, seal the edges. Re-roll the remaining scraps of pastry and cut decorations for the top.

Finally, glaze with beaten egg and bake in a moderately hot oven (190 c, 375 f, gas 5) for 45 minutes. Serve either hot or cold.

SERVES 6 TO 8

Crab and Artichoke Casserole

1 (369-g/14-oz) can artichoke hearts	SAUCE
	15 g/½ oz butter
350 g/12 oz fresh, cooked or canned crab meat	15 g/½ oz plain flour
	300 ml/½ pint single cream
100 g/4 oz mushrooms	4 tablespoons milk
25 g/1 oz butter	salt and pepper to taste
Worcestershire sauce	4 tablespoons dry sherry
50 g/2 oz Parmesan cheese	

Drain the artichoke hearts and arrange in a greased casserole. Using the metal blade, coarsely chop the crab meat and sprinkle over the artichokes. Fit the slicing plate and slice the mushrooms. Sauté in butter for 5 minutes then add Worcestershire sauce to taste. Arrange the mushrooms over the crab meat. Replace the metal blade and finely chop the Parmesan cheese. Set aside.

For the sauce, melt the butter and stir in the flour. Cook, stirring, for 1 minute. Slowly stir in the cream and milk. Season with salt and pepper and cook, stirring, until thick and bubbling. Add the sherry, then pour the sauce over the mushrooms. Sprinkle with Parmesan cheese and bake in a moderately hot oven (190 c, 375 f, gas 5) for 20 minutes.

SERVES 4

Tuna Mediterranean

A flavourful oven-to-table dish.

2 (198-g/7-oz) cans tuna	½ small onion, cut up
50 g/2 oz black olives, stoned	50 g/2 oz mushrooms
	100 g/4 oz Cheddar cheese
½ small green pepper, deseeded	250 ml/8 fl oz soured cream
	½ teaspoon oregano
100 g/4 oz cashew nuts	150 g/5 oz macaroni, cooked

Drain the tuna, flake and set aside. Using the metal blade, coarsely chop the olives. Transfer to a large mixing bowl. Chop the green pepper and add to the olives. Coarsely chop the cashew nuts, then the onion and finally, the mushrooms. Add to the olives. Fit the shredding plate, shred the cheese and set aside. Add the soured cream, oregano and tuna to the chopped vegetable. Toss to mix well. Stir in the cooked macaroni and turn into a greased 1.5-litres/2¾-pints baking dish or casserole. Sprinkle the shredded cheese on top and bake in a moderate oven (180 c, 350 f, gas 4) for about 25 minutes.

SERVES 4 TO 6

Salmon Steaks with Capers

A succulent dish with capers, lemon and wine. Try this with swordfish steaks too, if obtainable.

1 small onion, quartered	3 tablespoons capers, drained
1 carrot, cut into pieces	salt and pepper to taste
1 small fennel bulb, quartered	4 salmon steaks, cut about 2.5 cm/1 in thick
1 lemon, peeled, deseeded and cut into quarters	1 large lemon, cut in half lengthwise
100 g/4 oz butter or margarine	250 ml/8 fl oz dry white wine parsley to garnish

Using the metal blade, chop the onion and set aside. Chop the carrot, fennel and lemon. Melt half the butter in a frying pan, add the onion and cook until soft. Add the carrot, fennel and the lemon. Cook, stirring, for about 12–15 minutes. Add the capers and cook for 2 minutes more. Season to taste with salt and pepper, then spread evenly over the base of an ovenproof dish or casserole.

Wipe the fish dry and place in a single layer over the vegetables. Trim away the ends of the lemon halves, pack in the feed tube and use the slicing plate to slice neatly. Arrange the lemon slices over the fish and dot with the remaining butter. Pour in the wine, cover tightly and bake in a moderate oven (180c, 350F, gas 4) for about 20 minutes. Uncover and bake for a further 10 to 12 minutes. Garnish with parsley and serve.

SERVES 4

Salmon Steaks with Capers

Fish Lasagne

2 onions, quartered	salt and black pepper
2 cloves garlic	200 ml/7 fl oz parsley, stems removed
3 tablespoons oil	
450 g/1 lb white fish (e.g. cod or haddock)	450 ml/$\frac{3}{4}$ pint béchamel sauce (page 101)
1 (397-g/14-oz) can tomatoes	50 g/2 oz Cheddar cheese
4 tablespoons concentrated tomato purée	1 teaspoon mustard powder
	cayenne to taste
$\frac{1}{2}$ teaspoon oregano	225 g/8 oz lasagne
2 bay leaves	

Using the metal blade, chop the onions and garlic. Sauté in heated oil until tender. Cut the fish into bite-sized pieces and process in batches until finely minced. Add to the onions. Chop the tomatoes in the processor and add to the fish. Add the tomato purée, oregano, bay leaves and seasonings. Simmer for 30 minutes. Lastly, chop the parsley in the processor and add to the fish.

Meanwhile, fit the shredding plate, shred the cheese and add half to the béchamel sauce. Add the mustard and cayenne and set aside. Cook the lasagne in plenty of boiling, salted water until tender. Drain and rinse under cold water.

To assemble the dish, place a layer of lasagne in a greased ovenproof dish. Cover with a layer of fish, then a layer of béchamel sauce. Repeat these layers, making sure that the top layer has plenty of sauce. Sprinkle with the remaining cheese and bake in a moderate oven (160c, 325F, gas 3) for about 25 to 30 minutes until heated through and bubbling. Quickly brown under the grill and serve.

SERVES 6

This dish freezes well. Freeze, covered, before baking in the oven. Thaw before heating.

Hake with Fennel and Pernod

675 g/1$\frac{1}{2}$ lb hake, or any other firm white fish such as haddock	1 clove garlic
	25 g/1 oz butter
	squeeze of lemon juice
1 large fennel bulb	salt and black pepper
2 tablespoons parsley, stems removed	2 tablespoons Pernod
8 chives, cut into 1 cm/$\frac{1}{2}$ in lengths	

Place the fish on a large piece of heavy aluminium foil, dull side upwards. Fit the slicing plate to the processor and slice the fennel. Change to the metal blade and chop the parsley, chives and garlic. Add the butter, lemon juice and seasonings and pulse a few times. Arrange the fennel on top of the fish and dot with the butter mixture. Close the foil and bake the fish in a moderate oven (180c, 350F, gas 4) until cooked and the fish flakes easily. Cooking time will depend on the size and thickness of the pieces of fish. Unwrap and flambé with the Pernod. Serve immediately.

This dish may be prepared in advance up to the cooking stage. Refrigerate until required.

SERVES 3

Herbed Langoustines

A little extravagant, but these grilled langoustines, basted with a heavenly herb sauce, will make a truly memorable meal.

1 kg/2 lb langoustines or small lobsters	225 g/8 oz butter
3 sprigs parsley, stems removed	6 tablespoons oil
2 cloves garlic	2 tablespoons olive oil
2 teaspoons fresh thyme, stems removed	2 teaspoons paprika
2 teaspoons fresh tarragon, stems removed	salt and black pepper
	pinch of cayenne
	½ teaspoon mustard powder
	1 teaspoon Worcestershire sauce

Take a whole langoustine and place it on its back, stretching out the tail. Now, with a pair of pointed scissors snip away the entire membranous undershell, leaving the head section intact. Make a 5-mm/¼-in cut down the centre of the exposed flesh to allow the sauce to soak in. Turn the langoustine over and using the scissors, cut along the centre of the back up to the head. Using the tips of the scissors lift out the 'vein' or alimentary canal that lies immediately below.

Fit the metal blade to the processor. With the machine running, add the parsley, garlic and herbs. After a few seconds, add the butter and process until well combined, scraping down the sides with a spatula when necessary. Add all the remaining ingredients, except the langoustines, and process for a few seconds. Turn into a saucepan and warm the mixture over a low heat. Brush the sauce over the flesh of the langoustines, cover them and allow to stand for at least 2 hours. Brush once more, then place, flesh side uppermost, under a preheated grill and grill until just cooked. If the langoustines are particularly large it may be necessary to turn them over. Baste occasionally with the sauce during cooking. Serve with rice, a mixed salad and the remaining sauce.

SERVES 2 TO 3

Sole Bombay

4 soles, cleaned	15 g/½ oz plain flour
a little lemon juice	200 ml/7 fl oz chicken stock
salt and black pepper	2 teaspoons desiccated coconut
plain flour to coat	
about 100 g/4 oz butter	salt and pepper
SAUCE	3 tablespoons single cream
1 onion, quartered	GARNISH
1 apple, peeled, cored and quartered	1 green pepper, deseeded
	4 bananas
15 g/½ oz butter	25 g/1 oz butter
½–1 teaspoon curry powder	paprika

First make the sauce. Fit the metal blade to the processor and finely chop the onion and apple. In a heavy-based pan, heat the butter and carefully sauté the onion and apple, do not allow to brown. Add the curry powder and simmer gently for 5 minutes. Sprinkle in the flour, then add the chicken stock, coconut and seasonings. Bring to the boil, stirring well. Cover and simmer until the vegetables are soft and the sauce is of a pouring consistency. Return the sauce to the processor and pulse until smooth. Strain before adding the cream. The sauce may be made in advance; reheat to use, but do not boil.

Season the soles with lemon juice, salt and black pepper. Coat lightly with flour. Heat the butter until foaming, add the soles and fry until golden brown on both sides. Remove from the heat, drain and place on a warm serving platter. Mask with sauce.

Meanwhile, prepare the garnish. Fit the slicing plate to the processor, cut the green pepper in half lengthwise and place in the feed tube. Slice thinly. Blanch in boiling water for 4 minutes, drain and refresh in cold water. Peel the bananas and slice, using the slicing plate. Heat the butter and sauté the bananas for about 3 minutes. Add the green pepper and heat through. Arrange on top of the fish and sprinkle with paprika.

SERVES 4

Poultry

From the cook's point of view, poultry is often a good choice when entertaining. Not only is it less expensive than meat, but it is easy to prepare and extremely versatile. Soups, casseroles, curries and pies are just a few appetising dishes that make the best use of chicken, turkey or duck. Most kinds of poultry can be roasted to succulent brown perfection, while chicken and duck can also be fried to a tender, golden crispness. Use your food processor to pamper poultry by creating an unusual sauce, coating, stuffing or topping. The following recipes give a fresh, new approach to preparing these all-time favourite dishes, proving that ideas for serving poultry are almost endless.

Chicken à l'Orange

1 large chicken
salt and black pepper
1 teaspoon paprika
1 teaspoon mustard powder
50 g/2 oz plain flour
3 tablespoons oil
2 onions
1 large green pepper, halved
  and deseeded
225 g/8 oz mushrooms

3 sticks celery
1 tablespoon brown sugar
300 ml/½ pint chicken stock
1 tablespoon soy sauce
juice of 2 oranges
3 tablespoons dry sherry
GARNISH
slices of orange
parsley

Wipe and joint the chicken. Combine the seasonings with the flour and use to coat the chicken pieces. Heat the oil and brown the joints well. Remove from the pan and set aside. Fit the slicing plate to the processor and slice the onions, green pepper, mushrooms and celery. Add to the pan and sauté. Stir in any remaining flour and add the brown sugar and liquids. Bring to the boil before adding the chicken. Cover the pan and either simmer very slowly or place in a cool oven (150c, 300F, gas 2) for 1 hour. Garnish with slices of orange and parsley.

SERVES 6
This dish freezes well.

Chicken à l'Orange and Broccoli and White Wine Soup (page 35)

Cheesy Chicken Lasagne

150 g/5 oz lasagne
1 large onion, quartered
1 green pepper, deseeded
1 tablespoon oil
2 rashers bacon
1 (397-g/14-oz) can tomatoes
2 tablespoons concentrated
    tomato purée
½ teaspoon oregano
salt and black pepper

½ cooked chicken, diced
1 egg
225 g/8 oz cream cheese
4 tablespoons single cream
25 g/1 oz Parmesan cheese,
    shredded
2 tablespoons chopped parsley
100 g/4 oz mozzarella
    cheese, well chilled

Cook the noodles in plenty of boiling, salted water until tender. Drain and rinse in cold water. Using the metal blade, chop the onion and green pepper. Sauté in a little heated oil. Chop the bacon in the processor, add to the pan and cook for 5 minutes. Add the tomatoes, tomato purée, herbs and seasonings. Simmer for 10 minutes, then add the chicken. In a separate bowl, combine the egg, cream cheese, cream, Parmesan cheese and parsley. Fit the slicing plate and slice the mozzarella cheese thinly. Place half the lasagne in a greased ovenproof dish. Cover with half the chicken, then half the cheese mixture. Add a few slices of mozzarella. Repeat these layers, covering the top well with mozzarella. Bake, covered in a moderate oven (180 c, 350 f, gas 4) for 35 to 40 minutes. Allow to stand for 10 minutes before serving.

SERVES 4

This dish freezes well for up to two months. Freeze before baking.

Chicken Cacciatore

1 chicken, jointed
plain flour to coat
salt and black pepper
3 tablespoons oil
2 onions, quartered
2–3 cloves garlic
3 tablespoons concentrated
    tomato purée

150 ml/¼ pint white wine
150 ml/¼ pint chicken stock
½ teaspoon oregano
1 bay leaf
2 tablespoons brandy
50 g/2 oz Cheddar cheese
15 g/½ oz Parmesan cheese
350 g/12 oz spaghetti

Toss the chicken joints in well-seasoned flour. In a large, heavy bottomed sauté pan, heat the oil and brown the joints well. Set aside to drain. Fit the metal blade to the processor and finely chop the onions and garlic. Sauté in heated oil until the onions are transparent. Add all the ingredients except the brandy, cheeses and spaghetti. Simmer, covered, for at least 1 hour, stirring from time to time. When cooked, stir in the brandy and remove the bay leaf. Fit the shredding plate to the processor and shred the Cheddar cheese and Parmesan cheese. Cook the spaghetti in plenty of rapidly boiling, salted water until tender. Drain and rinse in cold water. Reheat with a knob of butter. Serve the chicken with the spaghetti and sprinkle the cheese on top.

SERVES 4 TO 6

Chicken Valencia

8 chicken thighs
40 g/1½ oz plain flour
1 teaspoon paprika
salt and black pepper
2 tablespoons oil
1 small onion, quartered
1 clove garlic
6 tablespoons white wine
300 ml/½ pint chicken stock
1 cm/½ in stick cinnamon
STUFFING
100 g/4 oz raisins

2 tablespoons sherry
40 g/1½ oz ham
1 slice bread, cubed
rind of 1 lemon
1 tablespoon parsley, stems
    removed
2 tablespoons melted
    margarine
1 teaspoon tarragon
GARNISH
8 slices of orange
parsley

First make the stuffing. Soak the raisins in sherry for half an hour. Fit the metal blade to the processor, add the ham, bread, lemon rind and parsley and pulse until fine. Remove from the bowl and add the margarine, tarragon and a third of the raisins. Mix well.

Make a slit in one side of each chicken thigh, push in a little stuffing and secure with a cocktail stick. Toss the joints in the flour, paprika and seasonings. Heat the oil in a frying pan, brown the chicken on all sides, then drain. Place in an ovenproof casserole. Using the metal blade, finely chop the onion and garlic and sauté in the oil. Stir in any remaining flour. Add the wine, stock and cinnamon stick and bring to the boil. Pour the mixture over the stuffed chicken thighs. Cover and bake in a moderate oven (160 c, 325 f, gas 3) for 1 to 1½ hours. Remove the cinnamon stick and add the remaining raisins. Garnish with slices of orange and parsley.

SERVES 4 TO 6

This dish freezes well.

Chicken Cacciatore

46

Coated Chicken Galantine (page 50)

Chicken Galantine

A variation of boned chicken, filled with a surprise stuffing and served cold.

1 boned chicken (page 49)	5 slices salami
salt and black pepper	stuffed olives
STUFFING	STOCK
1 small onion, quartered	1 onion
a little oil	1 carrot
2 tablespoons parsley, stems removed	sprig of parsley
	stick of celery
350 g/12 oz sausage meat	salt
100 g/4 oz ham	a few black peppercorns
1 pickled walnut (optional)	bouquet garni
salt and black pepper	

Lay the boned chicken flat and season. Now make the stuffing. Using the metal blade and pulse button, finely chop the onion and sauté in a little oil. Chop the parsley and add the onion, sausage meat, ham and pickled walnut to the work bowl. Process until smooth, then season well. Pile half the stuffing along the centre of the chicken. Wrap the salami around the stuffed olives and lay in a row down the centre. Cover with the remaining stuffing. Roll up the chicken and sew together with thick spread. Now roll in a length of cloth and tie each end to hold its shape.

To make the stock, select a large saucepan, add the chicken carcase and sufficient boiling water to cover the chicken roll. Fit the slicing plate to the processor and slice the onion and carrot. Add to the saucepan, together with the parsley, celery, salt, bouquet garni and peppercorns. Bring to the boil, add the chicken roll and simmer for 2 hours. Remove the chicken roll from the stock and allow to cool in the cloth. Unroll from the cloth, neaten the shape slightly and remove the thread. Serve thinly sliced.

MAKES 18 TO 20 SLICES

Boned, Stuffed Chicken

Boned, stuffed chicken are very versatile and can be served either hot or cold. They look especially glamorous on a cold buffet table as each slice takes the same size and shape. When serving cold, cook the chickens the day before they are required. Being stuffed, there is no need to fear that the meat might dry out. If you are entertaining a large number of people and do not want to make last-minute preparations, bone and stuff fresh chickens a week or more in advance, then freeze. All that remains for you to do the day before your party is to thaw and cook the chickens.

1 large chicken
salt and black pepper
25 g/1 oz plain flour
1 roasting bag
1 tablespoon oil
STUFFING
3 slices bread, cubed
1 onion, quartered
2 tablespoons parsley, stems
   removed

4 mushrooms
2 tablespoons oil
1 chicken liver (from the
   boned chicken)
2 sausages, casings removed
½ teaspoon dried rosemary
1 egg
salt and black pepper

To debone the chicken, turn the bird breast downwards. Using a small, sharp knife, split the skin along the backbone from the neck to the tail. Starting at the tail gradually work the meat away from the bone. Using a cleaver, chop the ends off the drumsticks and the wing bones. Work the flesh off the thigh bone and continue over onto the drumstick. Be sure to cut the sinews at this point. Now pull the drumstick bone through the flesh, which will be turned inside out. Continue along the wing joint, cutting the flesh close to the bone, then ease off the wing. Work carefully down towards the breast. Stop cutting once you have reached the top of the breastbone. Repeat the boning process for the other side of the bird. This time, when you reach the breastbone, the bony carcass will fall away from the flesh.

To make the stuffing, crumb the bread in the processor and set aside. Finely chop the onion, parsley and mushrooms, then sauté in heated oil. Roughly chop the liver, add to the onion in the pan and sauté. Combine the onion and liver mixture with the breadcrumbs and the remaining stuffing ingredients. Mix well.

Lay the boned chicken flat on a board and season. Place the stuffing down the centre, wrap the flesh around and use the flaps of skin to neaten off the ends. Sew together with thick thread. Season and rub with flour. Place in a roasting bag, pour the oil over the chicken and seal loosely so that the steam can escape. Cook in a moderate oven (180 c, 350 f, gas 4) for 1 to 1½ hours. Remove the thread and serve hot or cold, cut into slices. If serving cold, open the bag and allow the chicken to cool in the bag before slicing. Accompany hot chicken with a mushroom sauce (see page 100) or hollandaise (see page 99).

SERVES 6 (12 TO 14 SLICES)

Fresh chickens may be boned, stuffed and frozen for up to one month. Thaw before cooking.

Sherried Chicken

A quick and easy dish, yet worthy of the best company.

1 chicken, about 1 kg/2 lb
   cut into serving portions
1 onion, quartered
225 g/8 oz mushrooms
1 (425-g/15-oz) can cream of
   mushroom soup

300 ml/½ pint soured cream
½ teaspoon dried tarragon
2 teaspoons lemon juice
4 tablespoons lemon juice
4 tablespoons dry sherry
salt and pepper to taste

Place the chicken pieces in a greased, shallow casserole. Using the metal blade, chop the onions and sprinkle over the chicken. Fit the slicing plate, slice the mushrooms and arrange on top of the onions. Replace the metal blade and process the soup, soured cream, tarragon, lemon juice, sherry and salt and pepper until well mixed. Pour over the chicken and bake, covered in a moderately hot oven (190 c, 375 f, gas 5) for 50 minutes.

SERVES 4 TO 6

Chicken à la Klinzman

A deliciously different chicken dish suitable for a large number of guests.

2 cooked chickens
2 sprigs parsley, stems
   removed
1 large onion, quartered
1 large green pepper, halved
   and deseeded
3 sticks celery
225 g/8 oz mushrooms
1 (269-g/9½-oz) can water
   chestnuts drained
100 g/4 oz fresh bean sprouts
100 g/4 oz butter
1 (425-g/15-oz) can cream of
   asparagus soup

4 eggs, slightly beaten
300 ml/½ pint velouté sauce
   (page 99)
4 tablespoons sherry
300 ml/½ pint soured cream
1 teaspoon dried tarragon
1 teaspoon freshly grated
   root ginger
salt and pepper to taste
225 g/8 oz crushed potato
   crisps

Remove the skin from the chicken, dice the flesh and set aside. Using the metal blade, chop the parsley and set aside. Chop the onion and add to the parsley. Fit the slicing plate and slice the green pepper, celery, mushrooms and water chestnuts. In a frying pan, heat the butter and sauté the onion and parsley until the onion is soft and transparent. Transfer to a large bowl. Sauté the sliced vegetables and bean sprouts in batches, adding more butter if required. Add to the onions. Now add the soup, eggs, velouté sauce and diced chicken to the vegetables and mix well. Stir in the sherry, soured cream, tarragon and grated ginger. Season well with salt and pepper.

Turn the chicken mixture into two large casseroles and top with crushed potato crisps. Bake in a moderately hot oven (190 c, 375 f, gas 5) for 35 to 40 minutes. Serve with yellow rice and a crisp salad.

SERVES 12

Coated Chicken Galantine

For that really special occasion, try this delicious stuffed chicken roll coated in tangy mayonnaise and attractively decorated.

1 boned chicken (page 49)	sprig of parsley
salt and black pepper	bouquet garni
STUFFING	a few black peppercorns
1 small onion, quartered	salt
2 tablespoons parsley,	COATING
stalks removed	7 tablespoons mayonnaise
2 sticks celery	(page 95)
a little oil	7 tablespoons chicken stock
1 slice bread, cubed	1 tablespoon powdered
350 g/12 oz sausage meat	gelatine
salt and pepper	3 tablespoons hot water
½ teaspoon dried mixed herbs	DECORATION
150 g/5 oz chicken livers	cucumber skin or lengths of
3 hard-boiled eggs	spring onion
STOCK	tomato skin
1 onion	sliced mushrooms
1 carrot	sliced carrot

Lay the boned chicken flat and season well. To make the stuffing, use the metal blade to finely chop the onion, parsley and celery. Sauté in a little oil. Finely crumb the slice of bread in the processor. Add the sautéed vegetables, sausage meat, seasonings and herbs to the work bowl and process to mix. Sauté the chicken livers. Lay half the stuffing down the chicken. Place a row of chicken livers down the centre, then a row of hard-boiled eggs. Pile on the remaining stuffing. Roll up and sew. Now roll the chicken in a length of cloth and tie each end so that it holds its shape.

To make the stock, fit the slicing plate and slice the onion and carrot. Select a large saucepan, add the chicken carcase, sliced vegetables, bouquet garni, peppercorns and salt. Finally, add the chicken roll and cover with boiling water. Simmer for 2 hours. Remove the chicken roll from the stock, cool in the cloth, then place on a wire rack.

To make the coating, thin the mayonnaise using half the measured chicken stock. Dissolve the gelatine in the hot water then, combine the gelatine with the remaining stock. Add to the mayonnaise and stir until it begins to thicken. Use this mixture to evenly coat the chicken. A better more even result is achieved by coating the chicken two or three times with a thin layer of mayonnaise rather than coating it once with a thick layer. If the mayonnaise thickens too quickly, stand it over hot water for a few seconds. Cut decorative motifs from the vegetables slices and arrange over the chicken before coating has set firmly. Chill in the refrigerator. To serve, thinly slice half the chicken and arrange the slices, together with the remaining portion of roll, on a bed of lettuce.

MAKES 18 TO 20 SLICES

Chicken with Spinach and Cheese

1.5 kg/3 lb chicken, boned	100 g/4 oz butter, softened
(page 49)	1 egg
2 teaspoons lemon juice	¼ teaspoon freshly grated
2 teaspoons dry sherry	nutmeg
450 g/1 lb fresh spinach	salt and pepper to taste
leaves, washed and stems	½ teaspoon paprika
removed	1 teaspoon oregano
100 g/4 oz Cheddar cheese	pinch of dried sage
50 g/2 oz Parmesan cheese,	pinch of dried thyme
cut into cubes	parsley to garnish
100 g/4 oz ricotta cheese,	
broken into chunks	

Place the boned chicken, skin side down, on a cutting board. Rub the inner surface with lemon juice and dry sherry. Allow to stand for 10 minutes before stuffing.

Cook the spinach with only the water that clings to the leaves until the leaves wilt. Cool then press out the excess moisture. Fit the shredding plate to the processor and shred the Cheddar cheese. Set aside. Using the metal blade, finely chop the Parmesan cheese and add to the Cheddar cheese. Now coarsely chop the spinach and add all the cheeses, the butter, egg, nutmeg, salt and pepper to the work bowl. Process until well mixed. Spread this mixture over the chicken to within 2.5 cm/1 in of the edges. Starting with one side, roll the chicken up and securely tie into shape with string. Combine the paprika, oregano, sage and thyme and sprinkle over the chicken. Place in a well-oiled roasting tin and bake in a moderate oven (180 c, 350 f, gas 4) for 1 to 1½ hours, basting frequently with the juices. Remove the string and allow to stand for several minutes before slicing.

SERVES 6

Walnut Chicken

8 boneless chicken breasts	3 slices bread, torn into
1.4 litres/2½ pints chicken	pieces
stock	½ teaspoon paprika
2 carrots, cut into pieces	salt and pepper to taste
2 onions, quartered	½ teaspoon dried sage
4 sprigs parsley	½ teaspoon dried thyme
2 sprigs thyme	1 tablespoon dry sherry
SAUCE	extra walnut halves and
75 g/3 oz walnuts	parsley sprigs to garnish
½ small onion	

Cut each chicken breast lengthwise into six strips and trim away the skin. Place the chicken, stock, carrots, onions, parsley and thyme in a large saucepan and bring to the boil over a medium heat. Reduce the heat and simmer for 12 to 15 minutes until the chicken is tender. Cool in the stock, then transfer the chicken to a serving platter and chill. Skim the fat off the cold stock and strain. Discard the vegetables. Now heat the stock and boil vigorously until reduced to about 450 ml/¾ pint.

To make the sauce, fit the metal blade to the processor and place the walnuts, onion, bread and reduced stock in the work bowl. Process until the mixture is smooth. Add the paprika, salt, pepper, sage, thyme and sherry. Process for 4 to 5 seconds to combine well, then set aside to cool. Spoon this sauce over the chilled chicken and garnish with walnut halves and parsley.

SERVES 8 TO 10

Hot Chicken Salad

450 g/1 lb cooked chicken, skin removed
6 sticks celery
1 (269-g/9½-oz) can water chestnuts, drained
½ small onion, cut into pieces
100 g/4 oz flaked almonds
1 (425-g/15-oz) can cream of chicken soup
300 ml/½ pint mayonnaise (page 95)
salt and pepper to taste
2 teaspoons lemon juice
1 small packet potato crisps, crushed

Cut the chicken into bite-sized pieces and set aside in a mixing bowl. Use the slicing plate to slice the celery, then the water chestnuts and add both to the chicken. Fit the metal blade and finely chop the onion. Add to the chicken, along with the almonds, chicken soup and mayonnaise. Combine well and season with salt, pepper and lemon juice. Turn the mixture into a greased casserole and top with crushed potato crisps. Bake uncovered, in a moderate oven (180 c, 350 f, gas 4) for 15 to 20 minutes, or until nicely browned.

SERVES 8

Moulded Chicken Salad

2 tablespoons powdered gelatine
3 tablespoons hot water
900 ml/1½ pints chicken stock
2 tablespoons dill pickle liquid
1 tablespoon lemon juice
350 g/12 oz cooked chicken, cut into pieces
2 slices white bread, cubed
2 sticks celery
1 large dill pickle
6 spring onions, cut into small pieces
2 sprigs parsley, stems removed
6–8 stuffed olives
1 tablespoon fresh dill or 1 teaspoon dried dill
½ teaspoon dried tarragon
½ teaspoon oregano
pepper to taste
lettuce and parsley to garnish

Dissolve the gelatine in the hot water over a basin of boiling water then add 150 ml/¼ pint chicken stock and the dill pickle liquid. Bring the remaining chicken stock to the boil and add to the gelatine mixture. Add the lemon juice and chill until thickened, but not completely set.

Using the metal blade, finely chop the chicken and set aside. Crumb the bread and add to the chicken. Now chop the celery, dill pickle, spring onion, parsley, olives, herbs and pepper. Combine with the chicken, then stir the mixture into the jellied stock. Turn into 1.4-litres/2½-pints mould and chill until set (3 to 4 hours). Unmould on a lettuce-lined platter and garnish with parsley.

SERVES 6 TO 8

Moulded Chicken Salad

Curried Chicken

4 poussins, or 10 chicken portions	200 ml/7 fl oz oil
3 cloves garlic	3 tablespoons olive oil
3 bay leaves	juice of 1 lemon
2 teaspoons caraway seeds	curry paste (or powder) to taste
1 tablespoon paprika	salt and black pepper

Use a pair of kitchen shears and a cleaver or sharp knife to split the baby chickens down the middle of the breastbone. Fit the metal blade to the processor and with the machine running, add the garlic, bay leaves, caraway seeds and paprika. Pour in the oils and lemon juice, season well and add the curry paste to taste. Blend well. Pour over the chicken and allow to marinate for about 8 hours, turning from time to time. Drain the chicken and place on a rack over a roasting pan and bake in a moderately hot oven (200c, 400f, gas 6) for 20–30 minutes. Whilst cooking, brush the chicken frequently with the marinade and turn when brown. Serve with a crisp green salad and potatoes or rice of your choice.

SERVES 4

Stir-Fried Chicken and Cucumber

1 tablespoon cornflour	2 onions, halved lengthwise
4 tablespoons dry sherry	3 sticks celery
salt and black pepper	2 leeks
3 chicken breasts	2 courgettes
1 clove garlic	1 medium-sized cucumber
1 small piece root ginger	4 tablespoons sunflower or peanut oil
2 tablespoons soy sauce	
4 tablespoons water	225 g/8 oz frozen corn
pinch of cayenne	

In a bowl, combine the cornflour and sherry and season well. Remove the skin and bones from the chicken breasts and cut into 2.5-cm/1-in cubes or thin slices. Add to the sherry and allow to stand for 30 minutes. Meanwhile fit the metal blade to the processor, add the garlic, fresh ginger, soy sauce, water, and cayenne, pulse to combine well. Set aside in a small bowl. Now fit the slicing plate. Slice the onion, celery, leeks and courgettes. Set aside. Peel, halve and seed the cucumber, cut into 10 cm/4 in lengths, pack snugly into the feed tube and slice. Pat dry and reserve. Using a wok or cast iron frying pan, heat the oil. Drain the chicken and stir-fry quickly and evenly. Cook for about 10 minutes. If the pan is not large enough remove the chicken and drain. Now add all the vegetables and stir-fry quickly over a high heat until just tender, about 5 minutes. Remember stir-fried vegetables should be crisp. Add the chicken, the remaining marinade and the mixture. Bring to the boil vigorously, toss well to combine and serve immediately.

SERVES 4

Note: Stir-fry dishes are popular, economical and healthy. They are ideal when catering for a large crowd. Using your processor, slice a large selection of crisp seasonal vegetables in a moment. Boned chicken or meat may be partially frozen, then sliced.

Creamed Chicken Liver Pasta

The tasty sauce can be prepared ahead of time and warmed up while the pasta is cooking.

350 g/12 oz tagliatelle or spaghetti	6 spring onions, cut into small pieces
50 g/2 oz butter	2 sprigs parsley, stems removed
100 g/4 oz Parmesan cheese, cut into cubes	5 medium tomatoes, peeled and deseeded
SAUCE	
1 onion, quartered	$\frac{1}{2}$ teaspoon dried sage
50 g/2 oz butter	$\frac{1}{2}$ teaspoon dried mixed herbs
225 g/8 oz chicken livers	2 tablespoons brandy
300 ml/$\frac{1}{2}$ pint single cream	salt and pepper to taste

First make the sauce. Using the metal blade, chop the onion and sauté in half the butter until transparent. Remove from the pan and add the chicken livers. Fry until the livers just lose their pinkness. Purée the livers and onion in the processor, then add half the cream. Process until the mixture is smooth and set aside. Chop the spring onions and parsley in the processor, then sauté in the remaining butter until the onions are transparent. Add the remaining cream and the chicken liver purée to the pan. Use the processor to coarsely chop the tomatoes, then add them to the liver mixture. Stir in the sage, mixed herbs and brandy. Season to taste with salt and pepper. Simmer the sauce over a medium heat until the mixture thickens slightly and the tomatoes are cooked.

Cook the pasta in plenty of rapidly boiling, salted water until just tender. Drain and stir in the butter. Using the metal blade, chop the Parmesan cheese until it resembles fine crumbs. Top the hot pasta with the chicken liver sauce and serve the Parmesan cheese separately.

SERVES 4 TO 6

Roast Turkey with Walnut and Apricot Stuffing ☯

1 (4 to 5-kg/9 to 11-lb) turkey	100 g/4 oz walnuts
salt and black pepper	1 turkey liver (from the above bird)
oil for basting	2 eggs
WALNUT AND APRICOT STUFFING	1 teaspoon dried thyme
14 dried apricots	1 tablespoon soy sauce
8–10 slices white bread, cubed	SAUSAGEMEAT STUFFING
1 large onion, quartered	450 g/1 lb pork sausagemeat
6 tablespoons oil	1 small onion, quartered
1 small bunch parsley, stems removed	sprig of parsley, stems removed
	$\frac{1}{2}$ teaspoon dried sage
	1 egg

If the turkey has been frozen, allow to thaw completely. Rinse out and pat dry. Season the inside cavity.

To make the nut stuffing, soak the apricots in warm water for 1 hour. Using the metal blade, crumb the bread in batches, then turn into a large mixing bowl. Place the onion in the work bowl and pulse until finely chopped. In a frying pan, heat the oil and sauté the onion until transparent. Reserve the oil and add the onion to the breadcrumbs. Pulse the parsley and walnuts until finely chopped. Add to the breadcrumbs. Drain the soaked apricots and toss in a little flour before chopping them in the processor. Add to the breadcrumbs. Sauté the turkey liver in the remaining oil, then chop in the processor.

Add to the ingredients in the mixing bowl together with the eggs, herbs and seasonings. Stir well. Should the stuffing be a little dry, add a little milk. Fill the main cavity of the turkey with this stuffing.

To make the meat stuffing, place the sausagemeat in a bowl. Chop the onion and parsley in the food processor. Combine all the stuffing ingredients and mix well. Using your fingers, lift the skin off the flesh of the neck cavity as far up onto the breast as possible. Push the stuffing into this cavity and press the outside to shape evenly. Secure the opening with small skewers.

Truss the turkey by securing the wings and legs with string or skewers and cover the drumstick ends with foil. Season well and brush liberally with oil. Cook in a moderate oven (160c, 325 F, gas 3) for about $2\frac{1}{2}$ hours. To test if the bird is cooked, press the drumstick between your fingers – it should feel soft and move up and down easily. Allow the bird to stand in a warm place for 15 minutes before carving. Make a gravy in the normal way, scraping all the residue from the roasting tin into the liquid.

SERVES 10 TO 12

Roasting times for turkey

3–4 kg/6–9 lb	$2\frac{1}{4}$–$2\frac{1}{2}$ hours
4–6 kg/9–13 lb	$2\frac{1}{2}$–3 hours
6–7 kg/13–15 lb	3–$3\frac{1}{4}$ hours
7–9 kg/15–17 lb	$3\frac{1}{4}$–$3\frac{1}{2}$ hours
10–12 kg/21–27 lb	$3\frac{1}{2}$–4 hours

Roast Turkey with Walnut and Apricot Stuffing

Almond Turkey Casserole

Transform turkey leftovers into this scrumptious casserole.

350 g/12 oz tagliatelle or any other pasta	100 g/4 oz Cheddar cheese
3 sticks celery	½ small green pepper, deseeded
25 g/1 oz butter	100 g/4 oz almonds
25 g/1 oz plain flour	350 g/12 oz cooked turkey, diced
pinch of mustard powder	
salt and pepper to taste	50 g/2 oz chopped pimiento (canned red pepper)
600 ml/1 pint milk	
2 teaspoons Worcestershire sauce	2 slices white bread, torn into pieces

Cook the pasta in plenty of rapidly boiling, salted water until just tender. Drain well, rinse and set aside. Meanwhile, fit the slicing plate to the processor and slice the celery. In a large saucepan, melt 25 g/1 oz butter and sauté the celery, covered for 10 minutes, stirring frequently. Stir in the flour, mustard powder, salt and pepper. Gradually stir in the milk and cook, stirring all the time, until the mixture bubbles and thickens. Now add the Worcestershire sauce.

Fit the shredding plate to the processor, shred the cheese and set aside. Using the metal blade, chop the green pepper, then coarsely chop the almonds. Add the cheese, pepper, half the almonds, diced turkey, cooked pasta and chopped pimiento to the celery sauce. Mix well and turn into a greased ovenproof dish. Use the metal blade to crumb the bread. Sprinkle over the turkey mixture and top with the remaining almonds. Dot with the remaining butter and bake, uncovered, in a moderately hot oven (200 c, 400 f, gas 6) for about 15 to 20 minutes. Serve hot.

SERVES 6 TO 8

Turkey Tetrazzini

450 g/1 lb spaghetti	100 g/4 oz mushrooms, wiped clean
900 ml/1½ pints chicken stock	
75 g/3 oz butter	100 g/4 oz Emmental cheese
40 g/1½ oz flour	100 g/4 oz mature Cheddar cheese
300 ml/½ pint milk	
salt and pepper to taste	1.75 kg/4 lb cooked turkey, diced
1 large onion, quartered	
1 green pepper, deseeded and quartered	2 slices bread, torn into pieces

Cook the spaghetti according to the directions on the packet, using 300 ml/½ pint of the chicken stock with the boiling water. Drain well and set aside.

To make the sauce, melt 50 g/2 oz butter and stir in the flour. Cook stirring, for 2 minutes. Gradually stir in the remaining stock and the milk and cook, stirring, until bubbling and thick. Season to taste with salt and pepper. Using the metal blade, chop the onion and green pepper. Fit the slicing plate and slice the mushrooms. In a frying pan, heat 25 g/1 oz butter and sauté the onion, green pepper and mushrooms for 5 minutes. Add to the sauce. Now fit the shredding plate and shred the cheeses. Add the diced turkey, cooked spaghetti and most of the shredded cheese to the sauce. Mix well. Turn the mixture into a large, greased casserole and sprinkle with the remaining cheese. Using the metal blade, crumb the bread, then sprinkle over the turkey mixture. Bake, uncovered, in a moderate oven (180 c, 350 f, gas 4) for 30 to 35 minutes. Serve hot.

SERVES 6 TO 8

Duck with Grapefruit Sauce

Duck makes a rich and succulent main course.

1 duck	1 teaspoon dried sage
pinch of ground ginger	1 egg
a little plain flour	1 tablespoon Cointreau
2 teaspoons butter	salt and pepper
STUFFING	GRAPEFRUIT SAUCE
3 slices brown bread, cubed	25 g/1 oz plain flour
2 pieces orange rind	7 tablespoons water
1 onion, quartered	6 tablespoons orange juice
2 tablespoons parsley, stalks removed	julienne strips of orange and grapefruit rind
1 tablespoon oil	1 (410-g/14½-oz) can grapefruit segments, drained
1 duck liver	
1 teaspoon chicken stock powder	

First make the stuffing. Fit the metal blade to the processor and add the bread and orange rind. Pulse until finely crumbed, then transfer to a mixing bowl. Add the onion and parsley to the processor and pulse to chop. Sauté in heated oil, then add to the breadcrumbs. Sauté the duck liver, chop roughly in the processor, then add to the ingredients in the mixing bowl. Now add the stock powder, sage, egg, Cointreau and seasonings. Combine well.

Rinse the duck and pat dry. Season the cavity, then fill with stuffing. Truss the duck, lightly prick the skin with a fork and sprinkle with seasoning and ginger. Rub all over with flour and butter. Place the duck on the rack of a roasting tin which has a little water added. Roast in a moderate oven (180 c, 350 f, gas 4). Allow about 20 to 25 minutes per 450 g/1 lb of stuffed duck or 20 minutes per 450 g/1 lb of unstuffed duck. When cooked, remove the duck from the pan and keep warm.

To make the sauce, drain off most of the fat from the pan and add the flour. Stir and allow to brown. Add the water and orange juice and boil well. Meanwhile, cook the julienne strips in boiling water for 5 minutes, then drain. Add the julienne strips and grapefruit segments to the sauce. To simplify serving, carve the duck and place the meat in a shallow casserole. Pour the sauce over, cover and keep warm until required, or serve immediately.

SERVES 3 TO 4

Mandarin Duck

Mandarin Duck ☯

1 large duck	½ teaspoon of dried thyme
1 small carrot, cut into pieces	pinch of nutmeg
	3 tablespoons honey
1 stick celery, cut into pieces	2 tablespoons beer or brandy
	2 egg yolks
¼ small onion	6 tablespoons single cream
3 sprigs parsley, stems removed	2 (312-g/11-oz) cans mandarin oranges
150 g/5 oz noodles, cooked and coarsely chopped	4 tablespoons port
	2 teaspoons lemon juice
1 onion, quartered	salt and pepper to taste
1 tablespoon chopped parsley	parsley to garnish

Place the duck giblets in a saucepan. Add the carrot, celery, onion, parsley, salt, pepper and water to cover. Bring to the boil, cover and simmer for about 25 minutes. Strain the stock and reserve. Fit the metal blade to the processor, chop the giblets coarsely and add to the chopped noodles. Chop the onion and add to the noodle mixture together with the parsley, thyme and nutmeg. Mix well. Mix half the honey with half the

beer or brandy and add to the noodle mixture, together with the egg yolks and cream. Mix well.

Wipe the duck clean and stuff the cavity with the noodle mixture. Place the duck, breast side down, in a roasting tin. Add water to the pan to a depth of 1 cm/½ in. Roast in a moderate oven 180 c, 350 f, gas 4) for 25 minutes, basting frequently. Turn the duck breast side up, pour the remaining honey and beer or brandy over and roast for a further 25 minutes. When the duck is cooked, place on a serving platter and keep warm.

To make the sauce, drain the mandarin oranges and reserve a few segments for garnishing. Purée the remaining segments in the processor, transfer to a saucepan and add the port and 250 ml/8 fl oz reserved giblet stock. Boil the mixture until reduced and thickened. Now add the lemon juice and season with salt and pepper.

To serve, pour some of the mandarin sauce over the duck and garnish with reserved mandarin segments and parsley. Serve the remaining mandarin sauce separately.

SERVES 4

Meats

Revitalise your favourite meat recipes with processor magic. Sauces, stuffings, marinades and even pastry will give a new look and flavour to all kinds of meat dishes. Many traditional dishes began as simple peasant fare, carefully prepared by cooks who spent hours chopping, slicing and mincing. Nowadays, the food processor handles these preparations in a fraction of the time.

  Investigate shortcuts in your favourite recipes to see where your processor can save time and effort, then rearrange your recipes accordingly. In addition, we have selected a variety of delicious meat recipes, both simple and elaborate, to suit your style of entertaining.

Fillet in Phyllo Pastry

This is one of those impressive, special occasion dishes. The steak parcels can be made early in the day and be kept in the refrigerator until required. Although a lot of work is involved, it is ideal for a formal dinner party because each portion is ready to serve and will keep hot for a long time. Phyllo pastry can be obtained from Greek shops or delicatessens.

4 thick slices of fillet steak	8 mushrooms
a little oil	1 teaspoon plain flour
1 small onion, quartered	1 tablespoon brandy
3 sticks celery	8 sheets phyllo pastry
2 tablespoons parsley, stems removed	4 slices pâté
	100 g/4 oz butter, melted

Trim the meat and set aside. Take a heavy-based frying pan and heat until a haze forms. Brush with a little oil. Brown the meat well on both sides for a minute or two to seal, but do not cook through. Cool completely. Fit the metal blade to the processor and chop the onion, celery, parsley and mushrooms. Add a little more oil to the pan and sauté the chopped vegetables. Sprinkle with flour, add brandy and season. Set aside and cool.

Cut the sheets of phyllo in half. Brush one piece with melted butter, place another sheet of pastry on top. Repeat, so that four pieces of pastry are pasted together. For each serving, place one slice of fillet at the end of a stack of pastry, top with a little of the vegetable mixture, then slice of pâté. Roll the meat and pastry over, then brush the underside of the pastry with more butter. Roll over again. Always brush butter over any surface which is dry. Fold in the two open edges, then fold over again, making sure the main edge is concealed underneath. Brush the parcel with melted butter. Repeat with the remaining ingredients, making four parcels. Place these on a greased baking sheet and bake in a moderate oven (180c, 350f, gas 4) for 15 to 20 minutes. Remove from the oven and serve immediately, garnished with watercress or parsley.

To prepare this dish in advance, complete the pastry packages and place on the greased baking sheet. Cover with cling film and refrigerate until 20 minutes before serving. Brush once more with melted butter and bake.

SERVES 4

Sweet and Sour Meatballs

Sweet and Sour Meatballs

450 g/1 lb beef or pork, cubed	2 carrots
1 tablespoon soy sauce	3 gherkins
1 clove garlic, crushed	$\frac{1}{2}$ (425-g/15-oz) can pineapple chunks
1 tablespoon dry sherry	7 tablespoons pineapple juice
salt and black pepper	7 tablespoons water
a little plain flour	1 tablespoon soft brown sugar
oil for frying	1 tablespoon tomato ketchup
SAUCE	3 tablespoons white wine vinegar
1 green pepper	
$\frac{1}{2}$ small onion, halved	1 tablespoon cornflour
1 tablespoon oil	

Using the metal blade, finely chop the meat in batches. Add the soy sauce, garlic, sherry and seasoning. Pulse a few times to combine. Form into small balls, toss lightly in flour and fry in a little oil until brown and cooked through. Transfer to a serving platter and keep warm.

To make the sauce, use the metal blade and pulse to chop the green pepper and onion. Heat the oil in a saucepan and sauté. Fit the slicing plate and thinly slice the carrots and gherkins. Add to the pan together with all the remaining ingredients, except the vinegar and cornflour. Bring to the boil and simmer for 5 minutes. Mix the cornflour and vinegar, adding a little of the boiling liquid to the mixture. Add the cornflour mixture to the sauce and cook, stirring, until it thickens. Pour over the meatballs and serve with rice.

SERVES 4

Hungarian-Style Goulash

A special main dish to serve with noodles and dark bread.

1 kg/2 lb chuck steak, cut into 5-cm/2-in cubes	1 teaspoon castor sugar
2 tablespoons oil	1 tablespoon chopped parsley
1 onion, cut in half lengthwise	450 ml/$\frac{3}{4}$ pint beef stock
1 clove garlic, crushed	salt and pepper to taste
1 tablespoon sweet paprika	1 red or green pepper, deseeded and halved
1 tablespoon plain flour	2 tomatoes, peeled and quartered
1 tablespoon tomato purée	250 ml/8 fl oz soured cream

Brown the meat on all sides in hot oil, then place in a large casserole. Fit the slicing plate to the processor, slice the onion and add to the frying pan along with the garlic. Fry until the onion is soft, then add to the meat. Sprinkle the paprika into the frying pan and cook, stirring for 1 minute. Now stir in the flour, tomato purée, sugar and chopped parsley. Slowly stir in the stock and cook, stirring, until the mixture thickens. Season with salt and pepper and pour over the meat. Cover the casserole tightly and place in a moderate oven (160c, 325 f, gas 3) for 1$\frac{3}{4}$ hours, or until the meat is tender. Using the slicing plate, slice the pepper and add to the meat. Fit the metal blade and coarsely chop the tomatoes. Add to the casserole and continue to cook for a further 25 minutes. Just before serving, stir in the soured cream.

SERVES 6

Fillet Combo

1 kg/2 lb fillet steak
25 g/1 oz butter
salt and black pepper
25 g/1 oz plain flour
1 quantity of Quick Puff
  Pastry (page 132)
1 beaten egg for glazing
FILLING
1 small onion, quartered
25 g/1 oz butter

350 g/12 oz peeled prawns
25 g/1 oz plain flour
6 tablespoons single cream
2 teaspoons concentrated
  tomato purée
3 tablespoons whisky
½ teaspoon paprika
dash of Tabasco sauce
1 tablespoon lemon juice

Trim the fillet and tie into shape with string. Rub with flour and brown the fillet all over in heated butter to seal. Place on a roasting rack and cook in a hot oven (220 c, 425 f, gas 7) for 10 minutes. Cool and remove string.

To make the filling, fit the metal blade to the processor and chop the onion. Melt the butter and sauté the onion until soft. Add the prawns and cook for 5 minutes. Sprinkle with flour, remove from the heat and add all the remaining filling ingredients. Stir carefully and heat until just boiling. Place in the processor and process until smooth. Cool before using.

Roll the pastry out fairly thinly so that it is at least 6 cm/2½ in longer at each end than the meat and is wide enough to overlap by at least 6 cm/2½ in on the top. Cut the fillet into 2.5 cm/1 in thick slices and spread each slice thickly with filling. Replace the slices, forming a whole fillet. Cut the

pastry as indicated on the diagram. Lay the fillet down the centre on the uncut portion. Now plait the strands over the top of the fillet. Brush well with lightly beaten egg. Bake in a moderately hot oven (200 c, 400 f, gas 6) for 40 minutes. Serve immediately.

This dish may be prepared a few hours in advance. Be sure that the meat and filling are cold before wrapping them in the pastry. Cover and set aside in the refrigerator until placing in the oven 40 minutes before serving.

SERVES 6

1. Place fillet on prepared pastry.

2. Plait as directed above.

Beef Stroganoff

Rich, creamy stroganoff makes meat stretch a long way.

675 g/1½ lb lean rump steak
salt and pepper
75 g/3 oz plain flour
50 g/2 oz butter
1 large onion, quartered
1 clove garlic

225 g/8 oz mushrooms
1 tablespoon concentrated
    tomato purée
250 ml/8 fl oz stock
3 tablespoons dry sherry
300 ml/½ pint soured cream

Cut the meat into thin strips and dredge in half the seasoned flour. Melt 25 g/1 oz butter in a large saucepan, and brown the meat lightly on all sides. Transfer to a plate and keep warm. Fit the metal blade to the processor, chop the onions and garlic and add to the pan. Using the slicing plate, slice the mushrooms and add to the onions. Fry until the onions are soft. Set aside and keep warm. Add another 25 g/1 oz butter to the pan and heat to melt. Stir in the remaining flour and cook, stirring, for 2 minutes. Add the tomato purée and the stock. Cook stirring, until the mixture thickens. Return the meat and vegetables to the pan. Stir in the dry sherry and soured cream. Heat through, but do not boil. Serve with noodles or hot rice.

SERVES 4

Lamb in Tarragon Cream

1 kg/2 lb boneless lamb,
    cubed
salt and black pepper
a little plain flour
1 tablespoon butter
1 tablespoon oil
1 large onion, quartered
1 clove garlic
300 ml/½ pint beef and
    chicken stock combined

6 tablespoons white wine
2 teaspoons dried tarragon or
    1 tablespoon fresh
    tarragon
1 tablespoon French mustard
200 ml/7 fl oz single cream
1 tablespoon chopped parsley

Toss the lamb in the salt, pepper and a little flour. Heat the butter and oil in a cast iron casserole, add the meat and brown well. Using the metal blade, finely chop the onion and garlic. Add to the meat and cook for a few minutes. Pour in the stock and wine. Cover and place in a cool oven (150 c, 300 F, gas 2) for 1½ hours. Remove from the oven and add the tarragon, mustard and cream. Stir well. Return to the oven for 1 hour. Sprinkle with chopped parsley and serve with boiled potatoes.

SERVES 4

This dish will freeze well for a month. Cook for 30 minutes less than required time, then cool and freeze. If the sauce is a little thin when the dish is reheated, work an equal quantity of butter and flour together and stir in a little at a time to thicken.

Best-Ever Hamburgers

1 kg/2 lb lean beef, cut
    into cubes
½ small onion, cut in half
salt and freshly ground
    black pepper to taste

½ teaspoon mixed herbs
1 teaspoon Worcestershire
    sauce
25 g/1 oz butter, softened

Using the metal blade, chop the meat in four batches. Process for about 6 seconds per batch. Turn the meat into a large mixing bowl. Place the onion in the processor and chop finely. Add to the meat and mix well. Season with salt, pepper, herbs and Worcestershire sauce. Mix in the soft butter and shape into 6 hamburger patties, pressing the mixture together gently. Fry, grill or barbecue until done.

MAKES 6 HAMBURGERS

Note: To make cheeseburgers, use the shredding plate to shred 100 g/4 oz Cheddar cheese. Sprinkle the cheese over the hamburgers about 1 minute before serving.

Beer Curry

3 tablespoons oil
450 g/1 lb lean lamb, cut
    into bite-sized pieces
1 onion, quartered
1 or 2 cloves garlic
1 teaspoon freshly grated
    root ginger
2 tablespoons mild curry
    powder
25 g/1 oz plain flour
1 large apple, peeled, cored
    and quartered
300 ml/½ pint beef or lamb
    stock

300 ml/½ pint beer
2 tablespoons mango chutney
2 teaspoons concentrated
    tomato purée
1 tablespoon honey
2 tablespoons lemon juice
7 tablespoons single cream
salt to taste
GARNISH
1 bunch spring onions, cut
    into pieces
225 g/8 oz peanuts
desiccated coconut

Heat the oil in a large saucepan and brown the lamb on all sides. Set aside and keep warm. Fit the metal blade to the processor and chop the onion and garlic. Add to the oil, together with the grated ginger, and fry until the onion is golden. Now add the curry powder and flour. Cook, stirring for 2 minutes. Chop the apple in the processor and add to the pan. Stir in the stock and beer. Add the chutney, tomato purée, honey and lemon juice. Lastly add the lamb and simmer over a low heat for 45 minutes or until the meat is tender. Just before serving, stir in the cream.

Using the metal blade, first chop the spring onions, then the peanuts. Garnish the curry with spring onions, peanuts and coconut. Serve with hot rice.

SERVES 4

Fillet Combo Served with Potato Crowns (page 86)

Steak with Oyster Butter

For this dish, choose your favourite cut of steak. For that really special occasion, a whole fillet is impressive.

1 kg/2 lb rump or fillet steak
smoked oyster butter (page 103)
salt and black pepper

Trim the steak and cut thickly into portions, unless you are using a whole fillet. Cut a deep pocket in the side of each portion. Fill generously with the oyster butter. Use two cocktail sticks to secure the edges. (If using a whole fillet, sew with thick thread.) Heat a heavy-based frying or grilling pan until a haze forms. Wipe the pan with a little oil. Season the steak and cook completely on one side before turning and cooking the other side. The length of the cooking time will depend on the thickness of the steak and on the degree of rareness required. To cook a whole fillet, heat a little butter in a frying or grilling pan and brown the stuffed fillet on all sides over a high heat. Then place on a rack in a hot oven (220 c, 425 f, gas 7) for approximately 30 minutes, depending on how rare you like your meat.

SERVES 4

Lamb with Mustard Crust

Mustard and beer give lamb a special flavour and make a delicious gravy. For a slightly fruity flavour, use Appletizer or similar apple juice drink instead of beer.

4 tablespoons brandy	a little melted butter
freshly ground black pepper	salt to taste
1.4 kg/3 lb leg of lamb, boned	100 g/4 oz Dijon mustard
	300 ml/½ pint beer
2 slices bread	250 ml/8 fl oz single cream
1 tablespoon fresh rosemary	1 teaspoon lemon juice
½ small onion, cut up	parsley sprigs to garnish
1 clove garlic	

Pour half the brandy over the inside leg of lamb and sprinkle generously with pepper. Allow to stand for 30 minutes.

Using the metal blade, chop the bread and rosemary finely. Set aside. Chop the onion and garlic and mix with the breadcrumbs. Moisten with a little melted butter and season to taste with salt. Press the mixture gently into the cavities of the lamb. Roll the lamb and secure with string. Using a paper towel, dry the outer surface of the lamb. Spoon the mustard on top and, using your hands, pat it over the surface, covering evenly. Place, uncovered, in a moderately hot oven (200 c, 400 f, gas 6) for 15 minutes. Reduce heat to moderate (180 c, 350 f, gas 4) and add 250 ml/8 fl oz beer. Cover and bake for 30 minutes per 450 g/1 lb weight, adding more beer if necessary. When the lamb is cooked, transfer it to a carving board and stand for a few minutes before carving.

To make the gravy, add the remaining beer and brandy to the pan juices. Bring to the boil and cook until the liquid is reduced by half. Remove from the heat, stir in the cream and lemon juice and season with salt and pepper to taste. Heat through, bring to the boil and thicken. Remove the string from the lamb and slice. Arrange on a warm serving platter, garnish with parsley and serve with gravy.

SERVES 8

Lamb with Orange

1 kg/2 lb shoulder of lamb, cut into 2.5 cm/1 in cubes	150 ml/¼ pint fresh orange juice
50 g/2 oz plain flour	1 tablespoon fresh rosemary
salt and pepper to taste	1 teaspoon fresh mint, chopped
50 g/2 oz butter	
2 onions, cut in half lengthwise	1 tablespoon chopped fresh parsley
3 sticks celery	2 large oranges
350 ml/12 fl oz chicken stock	mint sprigs to garnish

Dredge the lamb in flour seasoned with salt and pepper. Melt the butter and fry the lamb in batches until golden brown. Transfer to a casserole. Fit the slicing plate to the processor and slice the onions and celery. Fry until the onion is tender. Add the remaining seasoned flour, stock, orange juice, rosemary, mint and parsley. Bring to the boil, then pour over the lamb. Bake, covered, in a moderate oven (180 c, 350 f, gas 4) for about 50 minutes or until the lamb is tender. Now add the grated rind of two oranges. Using a sharp knife, peel the oranges and cut the flesh into segments. Add the orange segments to the lamb and heat through. Garnish with mint.

SERVES 4 TO 6

Lamb Provençale

1 leg of lamb	3 tablespoons parsley, stems removed
salt and black pepper	
a little flour to coat	200 ml/7 fl oz chicken stock
2 cloves garlic	sprig of fresh rosemary or ½ teaspoon dried rosemary
15 g/½ oz butter	
1 tablespoon oil	
6–8 potatoes	
1 bunch chives or spring onion tops, cut into 1 cm/½ in lengths	

Trim the lamb, removing any excess fat. Sprinkle with seasonings, rub with flour and spike all over with slivers of garlic. Heat the butter and oil in a deep ovenproof casserole. Brown the meat well on all sides. Remove from the heat and drain off excess fat. Using the slicing plate, slice the potatoes thickly, then rinse in cold water. Change to the metal blade and chop the chives or spring onion tops and the parsley. Continue with these layers until both the potatoes and the chives or spring onion are finished. Season lightly. Add the lamb and the stock. Place the rosemary on top of the lamb, cover and bake in a moderate oven (180 c, 350 f, gas 4) for 1½ to 2 hours, depending on the size of the lamb. Add a little more stock during cooking if necessary.

SERVES 6

Pork and Fennel Casserole

The pork and fennel are baked together and the lemony sauce enhances the flavour of both.

50 g/2 oz butter
1.5 kg/3½ lb pork shoulder,
   cut into 2.5-cm/1-in
   cubes
4 onions, quartered
salt and pepper to taste
1 fennel bulb, washed

LEMON PARSLEY SAUCE
350 ml/12 fl oz cooking
   liquid from the pork
25 g/1 oz butter
25 g/1 oz flour
2 egg yolks
2 teaspoons parsley, chopped
6 tablespoons fresh lemon
   juice

In a frying pan, melt the butter and fry the pork in batches until browned on all sides. Transfer to a casserole and keep warm. Using the metal blade, coarsely chop the onions and add to the frying pan. Cook over a low heat until the onions are transparent. Add to the pork. Season with salt and pepper and pour in enough water to cover the pork. Cover the casserole and bake in a moderate oven (160 c, 325 f, gas 3) for about 50 minutes.

Fit the slicing plate to the processor and slice the fennel, saving the feathery top to use as garnish. Arrange around the pork and continue to bake, covered, for a further 25 minutes. Drain the liquid from the pork and reserve. Place the pork and fennel on a heated serving dish, spoon over 3 tablespoons of the liquid, cover and keep warm while making the sauce.

To make the sauce, fit the metal blade to the processor and place the cooking liquid in the work bowl. Add the butter and flour and process to combine. Pour into a saucepan and heat, stirring, until the mixture thickens. Place the egg yolks and parsley in the work bowl. With the machine running, pour in the lemon juice, followed by the thickened sauce in a slow and steady stream. Process until well mixed. Finally, pour the sauce over the pork mixture and garnish with the fennel top.

SERVES 6

Lamb Provençale

Pork Chops with Apple and Curry Stuffing

6 thick pork chops
1 large apple, peeled, cored and cut into quarters
½ small onion, cut in half
2 sticks celery, cut into 2.5-cm/1-in pieces
75 g/3 oz butter
5 slices wholewheat bread, crumbled
5 tablespoons milk
1 teaspoon curry powder
½ teaspoon salt
pinch of ground ginger
50 g/2 oz plain flour
pinch of pepper

Cut deep slits in the sides of the pork chops and set aside. To make the stuffing, fit the metal blade and chop the apple, onion and celery together. Melt half the butter, add the apple mixture and cook until soft. Crumb the bread in the processor and transfer to a large bowl. Add the milk, apple mixture, curry powder, salt and ginger. Toss lightly to mix. Use this stuffing to stuff the pork chops. Secure with cocktail sticks or thread. Coat with flour mixed with pepper and fry in the remaining butter until well browned on both sides. Place in a greased casserole and bake, covered, in a moderate oven (160 c, 325 f, gas 3) for about 50 minutes. Remove the cocktail sticks or thread before serving.

SERVES 6

Surprise Pork Fillets

3 pork fillets
50 g/2 oz plain flour
salt and black pepper
1 teaspoon mustard powder
1 teaspoon paprika
40 g/1½ oz margarine
1 tablespoon oil
1 large onion
300 ml/½ pint chicken stock
3 tablespoons white wine
1 teaspoon sage
225 g/8 oz mushrooms
6 wedges of Emmental cheese
a little paprika

Rub the pork fillets with flour mixed with all the seasonings. In a heavy-based pan, heat the margarine and oil and brown the fillets all over. Set aside and keep warm. Fit the slicing plate to the processor and slice the onion. Sauté until tender, then add any remaining flour to the pan. Add the stock, wine and sage and bring to the boil. Now add the fillets. Cover and simmer very slowly for 30 minutes. Using the processor, slice the mushrooms. Stir into the pan and cook for a further 10 minutes. Remove the meat from the sauce and make a slit about 1 cm/½ in deep in each fillet. Cut the cheese wedges to fit and place them in the slits. Return the meat to the heat, cover and simmer for 10 minutes or until the cheese has just melted. Sprinkle with a little paprika and serve immediately.

This dish may be prepared in advance up to the stage where the mushrooms are cooked. Cool and refrigerate. Reheat for 20 minutes, then add the cheese and allow to melt before serving.

SERVES 4

Barbecued Ribs

Oven-baked ribs take the pressure off the hostess.

2 kg/4½ lb spare ribs
50 g/2 oz butter
1 large onion, quartered
2 sticks celery
2 tablespoons lemon juice
1 tablespoon orange juice
1 tablespoon malt vinegar
1 tablespoon soft brown sugar
pinch of cayenne
250 ml/8 fl oz tomato ketchup
1 teaspoon Worcestershire sauce
1 teaspoon mustard powder
250 ml/8 fl oz water
salt to taste

Cut the ribs into serving pieces and brown in butter on all sides. Transfer to a large baking pan.

Using the metal blade, coarsely chop the onions and add to the frying pan. Fit the slicing plate, slice the celery and add to the onions in the pan. Cook, stirring until the onions are tender. Add all the remaining ingredients, mixing well. Bring to the boil, then pour over the ribs. Cover and bake in a moderate oven (160 c, 325 f, gas 3) for 2 hours, basting every 30 minutes.

SERVES 6

Pork Chops with Apple and Curry Stuffing

Veal Parmesan

Veal Parmesan

Prepare the casserole and refrigerate for up to 24 hours before baking.

50 g/2 oz Parmesan cheese, cubed	TOMATO SAUCE
225 g/8 oz seasoned dried breadcrumbs	150 ml/¼ pint concentrated tomato purée
6 large veal schnitzels	1 teaspoon dried basil
1 beaten egg	1 teaspoon oregano
oil for frying	½ teaspoon dried tarragon
100 g/4 oz mushrooms	2 teaspoons sugar
100 g/4 oz mozzarella cheese, very well chilled	salt and pepper to taste
	150 ml/¼ pint dry white wine

To make the sauce, combine all the ingredients in a medium saucepan and simmer over a low heat for about 1 hour.

Using the metal blade, process the Parmesan cheese a few cubes at a time until very finely chopped. Add half the Parmesan to the dried breadcrumbs and set aside the remaining cheese. Dip the schnitzels into the beaten egg, then into the crumb mixture and fry one or two at a time in hot oil until golden brown on both sides. Transfer to a platter and keep warm. Continue frying until all the schnitzels are done. Fit the slicing plate, slice the mushrooms and set aside. Change to the shredding plate, shred the mozarella cheese and refrigerate until required.

To assemble the casserole, pour a third of the tomato sauce into a baking dish or casserole. Arrange three schnitzels on top and cover with half the mushrooms. Add half the mozzarella cheese and half the remaining Parmesan cheese. Spread with half the remaining tomato sauce. Arrange the remaining schnitzels, mushrooms and tomato sauce in layers. Finally, top with mozzarella cheese and sprinkle with the remaining Parmesan. At this point, the casserole can be refrigerated for up to 24 hours.

Cook in a moderate oven (180c, 350f, gas 4) for about 1 hour. Serve with freshly cooked noodles or rice.

SERVES 6

Veal Scallopine with Risotto

450 g/1 lb veal shoulder	RISOTTO
a little plain flour to coat	1 small onion, quartered
salt and pepper	100 g/4 oz butter
50 g/2 oz butter	225 g/8 oz long grain rice
150 ml/¼ pint sherry	450 ml/¾ pint beef stock
100 g/4 oz mushrooms	salt and pepper to taste
	50 g/2 oz Cheddar cheese

Cut the veal into 2.5-cm/1-in cubes, dredge in flour mixed with salt and pepper, and brown well in half the butter. Fit the slicing plate to the processor and slice the mushrooms. Add the sherry and the sliced mushrooms to the veal and simmer for 15 minutes.

To make the risotto, use the metal blade to chop the onion. Sauté in half the butter until soft. Add the rice and fry until lightly browned. Heat the stock to boiling and season. Add the rice and onions and simmer, covered, for 20 minutes or until the rice is tender and all the liquid is absorbed. Stir in the remaining butter and transfer to a warm serving platter. Fit the shredding plate to the processor and shred the cheese. Sprinkle over the rice and spoon the veal on top.

SERVES 4 TO 6

63

Veal Supreme

1 shoulder of veal, boned	STUFFING
salt and pepper	1 small onion, quartered
3 tablespoons oil	1 tablespoon oil
1 onion	50 g/2 oz ham
2 carrots	50 g/2 oz mushrooms
1 turnip	2 tablespoons parsley, stems
2 sticks celery	removed
150 ml/¼ pint concentrated	1 piece lemon rind
tomato purée	3 slices bread, cubed
300 ml/½ pint chicken stock	generous pinch of dried
300 ml/½ pint white wine	rosemary
juice of 1 lemon	1 egg
1 bay leaf	salt and black pepper

First make the stuffing. Fit the metal blade to the processor and chop the onion. Sauté in oil until transparent and transfer to a mixing bowl. Chop the ham, mushrooms, parsley and lemon rind. Add to the onion. Place the bread in the processor, pulse until fine and add to the onion mixture. Finally, add the rosemary, egg and seasonings and mix well.

Season the meat with salt and pepper. Place the stuffing on the meat, roll up and secure by stitching or tying. In an ovenproof casserole, brown the meat in hot oil. Set aside and keep warm. Using the slicing plate, slice the onion, carrots, turnip and celery. Sauté the vegetables in oil, then add all the remaining ingredients. Bring to the boil, add the meat and cover. Cook in a moderate oven (160 c, 325 f, gas 3) for 2 hours or until tender. Remove the meat from the casserole, slice and arrange on a warm serving platter. Thicken or thin down the sauce as required and pour over the veal.

SERVES 6

Veal Orloff

One of the great classics in cooking. This version is easily made, using your processor.

1.25 kg/2½ lb boned loin of	bouquet garni
veal	1 quantity of Mushroom
salt and black pepper	Purée (page 100)
25 g/1 oz butter	1 quantity of Onion Purée
2 tablespoons oil	(page 100)
1 large onion, quartered	1 quantity of Mornay Sauce
2 sticks celery	(page 101)
2 medium carrots	sautéed mushroom caps, plain
2 cloves garlic	or fluted, to garnish
900 ml/1½ pints veal stock	

Roll the loin of veal and tie with string at 5-cm/2-in intervals. Season lightly. Heat the butter and oil in a cast iron casserole, brown the veal well. Remove from the pan and set aside. Using the metal blade, chop all the vegetables coarsely. Add to the pan and sauté. Add 150 ml/¼ pint veal stock and the bouquet garni. Boil rapidly until reduced by half. Add another 150 ml/¼ pint stock and again reduce by half. Now add 450 ml/¾ pint stock and the meat. Cover and cook in a moderate oven (160 c, 325 f, gas 3) for 1½ hours. Transfer the veal to a chopping board, remove the string and slice 2.5 cm/1 in thick, keeping the slices in the correct order. To assemble, place a layer of

mushroom purée and onion purée between each slice. Place on an ovenproof platter, then mask the meat with any remaining purée. Pour the mornay sauce over the meat and bake in a moderate oven (160 c, 325 f, gas 3) for 10 minutes. Brown quickly under the grill. Garnish with mushroom caps which have been sautéed in a little oil or butter.

SERVES 6

Note: To make veal stock, place the bones and a few vegetables, water and seasoning in a saucepan or pressure cooker and simmer until cooked. Strain and use.

Venison Casserole

This recipe may also be used with great success for a leg of venison.

1 kg/1 lb venison	salt and black pepper
600 ml/1 pint buttermilk	a little oil
1 onion	1 quantity of Espagnole
1 carrot	Sauce (page 99)
1 stick celery	2 tablespoons sherry
3 allspice berries	3 tablespoons soured cream
1 bay leaf	2 tablespoons redcurrant
1 clove garlic, crushed	jelly or chestnut purée
3 black peppercorns	

Cube the venison, place in a large bowl and add the buttermilk. Fit the slicing plate to the processor, slice the onion, carrot and celery and add to the meat. Add the allspice, bay leaf, garlic and peppercorns. Cover and refrigerate for at least two days, turning the mixture from time to time. Drain the meat from the marinade and pat dry. Season with salt and black pepper. Heat a little oil in an ovenproof casserole and brown the meat on all sides. Add the espagnole sauce and sherry. Cover and place in a cool oven (150 c, 300 f, gas 2) for at least 2 hours. (The cooking time will be determined by the cut of venison being used.) Remove from the oven, stir in the soured cream and the redcurrant jelly or chestnut purée. Reheat before serving. If the sauce has become too thin, thicken with a little butter and flour, mixed together. For variation, add a little buttermilk to the casserole.

SERVES 4 TO 6

Savoury Venison Pie

Savoury Venison Pie ⚫

1 kg/2 lb shoulder of venison
4 rashers bacon, rind removed
25 g/1 oz butter
225 g/8 oz mushrooms
25 g/1 oz plain flour
salt and pepper
1 quantity of Rough Puff
  Pastry (page 133)
1 beaten egg

MARINADE
1 onion, quartered
2 sticks celery
6 coriander seeds, crushed
6 allspice berries, crushed
2 bay leaves
2 sprigs parsley
$\frac{1}{2}$ teaspoon marjoram
300 ml/$\frac{1}{2}$ pint dry red wine
6 tablespoons oil

To make the marinade, use the metal blade to chop the onion. Place in a large bowl. Fit the slicing plate and slice the celery. Add to the onions. Add the remaining marinade ingredients and mix well. Cut the venison into 2.5-cm/1-in cubes and add to the marinade, stirring well to coat the meat. Stand in the refrigerator for at least 8 hours. Gently lift out the venison pieces and strain the marinade, retaining the liquid.

Coarsely chop the bacon in the processor and fry over a low heat to render the fat. Add the butter to the pan. Using the slicing plate, slice the mushrooms. Add to the pan and sauté for 3 minutes. Add the flour and cook, stirring for 2 minutes.

Stir in the reserved marinade liquid, and cook, stirring, until bubbling and thick. Add the venison and season with salt and pepper. Simmer over a very low heat for 1 to $1\frac{1}{4}$ hours, then cool.

Spoon the cooled venison into a deep pie dish and place a pastry funnel in the centre. Roll out the pastry and cut 1-cm/$\frac{1}{2}$-in strips from the edge. Place the strips on the moistened edge of the pie dish. Moisten the pastry strips before placing the pastry on top. Trim the edges, then seal and scallop. Brush the top of the pastry with beaten egg and decorate with pastry leaves. Brush once more with beaten egg. Bake the pie in a hot oven (220c, 425f, gas 7) for 15 minutes. Reduce to a moderately hot oven (190c, 375f, gas 5) and bake for 30 minutes or until the pie is golden and crisp. Serve hot.

SERVES 6

Buffet and Party Presentations

Buffet entertaining is often the result of your guest list outgrowing your dining table. For a successful buffet, the food must look as appetising to the last person as it did to the first. Arrange single-serving foods in neat layers or rows, and breads and other suitable foods in wide baskets or large bowls. All foods should be attractively presented in such a way that guests are able to see at a glance what is being served.

Once guest numbers start creeping towards twenty or more, you will have to use every trick you can think of to simplify preparation and serving. Your food processor will be kept busy chopping, slicing and grating the array of ingredients required, keeping preparation time to a minimum.

Choosing suitable dishes is especially important. Quiches, mousses, casseroles and salads require no last-minute preparation, can be kept waiting and still taste and look terrific. Casseroles can be assembled and refrigerated, then cooked just before serving. It may be an idea to make serveral medium-sized casseroles rather than one large one, so that as one dish empties, it can be replaced with another hot, full dish.

Entertain in the style to which you are accustomed, so do not plan a formal meal if you enjoy casual occasions. To make sure everything proceeds smoothly, carefully plan the arrangement of the table. Dinner plates, main dish, vegetables, salads, rolls or bread, cutlery and napkins should all be placed in a logical sequence. Allow sufficient room near each serving dish to enable guests to set down their plates while they serve themselves. If space permits, place the table so that guests can walk around it. For a large party, divide the table arrangement into two lines, one on either side of the table. This will require a double setting of casseroles, salads, vegetables, plates and so on.

Brighten up the table with colour co-ordinated napkins, candles and a decorative centrepiece. As an alternative to fresh flowers, try grouping together several green and flowering houseplants in baskets or bowls, or using a selection of interesting fruits or vegetables. These make low-cost centrepieces which can be used again.

It can be awkward if everyone has to stand for an entire evening, so make sure there is a place for each guest to sit comfortably. You may have to bring in extra chairs or arrange large cushions on the floor. Empty plates and glasses should be removed as soon as possible.

Further ideas on menu planning for the buffet or large party are given at the front of this book.

1. Mushroom quiche (page 68)
2. Shrimp quiche (page 39)
3. Spinach quiche (page 69)
4. Cheese and leek quiche (page 67)
5. Ham and pineapple quiche (page 67)
6. Smoked salmon quiche (page 39)

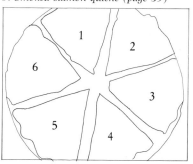

Ham and Pineapple Quiche

50 g/2 oz Parmesan cheese
350 g/12 oz cooked ham, cut
   in large cubes
2 tablespoons fresh mint
1 large pineapple, peeled
   and cored
8 eggs
450 ml/¾ pint evaporated
   milk

300 ml/½ pint single cream
salt and pepper to taste
1 teaspoon mustard powder
2 (23-cm/9-in) unbaked
   shortcrust pastry shells,
   made with pineapple
   juice instead of water
   (page 131)

Using the metal blade, chop the Parmesan cheese until it has the texture of fine crumbs and set aside. Coarsely chop the ham in the processor and turn into a large mixing bowl. Chop the mint and add to the ham. Cut the pineapple into wedges to fit the feed tube and use the chipper plate to dice. Add to the ham. In a bowl, mix together the eggs, evaporated milk, cream, salt and pepper and mustard powder. Add to the ham and mix well. Spoon the mixture into the pastry shells and sprinkle with Parmesan cheese. Bake in a moderate oven (180 c, 350 f, gas 4) for 35 to 45 minutes or until set and nicely browned.

SERVES 12

Cheese and Leek Quiche

Double up on this recipe for a buffet party.

3 large leeks, well washed
50 g/2 oz butter
7 tablespoons water
100 g/4 oz Cheddar cheese
250 ml/8 fl oz single cream
4 eggs

salt and pepper to taste
pinch of nutmeg
1 (23-cm/9-in unbaked
   shortcrust pastry shell
   (page 131)

Fit the slicing plate to the processor and slice the leeks. Melt the butter in a frying pan, add the leeks and fry until golden. Add the water and simmer until it evaporates (about 8 minutes). Set aside to cool. Using the shredding plate, shred the cheese and set aside. Change to the metal blade and process the cream, eggs, salt, pepper and nutmeg until well mixed. Pour the mixture over the cheese, add the leeks and turn into the pastry shell. Bake in a moderate oven (180 c, 350 f, gas 4) for 35 to 40 minutes or until set.

SERVES 6 TO 8

Egg and Ham Mousse

15 hard-boiled eggs	2 teaspoons gelatine
450 g/1 lb cooked ham	3 tablespoons hot water
5 tablespoons green peppercorns	600 ml/1 pint chicken stock
1 bunch spring onions	salt and black pepper
3 sprigs parsley, stems removed	450 ml/¾ pint double cream
3 tablespoons lemon juice	GARNISH
	10 stuffed olives, sliced
	2–3 hard-boiled eggs

Fit the shredding plate to the processor and shred the eggs. Transfer to a large mixing bowl. Using the metal blade, finely chop the ham, peppercorns, spring onions and parsley. Add to the shredded eggs, then add the lemon juice. Dissolve the gelatine in the hot water over a basin of boiling water then add 150 ml/¼ pint chicken stock. Add the remaining stock to the egg mixture and season. Using a whisk, lightly whip the cream. Stir the dissolved gelatine into the egg mixture and fold in the cream. Pour into a mould or soufflé dish. Chill well. If moulded, turn out onto a bed of shredded lettuce. Garnish with sliced, stuffed olives and chopped, hard-boiled eggs. Serve with Melba toast or wholewheat bread.

SERVES 20

This dish will freeze for up to 3 weeks.

Mushroom Quiche

225 g/8 oz mushrooms	4 egg yolks
1 onion, quartered	salt and pepper
25 g/1 oz butter	pinch of nutmeg
100 g/4 oz Gruyère cheese	1 (23-cm/9-in) unbaked
25 g/1 oz plain flour	shortcrust pastry shell
5 tablespoons milk	(page 131)
300 ml/½ pint single cream	mushroom slices and parsley to garnish

Fit the slicing plate, slice the mushrooms and set aside. Using the metal blade, chop the onion. Melt the butter in a medium saucepan, add the onion and sauté until the onion is soft (about 3 minutes). Add the flour to the onion and stir over a medium heat for 1 minute. Pour in the milk and bring to the boil, stirring. Remove from the heat, stir in the cream, beaten egg yolks, salt, pepper and nutmeg. Using the shredding plate, shred the Gruyère cheese. Add three-quarters of the cheese to the sauce. Arrange the sliced mushrooms in the bottom of the pastry shell, pour the sauce over and sprinkle with the remaining cheese. Bake in a moderately hot oven (190 C, 375 F, gas 5) for 25 minutes or until set. Garnish with mushroom slices and parsley.

SERVES 6 TO 8

Egg and Ham Mousse

Spinach Quiche

Double the recipe for a large crowd.

350 g/12 oz frozen spinach, thawed
50 g/2 oz Cheddar cheese
1 packet thick onion soup mix
250 ml/8 fl oz soured cream
100 g/4 oz cottage cheese
100 g/4 oz feta cheese, crumbled

3 eggs, beaten
pepper to taste
1 (23-cm/9-in) unbaked shortcrust pastry shell (page 131)

Drain the spinach well, pressing out all the moisture. Fit the shredding plate to the processor, shred the Cheddar cheese and set aside. Add the onion soup mix to the soured cream and stand for 15 minutes. Now add the soured cream mixture to the spinach along with the cottage cheese, feta cheese, beaten eggs and Cheddar cheese. Season to taste with pepper. Pour into the pastry shell and bake in a moderately hot oven (190 c, 375 f, gas 5) for 35 to 40 minutes or until set.

SERVES 6 TO 8

This quiche freezes well for up to two weeks.

Prawn and Ham Creole

Make the sauce the day before, if liked, and reheat before serving.

1 kg/2 lb cooked ham, diced
1.4 kg/3 lb peeled prawns
hot cooked rice
parsley to garnish
CREOLE SAUCE
1.4 kg/3 lb tomatoes, peeled and deseeded
2 large green peppers, deseeded and cut into chunks
2 large onions, quartered
3 sprigs parsley, stems removed

2 cloves garlic
50 g/2 oz butter
40 g/1½ oz flour
450 ml/¾ pint tomato juice
450 ml/¾ pint chicken stock
1 (142 g/5 oz) can concentrated tomato purée
1 teaspoon salt
pepper to taste
1 tablespoon chilli powder
1 tablespoon sugar
1 teaspoon dried thyme

To make the sauce, use the metal blade to coarsely chop the tomatoes, then transfer them to a large mixing bowl. Chop the green peppers, onion, parsley and garlic together and add to the tomatoes. In a saucepan, melt the butter, stir in the flour and cook for 1 minute. Slowly stir in the tomato juice and chicken stock. Add the tomato purée, salt, pepper, chilli powder, sugar, dried thyme and chopped vegetables. Bring to the boil, reduce the heat and simmer, covered, for 25 minutes. At this point, the mixture may be cooled and refrigerated.

To serve, reheat the sauce, add the ham and prawns and simmer for 10 minutes or until the prawns are cooked. Serve with hot rice and garnish with parsley.

SERVES 20

Surprise Party Dish

The surprise is for the hostess. Make this dish the day before and allow the flavour to mature overnight in the refrigerator.

450 g/1 lb brown rice
2 litres/4 pints boiling water
2 kg/4 lb lean beef, cut into large cubes
2 onions, quartered
1 clove garlic
6 sticks celery, cleaned and trimmed

450 g/1 lb mushrooms
40 g/1½ oz butter
4 (425-g/15-oz) cans of cream of chicken soup
4 beef stock cubes
salt and pepper to taste
2 bay leaves
½ teaspoon dried mixed herbs
100 g/4 oz slivered almonds

Rinse the rice in cold water, then drain. Pour half the boiling water over the rice and stand for 15 minutes. Do not cook. Drain the rice well. Using the metal blade, process the beef in batches for about 6 seconds per batch. Transfer to a large mixing bowl. Chop the onion and garlic and add to the meat. Fit the slicing plate, slice the celery and mushrooms and set aside. Now brown the meat and onions in the butter. Add the mushrooms, celery, rice and soup. Dissolve the stock cubes in the remaining boiling water and add to the meat mixture, seasoning to taste with salt and pepper. Add the bay leaves and mixed herbs and stir in the almonds. Place the mixture in two large casseroles, cover and refrigerate overnight. Bake, uncovered, in a moderate oven (180 c, 350 f, gas 4) for 10 minutes. Serve hot.

SERVES 20

Reuben Casserole

1.75 kg/4 lb corned beef, cooked and cooled
1 kg/2 lb sauerkraut, drained
6 firm tomatoes, cut in half lengthwise
6 tablespoons Thousand Island Dressing (page 95)

100 g/4 oz butter
400 g/14 oz Gruyère cheese
20 wholewheat savoury biscuits
1 teaspoon caraway seeds

Slice the corned beef very thinly. layer the sauerkraut and the meat in each of two large casseroles, ending with a layer of sauerkraut. Using the slicing plate, slice the tomatoes and arrange in a layer over the sauerkraut. Spread with dressing and dot with butter. Using the shredding plate, shred the Gruyère cheese and sprinkle over the tomatoes. Fit the metal blade to the processor, add the savoury biscuits and pulse to finely crumb. Mix with the caraway seeds and sprinkle over the casseroles. Bake in a moderately hot oven (190 c, 375 f, gas 5) for about 25 to 30 minutes.

SERVES 20

Deep Dish Pizza Pie

Deep Dish Pizza Pie

Make two of these for a buffet party.

1 quantity cheese scone dough (page 125)	225 g/8 oz mozzarella cheese, chilled
450 g/1 lb lean beef	1 (142-g/5-oz) can concentrated tomato purée
1 onion, quartered	
2 cloves garlic	½ teaspoon dried mixed herbs
1 green pepper, halved and deseeded	½ teaspoon oregano
100 g/4 oz mushrooms	salt and pepper to taste

Make the scone dough, roll out and line the base and sides of a casserole or gratin dish.

Using the metal blade, process the beef in batches until coarsely minced (about 4 seconds per batch) and set aside. Chop the onion and garlic for 3 seconds. Cut the green pepper into chunks and add to the onion. Process until the vegetables are finely chopped. Set aside with the meat. Using the slicing plate, slice the mushrooms and set aside. Fit the shredding plate, shred the mozzarella cheese and place in the refrigerator until required. Sauté the minced beef with the onion, garlic and green pepper until the meat is lightly browned. Spread the tomato purée evenly over the base of the scone dough and top with the meat mixture. Sprinkle with herbs and top with sliced mushrooms. Finally, season to taste and sprinkle the mozzarella cheese on top. Bake in a hot oven (220 c, 425 f, gas 7) for about 20 minutes or until the crust is golden brown.

SERVES 8

Cashew Nut Casserole

A rich, tasty casserole you will make again and again.

1.75 kg/4 lb lean beef, cut into large cubes	3 (425-g/15-oz) cans cream of mushroom soup
4 onions, quartered	350 ml/12 fl oz soured cream
350 g/12 oz ripe olives	5 tablespoons dry sherry
350 g/12 oz mushrooms	salt and pepper to taste
450 g/1 lb Cheddar cheese	100 g/4 oz cashew nuts
450 g/1 lb noodles	1 packet plain potato crisps

Fit the metal blade to the processor and process the beef in batches for about 6 seconds per batch. Transfer to a large frying pan and fry until the meat is lightly browned (about 10 to 15 minutes). Chop the onions in the processor and add to the meat. Coarsely chop the olives and set aside. Using the slicing plate, slice the mushrooms and add to the olives. Now fit the shredding plate, shred the cheese and set aside. Lastly, cook the noodles in plenty of rapidly boiling, salted water until just tender, then drain.

To assemble the dish, mix together the beef, onions, olives, mushrooms, cheese, soup, soured cream and sherry. Season to taste with salt and pepper. Layer this mixture with the noodles in two large casseroles. Top with the cashew nuts and crushed potato crisps. Bake, uncovered, for 45 to 50 minutes. Serve hot.

SERVES 16

Spanikopita (Greek Cheese Pie)

3 onions, quartered
100 g/4 oz margarine
1.75 kg/4 lb fresh spinach
750 ml/1¼ pints milk
1.4 kg/3 lb dried
    breadcrumbs
175 ml/6 fl oz mint leaves,
    stems removed
450 g/1 lb cream cheese

6 eggs
salt and pepper to taste
350 g/12 oz Cheddar cheese
350 g/12 oz feta cheese
400 g/14 oz butter, melted
18–20 sheets phyllo pastry,
    halved (available from
    Greek shops or
    delicatessens)

Using the metal blade, finely chop the onions. Heat the margarine and sauté the onion until golden. Cook the well-washed spinach until tender, using only the water left clinging to the leaves. Drain well, remove the stalks, then process in batches until roughly chopped. Transfer to a large mixing bowl and add the onion. Combine the milk and breadcrumbs and allow to stand. Meanwhile, with the processor running, drop the mint leaves onto the metal blade and process until finely chopped. Add to the spinach. Now place the cream cheese, eggs and seasonings in the work bowl, and pulse to mix well. Add to the spinach. Fit the shredding plate and shred the Cheddar and feta cheeses. Add these to the spinach mixture. Stir in the milk and breadcrumbs mixture and mix well.

Brush three 25 × 30-cm/10 × 12-in ovenproof dishes with melted butter. Using a sharp knife, cut the phyllo slightly larger than the inside of the dish. Place one layer of pastry in the dish and brush with butter until there are seven layers altogether. Add one third of the spinach mixture and repeat the pastry and butter layers using six layers of pastry. Brush the final layer of pastry very well with melted butter. Repeat the process with the remaining two dishes. Place in a preheated oven and bake in a moderate oven (160 c, 325 f, gas 3) for 45 minutes. Serve, hot or warm, cut into squares.

This dish may be served as a buffet luncheon dish, as a vegetable dish or as a cocktail snack, cut into very small squares.

SERVES 20 AT A BUFFET

To freeze, assemble the casseroles, cover and freeze before cooking. Thaw at least 3 hours before baking.

Spanikopita

Nasi Goreng

Nasi Goreng 🌀

This traditional Indonesian fried rice dish is a buffet special. Not only is it different, but it is glamorous to look at and easy to eat standing up. The less adventurous will start off with 'just a little' to eat – but watch them rush back for more

450 g/1 lb rice
1 small head table celery,
   cleaned and cut into
   2.5-cm/1-in lengths
4 onions, quartered
8–10 cloves garlic
2 bunches spring onions, cut
   into 2.5 cm/1 in lengths
1.4 kg/3 lb raw, boneless
   meat (chicken, pork
   or beef)
salt and black pepper
soy sauce
24 peeled prawns
350 g/12 oz cooked ham
FRIKADELLA
350 g/12 oz minced meat
oil for frying
sambals Oelik and Badjak
   (obtainable from Indian
   shops or delicatessens)

OMELETTE
6 eggs
salt and pepper
4 tablespoons water
4 tablespoons oil
SAMBALS
fresh or pickled cucumber
   spears
pineapple rings, fresh or
   fried in butter
chopped tomato and onion
toasted coconut and peanuts
slices or fried chunks of
   banana
prawn crackers
GARNISH
1 fried egg per person
sprigs of parsley

Cook the rice, then chill overnight. Have three large bowls ready and place the chilled rice in one bowl. Using the metal blade and pulse button, chop the celery, leeks, onions, garlic and spring onions until medium-fine in texture. Place the chopped vegetables in the second bowl. Chop the parsley and set aside. Cut the meat into 1-cm/½-in cubes and place in the third bowl. Season with salt and pepper and add a little soy sauce. Cover the bowls and set aside. Now chop the prawns by hand. Dice the ham and set aside.

To make small frikadella, place the minced meat, salt and pepper to taste, a little soy sauce and a small quantity of chopped vegetables in the processor bowl and pulse a few times to mix. Form into small, bite-sized frikadella and brown in a little heated oil in a large, heavy frying pan. Remove from the pan, drain and set aside.

Heat a little more oil in the large frying pan, add about 1 teaspoon of the sambals Oelik and Badjak, then add one fifth of the meat and prawns. Sauté for 5 minutes. Now add one fifth of the vegetables and rice. Stir well, season and add more soy sauce and more of the sambals if necessary. The flavour of the mixture should be spicy, but not excessively hot. Cook for 7 to 10 minutes. Remove from the pan, place in a deep container and keep covered. Repeat the process with the remaining ingredients. Lastly, stir the chopped parsley, frikadella and ham into the meat mixture. Cover and refrigerate until required.

To serve Nasi Goreng, bake covered, in a moderate oven (160 c, 325 F, gas 3), until it has heated through. Meanwhile, make the omelette. Combine the eggs, seasonings and water. Heat the oil, pour in the egg mixture and allow to set, lifting the edges a few times. When cooked, turn out onto a board and cut into strips about 1 cm/½ in wide. Pile the Nasi Goreng onto a heated platter and garnish with a lattice of omelette strips and parsley. Serve a selection of sambals and fried eggs separately.

Traditionally, Nasi Goreng is served with a fried egg on top and is eaten from a soup plate with a spoon and fork. Serve beer rather than wine with the meal.

SERVES 20

Note: If the sambals Oelik and Badjak are unobtainable, substitute the following:

2–4 chillies
2 cloves garlic, chopped
2 onions, chopped
1 teaspoon caraway seeds
1 teaspoon ground coriander

100 g/4 oz raisins
salt and pepper
2 teaspoons brown sugar
4 small tomatoes, peeled
a little oil for frying

Fit the metal blade to the processor and place all the ingredients, except the oil, in the work bowl. Pulse until chopped. Heat a little oil in a saucepan, add the chopped ingredients and simmer until thick (about 20 minutes). Cool and refrigerate. This mixture will keep for up to two months.

Chicken and Prawn Curry

Curry lends itself to buffet meals. This is a wonderful variation.

3 large chickens, jointed,
    seasoned with salt and
    pepper
oil
3 large onions, quartered
8 cloves garlic
3 green peppers, deseeded and
    quartered
1 large piece of root ginger
40 curry leaves (optional)
6–7 tomatoes, skinned
curry powder to taste

4 tablespoons fish stock
1 tablespoon curry spices
    such as whole caraway,
    coriander, cumin,
    cardamom, cloves,
    cinnamon and fenugreek,
    tied in muslin
3 large aubergines
10 courgettes
575 g/1¼ lb peeled prawns
salt and black pepper

Fry the seasoned chicken in a little oil, then transfer to a large casserole. Using the metal blade, chop the onions, garlic, green peppers, ginger and curry leaves in batches. Chop the tomatoes and set aside separately. Add a little more oil to the frying pan. Sauté the chopped vegetables and curry powder. Add the fish stock, tomatoes and curry spices tied in a muslin bag, and bring to the boil. Pour over the chicken and bake, covered, for 1 hours in a cool oven (140c, 275 f, gas 1).

Meanwhile, cut the aubergines in quarters lengthwise. Fit the chipper plate and process. Remove from the work bowl. Sprinkle with salt and stand for 30 minutes. Drain and pat dry. Using the slicing plate and a firm pressure, slice the courgettes. Add the aubergines, courgettes and prawns to the casserole and season to taste. Return to the oven and bake for a further 30 minutes. Remove the spice bag before serving with rice and a selection of sambals.

SERVES 20

This dish freezes well, but be careful not to overcook before freezing.

Lamb with Yogurt and Spicy Rice

The combination of rice, nuts, spices and lamb makes this dish an easy winner for a large gathering.

900 g/2 lb rice
6 onions, quartered
oil for frying
150 g/5 oz almonds
150 g/5 oz raisins
1 large piece root ginger
8 cloves garlic
1 tablespoon caraway seeds
3 kg/6½ lb boneless lamb,
    cubed
cayenne to taste
2 sticks cinnamon

15 cloves
14 cardamom seeds
3 blades of mace
¼ teaspoon nutmeg
750 ml/1¼ pints chicken
    stock
750 ml/1¼ pints natural
    yogurt
1 teaspoon turmeric
salt to taste
parsley to garnish

Cook the rice in boiling, salted water for 10 minutes. Drain and set aside. Using the slicing plate, slice the onions. Heat a little oil in a pan and fry the onions until golden. Drain and set aside. Add the nuts and raisins to the pan and fry until golden. Add to the onions and reserve. Fit the metal blade and, with the processor running, drop the ginger, garlic and caraway seeds onto the metal blade. Add a little more oil to the frying pan and sauté the crushed ingredients. Add the lamb and cayenne and brown well. Place in one large or several smaller casseroles. Tie the cinnamon, cloves, cardamom seeds and mace in a piece of muslin and add to the meat. Add the rice, nutmeg, chicken stock, yogurt, turmeric and salt. Stir well. Cover and bake in a moderate oven (160c, 325 f, gas 3) until all the liquid has been absorbed. If necessary, add a little more chicken stock. To serve, remove the muslin bag and pile the lamb mixture onto a heated platter. Sprinkle with nuts and onions and garnish with sprigs of parsley and leaves cut out of heavy foil. Serve with a salad.

SERVES 20

This dish freezes well for a week.

Snacks and Suppers

The supper is gaining popularity for entertaining. It may be a slightly formal meal, a very casual affair or a spur of the moment get-together. The menu may consist of a casserole, salad and dessert or a hearty soup with homemade bread.

Casseroles lend themselves to informal entertaining and take the pressure off the hostess. No longer is it considered a hurried, last-minute family dish consisting of leftovers. Some casseroles require long, slow cooking, but need little attention during the process. They can be made in advance and refrigerated or frozen for later use. The casserole looks appetising, stays hot and is easy to serve.

Also included in this section are a variety of snack foods which can be served as appetisers with drinks, for a casual function or a fancy cocktail party.

Apple and Liver Spread 📍

A spicey spread with an unusual flavour combination.

450 g/1 lb chicken livers
50 g/2 oz butter
1 clove garlic
1 small onion, quartered
1 apple, peeled, cored and
   quartered
6 tablespoons double cream

1 tablespoon lemon juice
1 tablespoon dry sherry
salt and pepper to taste
pinch each of ground
   allspice, cloves and
   nutmeg

Sauté the livers in the butter until they lose their pink colour. Place the garlic, onion and apple in the work bowl and chop with the metal blade. Add to the livers and cook for about 5 minutes. Spoon half the liver mixture into the work bowl and add half the cream, lemon juice, sherry and seasonings. Process until smooth. Repeat with the remaining ingredients. Pour this mixture into a serving dish and refrigerate until needed. Serve with brown bread or savoury biscuits.

MAKES ABOUT 450 G/1 LB

Bacon Fingers 📍 📍

4 rashers bacon
225 g/8 oz Cheddar cheese
5 tablespoons chutney
a little double cream

3 slices of bread
butter
a little mustard powder

Fry the bacon until crisp, then drain. Using the metal blade, chop the bacon finely and set aside. Fit the shredding plate and shred the cheese. Replace the metal blade and combine the

A selection of snacks including Bacon Fingers, Stuffed Eggs and Apple and Liver Spread

cheese, chutney and enough cream to moisten. Pulse to mix well. Toast the bread under the grill on one side only. Spread the untoasted side with butter and sprinkle with a little mustard powder. Spread thickly with the cheese mixture. Finally, sprinkle the bacon down the centre of the cheese. Place under the grill for a few minutes until the cheese bubbles. Cool slightly, trim away the bread crusts and cut into fingers. Serve hot or cold.

MAKES 12 BACON FINGERS

Stuffed Eggs 📍

Stuffed eggs are always popular. Use them as snacks, starters or as a garnish. Make them this way and they will keep for hours.

6 eggs
about 6 tablespoons
   mayonnaise (page 95)
salt and black pepper to
   taste

1 teaspoon Worcestershire
   sauce
2 tablespoons tomato ketchup
   (optional)
12 shrimps to garnish

Hard-boil the eggs in gently simmering water for 10 minutes. Plunge into cold water, then peel. Trim both ends of the eggs so that each half will stand easily. Cut the eggs in half and scoop out the yolk. Place the yolks in the work bowl fitted with the metal blade. Cover the inside of an egg box with cling film and set the whites in the hollows. Cover with plastic and close the box. Store in the refrigerator until required. (Do not rinse out the egg whites as they will discolour.) Now add the mayonnaise, seasonings, Worcestershire sauce and tomato ketchup to the egg yolks and blend until smooth. This mixture can be stored in a sealed container in the refrigerator for up to 8 hours. Fit a piping bag with a medium-sized star nozzle. Fill the bag with the egg yolk mixture. Arrange the egg whites on a platter, and generously fill each one with swirls of filling. Decorate with shrimps.

MAKES 12 HALVES

Variations

Stuffed Eggs with Curry Filling

6 eggs, hard-boiled	salt and black pepper
1 teaspoon curry paste	1 teaspoon Worcestershire
about 6 tablespoons	sauce
mayonnaise (page 95)	slices of stuffed olive

Proceed as for stuffed eggs. Garnish with tiny sprigs of parsley.

Stuffed Eggs Riviera

6 eggs, hard-boiled	2 teaspoons mustard powder
25 g/1 oz stuffed olives	1 teaspoon brandy
25 g/1 oz capers	a little mayonnaise
100 g/4 oz tuna	salt and black pepper

Proceed as for stuffed eggs. Use a plain tube when piping the filling.

Stuffed Eggs with Sardines

6 eggs, hard-boiled	1 teaspoon mustard powder
1 slice onion	2 teaspoons lemon juice
1 tablespoon parsley, stems	about 6 tablespoons
removed	mayonnaise (page 95)
1 (120-g/4¼-oz) can	salt and black pepper
sardines	

Fit the work bowl with the metal blade and finely chop the onion and parsley. Proceed as for stuffed eggs. Use a plain nozzle when piping the filling.

Stuffed Eggs with Pickled Walnuts

6 eggs, hard-boiled	about 4 tablespoons
2 pickled walnuts	mayonnaise (page 95)
1 tablespoon bottled brown	parsley sprigs to garnish
sauce (eg HP sauce)	

Proceed as for Stuffed Eggs. Garnish with tiny sprigs of parsley.

Chequer Board

1 (100-g/4-oz) jar caviar	100 g/4 oz smoked salmon
1 marinated herring	2 tablespoons oil
2 eggs, hard-boiled	2 teaspoons lemon juice
1 loaf semi-frozen wholewheat	shredded lettuce to serve
bread	freshly ground black pepper
butter to spread	

Place the caviar in a sieve, rinse and drain. Fit the metal blade to the processor and place the caviar, herring and eggs in the work bowl. Pulse until well mixed. Allow the bread to thaw slightly, then slice thinly lengthwise. Spread each long slice with butter. Place smoked salmon on half the bread slices. Combine the oil and lemon juice and brush over the salmon. Trim the crusts and cut the bread into small squares. Spread the remaining bread slices with the caviar mixture, trim the crusts and cut into squares. With the slicing plate, shred the lettuce and scatter over a tray. Arrange the smoked salmon and caviar squares in a chequer board pattern on top of the shredded lettuce. Lastly, add a few grindings of black pepper, cover with cling film and refrigerate for not more than 3 hours.

COVER A TRAY MEASURING 33 × 23 CM/13 × 9 IN

Vegetarian Pâté

2 sticks celery, cut into	1 teaspoon sugar
short pieces	½ teaspoon dried basil
1 small green pepper,	pinch of ground cloves
deseeded and cut up	salt and pepper to taste
1 onion, quartered	2 teaspoons powdered
1 small cucumber, peeled,	gelatine
deseeded and cut up	3 tablespoons hot water
1 clove garlic	4 tablespoons white wine
1 (397-g/14-oz) can tomatoes	1 teaspoon lemon juice
2 tablespoons oil	parsley to garnish
1 tablespoon concentrated	mayonnaise to serve
tomato purée	(optional)
1 tablespoon white wine	
vinegar	

With the metal blade, chop the celery, green pepper, onion, cucumber and garlic together. Add the tomatoes and all the liquid from the can, the oil, tomato purée, vinegar, sugar, basil and cloves. Process until the mixture is smooth, scraping down the sides of the bowl when necessary. Season to taste with salt and pepper.

Dissolve the gelatine in the hot water over a basin of boiling water then add the wine and lemon juice. Add to the vegetable mixture and process for 4 to 5 seconds to mix well. Turn the mixture into a serving bowl or mould, and chill until set. Turn out and garnish with parsley. Serve with mayonnaise, if desired.

SERVES 6 TO 8

Chequer Board

Three Cheese Spread

100 g/4 oz Cheddar cheese	25 g/1 oz butter, softened
100 g/4 oz Parmesan cheese, cut into pieces	2 teaspoons powdered gelatine
100 g/4 oz blue cheese, crumbled	3 tablespoons hot water
2 teaspoons prepared English mustard	200 ml/7 fl oz dry white wine
dash of Tabasco sauce	250 ml/8 fl oz single cream
salt and pepper to taste	2 tablespoons mayonnaise (page 95)

With the shredding plate, shred the Cheddar cheese and set aside. Fit the metal blade and process the Parmesan cheese until it is finely crumbled. Add the Cheddar and cheeses, mustard, Tabasco, salt, pepper and softened butter. Process to mix well.

Dissolve the gelatine in the hot water over a basin of boiling water then add the wine, the cream and stir in the mayonnaise. Now add the gelatine mixture to the cheese in the work bowl and process until the mixture is smooth, scraping down the sides of the bowl when necessary. Turn the mixture into a mould or serving bowl and chill until set. Turn out the mould or serve the spread directly from the bowl. Accompany with savoury biscuits.

SERVES 12

Ham and Chicken Puffs

Filled choux pastries make wonderful snacks. Make the pastry cases 'bite-size' and use a selection of fillings to provide interesting variety. Larger puffs make excellent starters.

24 small choux pastry puffs (page 135)	250 ml/8 fl oz chicken stock
1 small onion, quartered	3 tablespoons single cream
2 sticks celery	3 tablespoons sherry
sprig of parsley, stems removed	salt and cayenne to taste
2 tablespoons oil	100 g/4 oz cooked chicken
50 g/2 oz plain flour	100 g/4 oz cooked ham
	parsley to garnish

Chop the onion, celery and parsley with the metal blade. Sauté in heated oil. Add the flour, then the chicken stock. Bring to the boil, stirring constantly until thickened. Remove from the heat and add the cream, sherry and seasonings. Using the metal blade and pulse, roughly chop the chicken and ham. Add the meats to the sauce, stir well and cool before using. Cut the puffs in half and fill generously. Replace the tops and serve on a flat platter, garnished with parsley.

MAKES 24 SMALL PUFFS

Aloha Spareribs

Serve these as a snack and supply plenty of paper serviettes.

1.4 kg/3 lb pork spareribs, cut into serving pieces	200 ml/7 fl oz white wine vinegar
2 litres/4 pints water	200 ml/7 fl oz water
6 tablespoons white wine vinegar	200 ml/7 fl oz pineapple juice
100 g/4 oz cornflour	1 large green pepper, deseeded and halved
3 tablespoons golden syrup	1 large onion, cut in half lengthwise
3 tablespoons soy sauce	
1 teaspoon salt	1 small pineapple, peeled and cut into wedges
6 tablespoons oil	
GLAZE	
100 g/4 oz sugar	

Trim the ribs. Bring the water and vinegar to the boil and add the ribs. Cover and bring back to the boil. Uncover and simmer for 15 minutes. Drain and cool. Mix the cornflour, syrup, soy sauce and salt. Spread over the ribs to coat well. Fry the ribs in hot oil until well browned on all sides.

To make the glaze, place the sugar, vinegar, water and pineapple juice in a large saucepan and bring to the boil. Add the ribs, cover and simmer for 30 minutes. Using the slicing plate, slice the green pepper halves in julienne strips. Slice the onion halves and pineapple wedges. Add to the spareribs and cook for 15 minutes more. Serve hot with the sauce.

SERVES 12

Anchovy Crisps

1 (50-g/1¾-oz) can anchovies	2 teaspoons lemon juice
1 hard-boiled egg yolk	1 teaspoon French mustard
25 g/1 oz butter, softened	15 thin slices white bread
	melted butter

Fit the metal blade to the processor and place the anchovies, egg yolk, butter, lemon juice and mustard in the work bowl. Pulse until smooth. Remove the crusts from the bread. Using a rolling pin, roll the slices very thin. Spread with the anchovy butter. Dampen one edge of each slice and roll up towards that edge. Brush the rolls generously with melted butter and arrange, seam side downwards, on a baking tray. Spike each roll with a toothpick to prevent it unrolling. Bake in a moderately hot oven (200 c, 400 f, gas 6) for about 15 to 20 minutes or until the rolls are golden brown. Remove the toothpicks and serve hot.

These may be made in advance, covered and kept in the refrigerator until required. Bake and serve piping hot.

MAKES 15 ROLLS

Olive Bites

100 g/4 oz Cheddar cheese	generous pinch of cayenne
25 g/1 oz butter	25 stuffed olives
50 g/2 oz plain flour	

Fit the shredding plate to the processor and shred the cheese. Now fit the metal blade, add the butter to the cheese and process for a few seconds. Sift the flour and cayenne, add to the butter and cheese in the work bowl. Process for a few seconds until the dough starts to hold together. Take about a teaspoon of the dough, flatten it into a circle and wrap it around an olive. Place on a non-stick baking tray. Repeat with the remaining pastry and olives. Bake in a moderately hot oven (200 c, 400 f, gas 6) for 15 minutes. Cool slightly before removing from the tray. Serve hot or cold.

These bites may be made and cooked a few days in advance. Store in an airtight container. To reheat, place in a moderate oven (160 c, 325 f, gas 3) for 3 to 5 minutes.

MAKES 25 BITES

Curried Sardine Crescents

1 quantity of Cream Cheese Pastry (page 131)	2 teaspoons lemon juice
1 tablespoon parsley	salt and black pepper
2 hard-boiled eggs	curry paste to taste
1 (124-g/4⅜-oz) can sardines	

Make up the pastry and chill well for at least one hour. Fit the metal blade to the processor, place the parsley, eggs and sardines in the work bowl and pulse to chop. Add the lemon juice, seasonings and curry paste to taste. Pulse to combine. Roll out the pastry until 5 mm/¼ in thick. Cut into 10-cm/4-in squares, then cut each square in half to form triangles. Place a

little filling in the middle of the diagonal of each triangle. Wet the tip of the triangle, roll up towards the tip and seal. Twist the ends to form a crescent shape. Place on a greased baking tray. Bake in a hot oven (220 c, 425 f, gas 7) for 10 minutes and serve hot.

MAKES 36 CRESCENTS

These crescents freeze perfectly. Freeze on a baking tray before cooking. When frozen, pack into airtight containers and keep for up to one month.

Cheesy Prawn Puffs

450 g/1 lb peeled prawns	PASTRY
100 g/4 oz Cheddar cheese	250 ml/8 fl oz fish stock
about 4 tablespoons single cream	50 g/2 oz butter
	100 g/4 oz plain flour
	oil for deep frying

Place the prawns in the work bowl and chop, using the metal blade. Fit the shredding plate and shred the cheese. Bind the cheese and prawns with the cream. For the pastry, heat the fish stock and the butter and allow to boil. Remove from the heat and add the sifted flour all at once. Stir well and return to the heat for a few seconds. Cool slightly, then roll out until 5 mm/¼ in thick. Using a biscuit cutter, cut into rounds. Place a little of the filling on each circle. Brush the edges of the pastry with water and fold in half, sealing well. Fry in deep, hot oil until golden brown. Drain and serve.

These may be made in advance, covered and placed in the refrigerator. Deep fry just before serving.

MAKES 20 PUFFS

Savoury Supper Bread

This bread makes an ideal accompaniment to casseroles and soups.

100 g/4 oz Cheddar cheese	1 teaspoon salt
2 sticks celery	1 tablespoon baking powder
50 g/2 oz salted nuts	1 teaspoon dried mixed herbs
1 tablespoon parsley, stems removed	100 g/4 oz margarine
1 tablespoon fresh chopped chives	200 ml/7 fl oz milk
225 g/8 oz plain flour	1 egg
	1 tablespoon melted butter

Fit the shredding plate to the processor, shred the cheese and set aside. Reserve half the cheese for the top. Using the metal blade, pulse to chop the celery, nuts, parsley and chives. Add to the cheese. Place the flour, salt, baking powder and mixed herbs in the work bowl and pulse four times to aerate. Add the margarine and pulse to rub in. Now add the cheese mixture. Combine the milk and egg and pour through the feed tube while the machine is running. Process until a stiff dough forms. Turn the dough into a deep, greased and lined, 23-

cm/9-in round cake tin. Sprinkle with the reserved cheese and drizzle with melted butter. Bake in a moderately hot oven (200 c, 400 f, gas 6) for 30 minutes.

SERVES 6 TO 8

Sukiyaki

450 g/1 lb rump steak, thinly sliced
2 tablespoons oil
5 sticks celery
150 g/5 oz mushrooms
1 large onion, cut in half lengthwise
2 green peppers, deseeded and quartered

1 bunch spring onions, cut into 1-cm/½-in lengths
250 ml/8 fl oz beef stock
1 tablespoon soy sauce
5 tablespoons water
40 g/1½ oz cornflour

Sauté the meat in oil until browned. Using the slicing plate, slice the celery, mushrooms and onion. Fit the metal blade and chop the green pepper. Add the sliced vegetables, green pepper and spring onions to the meat. Pour in the stock and soy sauce. Cover and cook over a low heat for 10 minutes. Combine the water with the cornflour and add to the meat mixture, stirring constantly until thickened. Serve with rice.

SERVES 6

Mushroom and Cheese Bake

4 slices day-old bread
butter
225 g/8 oz mushrooms
225 g/8 oz Cheddar cheese
½ small onion, halved
2 tablespoons parsley, stems removed
3 eggs

300 ml/½ pint milk
4 tablespoons single cream
salt and black pepper
½ teaspoon paprika
½ teaspoon mustard powder
1 teaspoon Worcestershire sauce
½ teaspoon dried thyme

Remove the crusts from the bread and spread butter on both sides of each slice. Dice into 1-cm/½-in cubes and place cubes in a 20-cm/8-in greased pie plate. Fit the slicing plate to the processor and slice the mushrooms. Arrange over the bread. Using the shredding plate, shred the cheese and sprinkle over the mushrooms. Change to the metal blade and finely chop the onion and parsley. Add all the remaining ingredients and pulse twice to mix. Pour over the cheese, cover tightly and refrigerate overnight. Bake in a cool oven (140 c, 275 f, gas 1) for 1½ hours. Serve immediately.

SERVES 4

Left: Sukiyaki, Right: Mushroom and Cheese Bake: Country Sausage Pie (page 80)

Moussaka

2 medium aubergines, cut in half	salt and pepper to taste
100 g/4 oz butter	SAUCE
450 g/1 lb lean lamb, cut into pieces	75 g/3 oz butter
2 tablespoons olive oil	25 g/1 oz flour
1 small onion, quartered	450 ml/¾ pint milk
3 tomatoes, peeled and quartered	3 eggs, beaten

Using the slicing plate, slice the aubergines and soak in salted water for 15 minutes. Drain and press out the excess water with a paper towel. Brown the aubergine slices in butter and set aside. Using the metal blade, mince the lamb in two batches. Brown the meat in heated olive oil. Chop the onion with the metal blade, add to the lamb and sauté. Lastly, chop the tomatoes, add to the lamb and season to taste with salt and pepper, cover the pan and simmer for 20 minutes. Arrange a layer of aubergine slices in a greased casserole. Cover with a layer of meat mixture. Repeat these layers until all the ingredients are used.

To make the sauce, melt the butter, stir in the flour and cook for 2 minutes. Pour in the milk and cook, stirring until the mixture thickens. Remove from the heat and stir a little sauce into the beaten eggs. Now add the egg mixture to the remaining sauce in the pan and mix well. Finally, pour the sauce over the ingredients in the casserole and bake, uncovered, in a moderate oven (180 c, 350 f, gas 4) for about 40 minutes. Serve hot.

SERVES 4

Italian Mostaccioli

450 g/1 lb extra large macaroni	5 tablespoons concentrated tomato purée
1 small green pepper, deseeded and quartered	150 ml/¼ pint water
1 small onion, quartered	1 bay leaf
2 tablespoons oil	salt and pepper to taste
675 g/1½ lb lean beef, cut into cubes	100 g/4 oz Parmesan cheese, cut into cubes
1 (397-g/14-oz) can tomatoes	450 g/1 lb sliced processed cheese

Cook the macaroni according to the directions on the packet and drain well. Place half the macaroni in a 23 × 33-cm/9 × 13-in baking dish. Using the metal blade, chop the green pepper and onion and sauté in oil for 5 minutes. Continuing to use the metal blade, mince the beef in batches, a third at a time. Add to the green pepper and onion and cook until just browned. Stir in the tomatoes, tomato purée, water and bay leaf. Season with salt and pepper. Bring to the boil and simmer for 20 minutes. Finely chop the Parmesan cheese with the metal blade. Pour half the meat sauce over the layer of macaroni, top with slices of processed cheese and sprinkle with Parmesan. Repeat these layers, ending with Parmesan. Bake, uncovered in a moderately hot oven (190 c, 375 f, gas 5) for about 25 minutes.

SERVES 8 TO 10

Country Sausage Pie

1 quantity of Crusty Pastry (page 133)	225 g/8 oz mushrooms
450 g/1 lb sausages	2 eggs
1 onion, quartered	200 ml/7 fl oz milk
2 tablespoons parsley, stems removed	½ teaspoon dried sage
a little oil	salt and black pepper
	75 g/3 oz Cheddar cheese
	1 beaten egg to glaze

Make the pastry and allow it to rest in the refrigerator. In a frying pan, brown the sausages using a little oil if necessary. With the metal blade, chop the onion and parsley. Remove the sausages from the pan and cut them into pieces. Add a little oil to the pan and sauté the onion and parsley. With the slicing plate, slice the mushrooms. Add to the onions in the pan and sauté for 3 minutes. In a bowl, combine the eggs and milk and add the sausages, mushroom mixture and sage. Season well. Now fit the shredding plate and shred the cheese. Add to the sausage mixture which should be completely cool. Grease a 25-cm/10-in diameter round or rectangular pie plate. Cut the pastry in half and roll out one half to line the pie plate. Carefully place it in position and trim the edges with a sharp knife. Pour the filling into the pastry. Roll out the remaining pastry to form the top. Wet the edges and place in position. Press the edges firmly together, trim and flute. Brush with beaten egg. Bake in a moderate oven (180 c, 350 f, gas 4) for 50 minutes. Serve hot or warm.

SERVES 6

This dish freezes very well for up to two months. Freeze before cooking and without glazing with beaten egg. Do not thaw before baking.

One Pot Sausage Supper

2 tablespoons oil	450 ml/¾ pint water
450 g/1 lb sausages	2 teaspoons chicken stock powder
1 onion, quartered	1 bay leaf
1 green pepper, peeled, deseeded and quartered	salt and black pepper
225 g/8 oz rice	1 (227-g/8-oz) can pineapple pieces, drained
2 tomatoes, peeled	
½ teaspoon curry paste	

Heat the oil in a heavy-based pan. Brown the sausages, drain and set aside. Using the metal blade, chop the onion and green pepper, add to the oil and sauté. Add the rice and sauté until opaque. Chop the tomatoes in the processor and add to the pan along with the sausages, curry paste, water, stock powder, bay leaf and seasonings. Cover and simmer until all the liquid has been absorbed and the rice is tender. Stir in the pineapple pieces and serve.

SERVES 4

Few people give vegetables their due and often the much neglected 'veges' arrive at the table soggy, overcooked and seasoned with only a dash of salt and a pat of butter. Not only do they look unappetising but most of their goodness has been destroyed. Generally the problem lies not with the vegetables themselves, but with the cook who treats them as an afterthought when planning meals.

Different methods of preparation and different combinations of vegetables will boost any meal, adding extra colour, texture and flavour. Here your food processor will be of the utmost assistance as it not only slices, shreds and chops raw vegetables and purées cooked ones, but also grates cheese and makes tasty sauces to enhance many vegetable dishes. Crisp, raw vegetable pieces, increasingly popular as low-calorie snacks, are great for dipping and serving with savoury spreads, so include a selection in your next party menu.

Remember, the quality of any vegetable dish begins with the quality of the vegetable itself. When selecting vegetables, look first for freshness. Vegetables should be comparatively dry, as any excess moisture hastens decay. Avoid using excessively bruised, wilted or badly damaged ones. Preserving quality is difficult as, even under ideal temperature and humidity conditions, most fresh vegetables remain in top condition for only a few days. Leafy vegetables tend to wilt and change colour due to loss of moisture from the tissues, while vegetables such as sweet corn, green beans and peas, lose their sweetness when their sugar converts to starch. Most fresh vegetables will remain crisp if placed in covered containers or plastic bags and stored in the refrigerator. Drain and dry lettuce, celery and other leafy vegetables before storing.

Before cooking, wash the vegetables thoroughly in a basin of cold water. Lift leafy vegetables and greens out of the water to allow any sand or grit to settle at the bottom of the basin, and drain upside down. For the best results, cook prepared or frozen vegetables in a little salted water until just tender, then drain. Avoid overcooking, as the vegetables will continue to cook for a while longer after they have been removed from the saucepan.

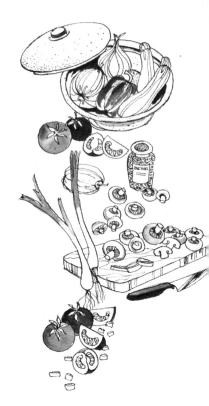

Baked Stuffed Artichokes

6 artichokes, fresh or canned	2 slices bread, cubed
10 peppercorns	2 cloves garlic
1 bay leaf	2 teaspoons mint leaves, stalks removed
2 teaspoons oil	3 tablespoons oil
wedge of lemon	1 tablespoon white wine
STUFFING	salt and black pepper

If using canned artichokes, level the base and push the leaves aside to make room for the stuffing. When fresh artichokes are available, prepare and cook in the following way: using a sharp knife or kitchen shears, trim 2.5 cm/1 in off the leaf tops. Bring to the boil sufficient water to cover the artichokes, then add the artichokes, peppercorns, bay leaf, oil and lemon. Boil for about 25 to 30 minutes or until tender – the outside leaves should peel away easily. Drain upside down and cool. Remove the tough outer leaves and cut the bases so the artichokes will stand level. Gently prise open the top and lift out the centre leaves. Use the end of a teaspoon to remove the hairy 'choke'. Brush the artichoke with lemon juice to prevent discoloration. To make the stuffing, fit the metal blade to the processor and process the bread until finely crumbled. With the machine running, drop in the garlic and mint leaves and process till fine. Heat the oil in a pan, sauté the crumb mixture and add the wine. Season well and press as much stuffing as possible into the centre of the artichokes. Push the remainder into the

spaces between the outside leaves. Arrange the artichokes in a baking dish and add 2 tablespoons boiling water. Cover the dish with aluminium foil and bake in a moderate oven (160 c, 325 f, gas 3) for 30 minutes. Serve hot.

SERVES 6

Courgette Sauté

This vegetable dish takes so little time that you can prepare it at the last minute

8 medium courgettes, ends removed	2 tablespoons lemon juice
100 g/4 oz butter or margarine	150 ml/$\frac{1}{4}$ pint soured cream
salt and freshly ground black pepper to taste	1 tablespoon chopped parsley
	2 teaspoons chopped chives

Using the shredding plate, shred the courgettes. Heat the butter in a large frying pan. Add the courgettes and sauté for 2 minutes, stirring continuously. Season with salt and pepper. Stir in the lemon juice, soured cream, chopped parsley and chives. Serve at once.

SERVES 6 TO 8

Broccoli Ring

Garnished with sliced tomatoes and parsley, this tasty dish makes a colourful addition to the dinner table.

450 g/1 lb frozen chopped broccoli thawed	2 cloves garlic
225 g/8 oz mature Cheddar cheese	4 tablespoons melted butter
	4 eggs, well beaten
2 sprigs parsley, stems removed	salt and pepper to taste
	sliced tomatoes and parsley to garnish

Generously coat the inside of a 1.4-litres/2½-pints ring mould with oil or melted butter. Drain the broccoli, squeeze out the excess moisture and place in a large mixing bowl. Using the shredding plate, shred the cheese and add to the broccoli. Change to the metal blade and chop the parsley, onion and garlic. Add to the broccoli and cheese. Now stir in the flour, melted butter, eggs, salt and pepper. Spoon this mixture into the prepared mould. Set the mould in a roasting tin filled with hot water to a depth of 2.5 cm/1 in. Bake in a moderate oven (180c, 350f, gas 4) for 20 to 25 minutes or until set. Allow to cool in the pan for about 5 minutes before unmoulding onto a warm serving platter. Garnish with sliced tomatoes and parsley.

SERVES 6

Aubergines in Cream

6 small aubergines	150 ml/¼ pint single cream
salt and black pepper	
50 g/2 oz butter	1 clove garlic, crushed
a little chicken stock	generous pinch of dried marjoram
25 g/1 oz plain flour	
	2 teaspoons chopped parsley

Wash the aubergines, remove the ends and cut to fit the feed tube. Using the chipper plate, dice the aubergines. Sprinkle with salt and allow to stand for 30 minutes. Dry with absorbent kitchen paper before gently frying in butter until golden. Add a little chicken stock, cover and simmer until tender. Sprinkle with flour, season and stir in the cream, garlic and marjoram. Simmer for a few minutes more. Sprinkle with parsley before serving.

SERVES 6

Celery with Pecan Nuts

Take care not to overcook the celery as this vegetable casserole should be firm and crunchy in texture.

½ small onion, cut up	50 g/2 oz butter
100 g/4 oz pecan nuts	25 g/1 oz plain flour
2 slices dry bread, broken up	450 ml/¾ pint milk
	salt and pepper to taste
1 large head celery, cleaned and trimmed	7 tablespoons single cream

Broccoli Ring

Fit the metal blade to the processor and chop the onion followed by the pecan nuts and bread, keeping the ingredients separate. Change to the slicing plate and slice the celery. Cook the celery in a little boiling, salted water until just tender. Drain well and place in a greased casserole dish.

Melt half the butter and sauté the onion until just tender. Remove from the heat and stir in the flour. Stir in the milk and bring to the boil. Cook, stirring until bubbly and thickened. Season with salt and pepper, then stir in the cream. Pour the sauce over the celery, mixing well. Sprinkle with chopped pecan nuts. Now melt the remaining butter and toss in the breadcrumbs. Sprinkle the buttered crumbs over the casserole and bake, uncovered, in a moderately hot oven (190c, 375f, gas 5) for about 15 minutes or until heated through and browned.

SERVES 8 TO 10

Cheesy Onions

Cheese gives onion a special flavour. This dish is an excellent accompaniment to roasts or grilled meats.

450 g/1 lb large onions, peeled	½ teaspoon dried dill or 1 teaspoon fresh dill
225 g/8 oz cheese, cut into pieces	1 teaspoon chopped parsley
	1 teaspoon Worcestershire sauce
100 g/4 oz butter, softened	
pinch of oregano	black pepper to taste

Cut the onion in half and slice, using the slicing plate. Arrange in a greased casserole dish. Fit the metal blade to the processor and place the cheese, butter, oregano, dill, parsley, Worcestershire sauce and pepper in the work bowl. Process for 6 to 8 seconds, scraping the bowl when necessary. Spread this mixture evenly over the sliced onion, and bake in a moderately hot oven (200c, 400f, gas 6) for 20 to 25 minutes or until melted and golden brown. If desired, place under the grill to brown the top. Serve immediately.

SERVES 6

Risotto Milanese

Risotto Milanese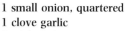

1 small onion, quartered	450 ml/¾ pint chicken
1 clove garlic	stock
2 sticks celery	salt and black pepper
50 g/2 oz mushrooms	25 g/2 oz Parmesan cheese,
25 g/1 oz margarine	shredded
225 g/8 oz rice	50 g/2 oz cashew nuts
pinch of turmeric	paprika to dust
1 bay leaf	

Fit the metal blade to the processor and chop the onion, garlic and celery. Using the slicing blade, slice the mushrooms. Heat the margarine in an ovenproof casserole and sauté the onion, garlic and celery. Add the mushrooms and rice and combine to sauté for 5 minutes more. Now add the turmeric, bay leaf, chicken stock and seasonings. Cover and bake until the rice is cooked. Add a little more liquid if necessary. Remove the bay leaf and stir in the Parmesan cheese and cashew nuts. Finally, dust with paprika and serve.

SERVES 4

Green Beans in Sherry Sauce

Dry sherry gives an unusual, tangy taste to green beans.

450 g/1 lb fresh green	25 g/1 oz sugar
beans	2 teaspoons cornflour
3 rashers bacon, rinds	3 tablespoons tarragon wine
removed	vinegar
1 onion	7 tablespoons dry sherry

Top and tail the beans and rinse in cold water. Use the slicing plate to slice the beans. Cook in a little boiling, salted water until just tender. Drain and keep warm. Fry the bacon until crisp. Fit the metal blade to the processor, chop the bacon and set aside. Cut the onion into quarters and chop coarsely in the processor. Sauté the onion in bacon fat until tender. Add the sugar, cornflour, vinegar and sherry to the pan. Cook until thickened, stirring constantly. Now add the bacon and the beans, stirring to mix. Serve hot.

SERVES 8

Cauliflower Polonaise

1 medium-sized cauliflower	1 teaspoon Worcestershire
1 tablespoon oil	sauce
1 medium onion, quartered	50 g/2 oz Cheddar cheese
1 (398-g/14-oz) can tomatoes	1 hard-boiled egg
1 teaspoon dried mixed herbs	2 tablespoons dried
salt and black pepper	breadcrumbs

Wash the cauliflower well and break into florets. Soak in salt water for 10 minutes, then drain. Cook in boiling, salted water until tender. Meanwhile, heat the oil in a small saucepan. Using the metal blade, chop the onion and sauté in the oil until transparent. Chop the canned tomatoes in the processor and add to the saucepan. Add the herbs, salt, pepper and Worcestershire sauce. Simmer until thick. Fit the shredding plate to the processor, shred the cheese and add half to the sauce. Now shred the hard-boiled egg. Add the breadcrumbs to the egg and remaining cheese. Arrange the cauliflower in an ovenproof dish and pour the sauce over. Top with the crumb mixture and place in a moderate oven (180 c, 350 f, gas 4) for 5 minutes.

SERVES 4 TO 6

Dilled Cauliflower

If you have never thought to serve cauliflower to your guests, try this recipe.

2 medium cauliflowers	225 g/8 oz mature Cheddar
salt and pepper to taste	cheese
450 ml/¾ pint soured	1 slice bread, cubed
cream	2 tablespoons sesame seeds
2 teaspoons dried dill or	
1 tablespoon fresh dill	

Break the cauliflowers into florets and cook in a small amount of boiling, salted water until just tender (about 10 to 12 minutes). Drain well. Arrange half the cauliflower in a large, greased casserole dish. Season with salt and pepper and pour half the soured cream over. Sprinkle with half the dill. Using the shredded plate, shred the cheese and sprinkle half over the soured cream. Fit the metal blade to the processor and crumb the bread. Sprinkle half over the cheese and top with half the sesame seeds. Repeat these layers, ending with shredded cheese and sesame seeds. Bake in a moderate oven (180 c, 350 f, gas 4) for 15 minutes until the cheese melts and the soured cream is bubbly.

SERVES 8 TO 10

Glazed Carrots

Ginger and orange impart a special flavour to this carrot dish.

8 medium carrots	1 teaspoon freshly grated
2 teaspoons sugar	root ginger
2 teaspoons cornflour	6 tablespoons orange juice
½ teaspoon salt	25 g/1 oz butter

Using the slicing plate, slice the carrots. Cook in a little boiling, salted water until just tender. Drain and keep warm.

Combine the sugar, cornflour and salt in a saucepan. Add the ginger, orange juice and butter. Cook, stirring, until the mixture thickens and bubbles. Pour over the hot carrots, mixing well. Serve hot.

SERVES 6 TO 8

Ratatouille

Ratatouille originates from the south of France, where traditionally dishes are rich in colour and flavour. Ideally, the separate vegetables should be distinguishable in the herby tomato sauce.

2 aubergines	5 tablespoons oil
4 large tomatoes, peeled	salt and black pepper
2 onions	½ teaspoon dried thyme
3 courgettes	generous pinch of oregano
2 cloves garlic	2 tablespoons concentrated
1 green pepper, deseeded	tomato purée
3 tablespoons parsley,	pinch of coriander
stems removed	

Fit the chipper plate to the processor and dice the aubergines. Sprinkle with salt and allow to stand for 30 minutes. Again using the chipper plate, chop the tomatoes. Fit the slicing plate and slice the onions and courgettes. Set aside. Using the metal blade and pulse, chop the garlic and green pepper. Set aside. Now chop the parsley. In a large shallow pan, heat the oil and sauté the onion, courgettes, garlic and green pepper. Drain and pat dry the aubergine and add to the pan. Sauté for 10 minutes. Add all the remaining ingredients, cover and simmer for 20 minutes. Serve hot as a vegetable or ice cold as a starter.

SERVES 6

This dish freezes well for up to three months. Reheat very carefully.

Oriental Peas

1 (269-g/9½-oz) can water	1 (425-g/15-oz) can cream
chestnuts, drained	of mushroom soup
150 g/5 oz mushrooms, wiped	7 tablespoons water
clean	350 g/12 oz frozen peas,
¼ small onion, cut up	thawed
50 g/2 oz fresh bean	salt and pepper to taste
sprouts	

Using the slicing plate, slice the water chestnuts and mushrooms. Fit the metal blade and chop the onion. Mix the water chesnuts, mushrooms and onion with the bean sprouts, soup and water. Stir in the peas and bring to the boil. Simmer until the peas are just tender. Season with salt and pepper and serve hot.

SERVES 4 TO 6

Spicy Peas

450 g/1 lb frozen peas
1 small onion, quartered
½ small green pepper,
  deseeded and cut up
1 tablespoon parsley,
  stems removed
25 g/1 oz butter

2 tablespoons chopped
  pimiento (canned red
  pepper)
1 small bay leaf
pinch of nutmeg
½ teaspoon salt
½ teaspoon vinegar
pinch of sugar

Cook the peas in a little salted water until just tender. Drain and keep warm. Meanwhile, fit the metal blade to the processor. Place the onion, green pepper and parsley in the work bowl and chop. Melt the butter in a medium saucepan, add the chopped onion, green pepper, parsley, pimiento and bay leaf. Cover and cook for 10 minutes. Remove the bay leaf and add the nutmeg, salt, vinegar and sugar. Stir in the hot, drained peas and serve immediately.

SERVES 6 TO 8

French Peas

25 g/1 oz butter
2 medium onions
2 heads round lettuce
450 g/1 lb peas
2 tablespoons water
sprig of mint

1 teaspoon sugar
salt and pepper to taste
1 tablespoon parsley, stems
  removed
75 g/3 oz ham

Heat the butter in a medium saucepan. Fit the slicing plate to the processor, slice the onions and add to the butter. Sauté until tender. Remove the outer leaves from the lettuce, cut out the main stalk and wash well. Dry, then slice, using the slicing plate. Add to the onion. Now add the peas, water, mint, sugar and seasonings. Cover with a piece of non-stick baking parchment and a lid. Simmer gently until cooked. Meanwhile, using the metal blade and pulse button, chop the parsley and ham. Remove the mint from the peas, add the parsley and ham and stir gently. Serve hot.

SERVES 4 TO 6

French Fried Potatoes

6 medium potatoes
oil for deep frying
salt

Using the chipper plate, cut the potatoes into chips. Soak in cold, salted water for 20 minutes, then drain well and pat dry. Heat the oil to 180 c/350 f and fry the potatoes, a few at a time, until tender. Remove and drain well. When all the potatoes are fried, heat the oil to 190 c/375 f and fry again in batches until crisp and golden brown. Drain well, sprinkle with salt and keep warm.

SERVES 4

Caraway Potatoes with Cheese

Mozzarella cheese makes a delicious 'sauce' for these scalloped potatoes. Remember, the cheese must be almost frozen to shred easily.

6 medium potatoes, peeled
225 g/8 oz mozzarella
  cheese, well chilled
2 eggs, beaten
450 ml/¾ pint single cream

5 tablespoons water
1 teaspoon onion salt
pepper to taste
1 teaspoon caraway seeds
40 g/1½ oz butter

Using the slicing plate, thinly slice the potatoes. Fit the shredding plate and shred the cheese. Alternate layers of potato and cheese in a greased casserole dish, ending with a layer of cheese. Mix together the eggs, cream, water, onion salt, pepper and caraway seeds. Spoon over the potato mixture and dot with butter. Bake in a moderate oven (160 c, 325 f, gas 3) for about 1 to 1¼ hours or until the potatoes are tender.

SERVES 6 TO 8

Potato Crisps ●

Quick and easy to make at home.

6 medium potatoes
oil for deep frying
salt

Cut the potatoes to fit the feed tube and, using the slicing plate, slice thinly. Soak in cold, salted water for 20 minutes, then drain well and pat dry. Heat the oil to 180 c/350 f and fry the potato slices, a few at a time, until tender. Remove and drain well. When all the potato slices are fried, heat the oil to 190 c/375 f and fry again in batches until crisp and golden brown. Drain well and sprinkle with salt. Store in a sealed, airtight container.

SERVES 4 TO 6

Potato Crowns ●

Crispy potato crowns add a touch of glamour to a formal meal.

450 g/1 lb potatoes
1 quantity of Choux Pastry
  (page 135)
40 g/1½ oz butter

1 egg yolk
salt and pepper
oil for deep frying

Boil the potatoes in their jackets until soft. Meanwhile, make the choux pastry and set aside. Peel the potatoes, cut into four and process for a few seconds. Add the butter and egg yolk and pulse to combine. Lastly, add the choux pastry and process until smooth. Season well. Cut squares of greaseproof or non-stick baking parchment and oil well. Fit a piping bag with a large star nozzle and fill with the potato mixture. Pipe circles of potato onto the paper. Heat the oil in a deep pan. Carefully drop the potato circles into the hot oil, cooking a few at a time.

French Fried Potatoes

Fry until golden, drain and serve as soon as possible.

The potato crowns may be made some hours before required. Only the frying need be done at the last minute.

SERVES 6 TO 8

Rosti

4 medium potatoes	salt and black pepper to
1 onion, quartered	taste
	100 g/4 oz butter

Cook the potatoes in their jackets in boiling, salted water until just tender. Drain, then chill for 3 hours. Peel the potatoes and, applying gentle pressure, shred with the shredding plate. Set aside. Using the metal blade, finely chop the onion and mix gently with the potato. Season with salt and black pepper. Melt about 25 g/1 oz butter in a small frying pan. Add a quarter of the potato mixture and press down firmly. Fry until golden on the underside, then carefully turn over and fry until golden on the other side. Remove and keep warm. Repeat, adding butter as required, until all the mixture has been fried. Serve hot.

SERVES 4

Soured Cream Scalloped Potatoes

This tasty potato casserole makes enough to serve a crowd.

8 medium potatoes	450 ml/¾ pint soured cream
1 large onion, quartered	4 tablespoons water
40 g/1½ oz butter	4 eggs, lightly beaten
1 tablespoon chopped chives	2 teaspoons salt
1 tablespoon dried dill or	pepper to taste
1 teaspoon chopped fresh	225 g/8 oz cheese
dill	

Fit the slicing plate to the processor and slice the potatoes. Cook in a little boiling, salted water until just tender. Drain carefully and arrange in a greased casserole dish. Using the metal blade, chop the onion. Heat the butter in a medium saucepan and sauté the onion until tender. Remove the pan from the heat and add the chives, dill and soured cream. Stir in the water, eggs, salt and pepper. Pour over the potatoes. Using the shredding plate, shred the cheese and sprinkle on top. Bake in a moderate oven (180 c, 350 f, gas 4) for 35 to 40 minutes or until set. Place under the grill to brown the top. Serve hot.

SERVES 10 TO 12

Purée of Brussels Sprouts

When fresh Brussels sprouts are in season, make up the purée and freeze for future use.

1.4 kg/3 lb fresh Brussels sprouts	½ teaspoon white pepper
100 g/4 oz butter, softened	pinch of freshly grated nutmeg
2 tablespoons cream	2 tablespoons lemon juice
1 teaspoon onion salt	

Wash and trim the sprouts and cook in boiling, salted water until tender, about 15 to 18 minutes. Using the metal blade, purée the well-drained sprouts in batches. At this point, the purée may be frozen for later use or kept refrigerated for 24 hours.

To prepare for serving, reheat the purée and stir in the butter, cream, onion salt and pepper. Mix well. Just before serving, add the nutmeg and lemon juice.

SERVES 8 TO 10

Carrot and Celery au Gratin

12 medium carrots, cleaned	pinch of mustard powder
4 sticks celery	250 ml/8 fl oz milk
1 large onion, quartered	250 ml/8 fl oz single cream
100 g/4 oz butter	pepper to taste
50 g/2 oz plain flour	225 g/8 oz Cheddar cheese
1 teaspoon salt	3 slices bread, cubed

Fit the slicing plate to the processor and slice the carrots, then the celery. Change to the metal blade and chop the onion. Cook the carrots in a little boiling, salted water until just tender; drain well. Meanwhile, heat 25 g/1 oz butter and sauté the onion and celery until just tender. Remove the vegetables with a slotted spoon and add to the carrots. Stir the flour into the butter and add the salt and mustard powder. Mix well. Pour in the milk and cream and cook, stirring, until bubbly and thickened. Season to taste with pepper. Fit the shredding plate, shred the cheese and add to the sauce. Stir to melt the cheese. To make buttered breadcrumbs, use the metal blade to crumb the bread. Combine the breadcrumbs with the remaining butter which has been melted and toss to mix well.

Arrange the carrots, onion and celery in a greased casserole dish. Pour the cheese sauce over and top with buttered breadcrumbs. Bake, uncovered in a moderate oven (180 c, 350 f, gas 4) for 35 to 40 minutes.

SERVES 8 TO 10

Deep-Fried Vegetables

These crispy vegetables may be served as a vegetable accompaniment or as a starter.

aubergines	BATTER
onions	75 g/3 oz plain flour
courgettes	25 g/1 oz cornflour
cauliflower	salt
button mushrooms	2 eggs
parsley sprigs to garnish	7 tablespoons water
oil for frying	

Using the slicing plate, slice the aubergines, then the onions fairly thickly. Sprinkle the aubergine slices with a little salt and allow to stand for 20 minutes.

To make the batter, fit the metal blade to the processor and add the flour, cornflour and salt to the work bowl. Pulse twice to aerate. With the machine running, add the eggs and water through the feed tube and process to mix well. Allow to stand for 20 to 30 minutes before coating the vegetables.

Cut the courgettes into 1 cm/½ in lengths and break the cauliflower into small florets. Choose small mushrooms and leave whole. Dry all the vegetables very carefully before dipping in batter and deep frying, a few at a time, in hot oil until golden brown. Drain on paper and serve immediately. For the garnish, fry a few sprigs of parsley. Parsley has a very high water content, therefore extreme care must be taken when frying it in hot oil.

Salads and Salad Dressings

Tempt your guests with sensational salads – crisp greens sprinkled with oil and vinegar, delectable fruit and vegetable combinations, chilled meat, poultry or fish salads and spicy rice or pasta combined with vegetables and a piquant dressing.

When it comes to making salads, your food processor will prove an invaluable asset. Dressings are emulsified in a whiz and ingredients are chopped, sliced, shredded or pureed in seconds. Because the processor is so quick, salads can be prepared just before serving, thus ensuring the ingredients retain their chill and crispness.

Here are pointers for perfect salads:

- Use fresh, crisp ingredients that are at their peak of goodness.

- Dry greens well so that the dressing will cling. Clean and chill salad ingredients before processing.

- Use a variety of greens such as round lettuce, curly endive or fresh, tender spinach leaves for added flavour. Use raw vegetables such as sliced mushrooms, cauliflower, fennel, leeks, radishes, courgettes and bean sprouts in addition to the usual tomato, cucumber and onion.

- Toss ingredients lightly or arrange on lettuce leaves. Never stir in the dressing.

- For perfection, chill the salad plates in the refrigerator until ready to use.

- Select the salad dressing carefully. A thin French or Italian dressing goes well with plain or mixed greens while a bold salad can hold a thicker, more robust dressing.

- Serve dressed salads as soon as possible.

Cauliflower, Mushroom and Courgette Salad

1 small cauliflower	6 tablespoons vinegar
6–8 courgettes	salt and black pepper
225 g/8 oz mushrooms	cayenne
2 sprigs parsley, stems removed	$\frac{1}{2}$ teaspoon sugar
	1 teaspoon mustard powder
2 cloves garlic	$\frac{1}{2}$ teaspoon thyme
250 ml/8 fl oz oil	2 tablespoons chopped chives

Break the cauliflower into small florets, then soak in salt water for 10 minutes. Using the slicing blade and a firm pressure, slice the courgettes thickly. Wipe the mushrooms with a damp cloth, then slice. Blanch the cauliflower and courgettes in boiling water for 4 minutes. Drain and refresh in cold water. Allow to drain for 5 minutes. Fit the metal blade to the processor and, with the machine running, drop the parsley and garlic through the feed tube onto the metal blade. Add the oil, vinegar and all the remaining ingredients. Process until well combined. Pour the dressing over the vegetables and chill for at least 4 hours before serving. This salad may also be made the night before. Seal and refrigerate until required. For variation, use blanched young green beans or lightly fried slices of aubergine.

SERVES 8

Green Bean Salad with Almond Dressing

1 kg/2 lb fresh green beans, topped and tailed	ALMOND DRESSING
	75 g/3 oz blanched almonds
3 cloves garlic, unpeeled	2 egg yolks
a little oil	6 tablespoons oil
salt to taste	2 tablespoons lemon juice
lettuce leaves to serve	$\frac{1}{2}$ teaspoon dried dill (optional)
	salt and pepper to taste

Place the beans in boiling, salted water with the garlic and simmer for 5 to 8 minutes until the beans are just tender. Reserve the garlic. Rinse the beans in cold water and drain well, then brush them with oil and sprinkle with salt. Now fit the metal blade to the processor, place the peeled, reserved garlic and the almonds in the work bowl and process until finely chopped. Add the egg yolks and process until very well mixed. While the machine is running, add the oil in a steady stream and process until the dressing is very thick. Lastly, add the lemon juice, dill, salt and pepper to taste. Pulse three or four times to mix well. To serve, place the green beans in bundles on lettuce leaves and spoon the dressing over.

SERVES 6

Beans Mimosa

Layered Vegetable Salad

This salad can be made up to 24 hours ahead of time and refrigerated until required.

1 head lettuce	1 quantity of mayonnaise
2 sticks celery	(page 95)
1 green or red pepper,	2 teaspoons sugar
deseeded and cut in half	50 g/2 oz Parmesan cheese,
1 small cucumber	cut into cubes
10 mushrooms	1 teaspoon salt
1 onion, cut in half	100 g/4 oz cooked ham,
lengthwise	cubed
1 (269-g/9½-oz) can water	2 hard-boiled eggs,
chestnuts, drained	quartered
1 large carrot	1 large tomato and parsley
450 g/1 lb frozen peas	sprigs to garnish

Separate the lettuce leaves, wash well and pat dry. Fit the slicing plate to the processor then, folding a few lettuce leaves at a time, place them in the feed tube and slice. Arrange in a large glass salad bowl. Now slice the celery and sprinkle over the lettuce. Slice the green pepper and arrange over the celery. Slice the cucumber and mushrooms and arrange on top of the green pepper. Slice the onion and sprinkle over the cucumber. Slice the water chestnuts and arrange over the onion. Using the shredding plate, shred the carrot and arrange over the water chestnuts. Top with frozen peas, spread with mayonnaise and sprinkle with sugar. Using the metal blade, finely chop the Parmesan cheese and sprinkle over the mayonnaise. Now sprinkle with salt. Using the metal blade, chop the ham and sprinkle over the salad. Chop the eggs and sprinkle on top of the ham. Lastly, cut the tomatoes into wedges. Garnish the salad with the tomato wedges and sprigs of parsley, cover and refrigerate for 24 hours.

SERVES 10 TO 12

Pawpaw and Avocado Salad

2 ripe avocados, peeled	1 tablespoon dry sherry
1 firm ripe pawpaw, peeled	2 teaspoons white wine
and deseeded	vinegar
3 tablespoons fresh lemon	salt and freshly ground
juice	pepper to taste
lettuce leaves to serve	7 tablespoons oil
50 g/2 oz walnuts	watercress to garnish

Slice the avocados and pawpaw and sprinkle with 1 tablespoon of the lemon juice. Place lettuce leaves on individual plates and arrange the avocado and pawpaw slices on top. Using the metal blade, coarsely chop the walnuts and set aside. Place the remaining lemon juice, sherry, vinegar, salt and pepper in the work bowl and process for 10 seconds. With the machine running, add the oil in a steady stream and process until well blended. Finally, add the walnuts and allow to stand for a few minutes. Spoon the dressing over the avocado and pawpaw and garnish with watercress.

SERVES 4

Cucumber Salad with Blue Cheese

1 slender cucumber	4 tablespoons oil
a little salt	4 tablespoons lemon juice
225 g/8 oz blue cheese, cut	freshly ground black pepper
into cubes	mint sprigs to garnish
½ small onion, cut up	

Using the tines of a fork, score the cucumber skin lengthwise. Use the slicing plate to slice the cucumber evenly. Sprinkle with salt and allow to stand for 20 minutes, then drain well. Fit the metal blade and process the cheese, onion, oil, lemon juice and black pepper until very well mixed. Combine the cucumber and cheese mixture, arrange in a shallow serving dish and garnish with mint sprigs. Chill for about 30 minutes before serving.

SERVES 6

Chive and Courgette Salad

3 large carrots	2 tablespoons chopped chives
4 courgettes	lettuce leaves to serve
225 g/8 oz mushrooms	
Vinaigrette Dressing (page	
96) to taste	

Cut the carrots and courgettes into lengths to fit sideways in the feed tube. Using the slicing plate, slice the carrots and courgettes into julienne strips, then slice the mushrooms. Blanch the vegetables for 1 minute in boiling, salted water. Plunge into cold water and drain well. Mix the vegetables with vinaigrette dressing and stir in the chopped chives. Spoon into lettuce leaves and arrange on individual plates.

SERVES 6

Artichokes Vinaigrette

Fresh artichokes have a very limited season. Served this way, they are at their best and very tasty.

8–10 artichokes	salt
1 slice lemon	150 ml/$\frac{1}{4}$ pint Vinaigrette
few peppercorns	Dressing (page 96)
2 cloves garlic	lettuce leaves to serve
6 tablespoons white wine	1 tomato, sliced, to garnish

To cook artichokes, trim away the tips of the leaves with a stainless steel knife. Place in a large saucepan, cover with boiling water and add a slice of lemon, peppercorns, garlic, white wine and salt. Simmer, covered, until the outside leaves peel off easily (about 25 to 30 minutes). Drain and cool upside down. Carefully lift out the centre leaves and reserve. Using the end of a teaspoon, remove the hairy 'choke'. Cut the bases so that each artichoke will stand upright. Peel off the tough outer leaves and spoon a little dressing into the middle of each artichoke. Replace the centre leaves and spoon more dressing over. Chill for at least 1 hour. Arrange flat lettuce leaves on a large platter or on individual plates. Stand the artichokes on the leaves and spoon over more dressing. Garnish with slices of tomato. The remaining dressing is served separately.

Artichokes are eaten with the fingers. Peel off the leaves one at a time and eat the small fleshy part at the base of each leaf. Towards the middle, the whole leaf may be eaten. Of course, the ultimate is found when eating the 'heart'.

This dish may be served either as a salad or as a starter. Allow approximately two per person when serving them as a starter.

SERVES 4 TO 5

Beans Mimosa

450 g/1 lb green beans	2 hard-boiled eggs
$\frac{1}{2}$ small onion, cut up	5 tablespoons French
1 clove garlic	Dressing (page 97)
2 tablespoons parsley,	lettuce leaves to serve
stems removed	parsley to garnish
2–3 gherkins	

String the beans and cut into approximately 7.5-cm/3-in lengths. Cook in boiling, salted water until just tender. Drain, refresh in cold water and cool. Using the metal blade, chop the onion and garlic. Add the parsley and gherkins and pulse until all the ingredients are finely chopped. Add to the cooled beans. Chop one hard-boiled egg finely and cut the remaining egg into wedges. Add the chopped egg and French dressing to the beans. Toss well. Line a platter with lettuce leaves and heap the bean salad on top. Garnish with egg wedges and parsley.

SERVES 6 TO 8

Layered Vegetable Salad

Avocado Mould with Mock Crayfish

AVOCADO MOULD
2 ripe avocado pears
1 slice onion
lemon juice
½ quantity of mayonnaise
    (page 95)
6 tablespoons chicken stock
dash of Tabasco sauce

salt and black pepper
1 tablespoon powdered
    gelatine
3 tablespoons hot water
GARNISH
lemon twists
parsley
paprika

Using the metal blade, purée the avocado and onion. Add the lemon juice, mayonnaise and half the chicken stock. Process until mixed, then season well. Combine the remaining chicken stock and the gelatine dissolved in 3 tablespoons hot water. With the machine running, pour the gelatine through the feed tube and mix well. Turn the mixture into a rinsed loaf tin or deep round cake tin and chill until set. To serve, turn out onto a large platter. Arrange the mock crayfish mixture around the mould and garnish with lemon twists, parsley and paprika.

MOCK CRAYFISH
450 g/1 lb monk fish
few peppercorns
1 clove garlic
generous pinch of salt
slice of lemon
5 tablespoons cream
150 ml/¼ pint mayonnaise
    (page 95)

a little tomato sauce
1 teaspoon Worcestershire
    sauce
cayenne
a few drops of cochineal
a little lemon juice

Cook the fish until tender in a little boiling water, to which the peppercorns, garlic, salt and a slice of lemon have been added. Drain, cool and cut the fish into bite-sized pieces. Using the nylon blade, process the cream until thick. Add the mayonnaise, cayenne, salt, a few drops of cochineal and lemon juice. Pulse a few times to combine. Pour over the fish and refrigerate for a few hours before serving.

SERVES 8 AS A STARTER

Spicy Cabbage Slaw

½ medium cabbage, cut into
    wedges
1 small onion, cut in half
    lengthwise
1 green pepper, cut in
    half and deseeded
2 sticks celery
2 carrots

DRESSING
150 ml/¼ pint white wine
    vinegar
5 tablespoons oil
3 tablespoons sugar
1 teaspoon salt
pinch of pepper
½ teaspoon chilli powder
dash of Tabasco sauce
½ teaspoon dried mixed herbs

For the salad, use the slicing plate to slice the cabbage, onion, pepper and celery. Fit the shredding plate and shred the carrots. Add to the cabbage mixture.

For the dressing, fit the metal blade to the processor and place all the ingredients in the work bowl. Process for 10 seconds to combine well. Pour over the vegetables, toss to mix, and cover. Refrigerate for at least 8 hours or overnight before serving. To serve, mix well, then drain.

SERVES 6

Macaroni Salad Supreme

Serve as a side dish or main dish for lunch.

450 g/1 lb macaroni,
    cooked and drained
4 hard-boiled eggs,
    quartered
4 rashers bacon, crisply
    fried
1 onion, quartered
100 g/4 oz stuffed olives, drained
2 medium carrots
2 stalks celery
1 (198-g/7-oz) can tuna,
    drained and flaked

DRESSING
450 ml/¾ pint mayonnaise
    (page 95)
150 g/5 oz sugar
1 tablespoon prepared mild
    mustard
2 teaspoons white wine
    vinegar
7 tablespoons milk

For the salad, place the macaroni in a large mixing bowl. Using the metal blade, first chop the eggs, then the bacon, followed by the onion and olives. Add these to the macaroni. Using the shredding plate, shred the carrots and add to the macaroni. Fit the slicing plate, slice the celery and add to the macaroni along with the tuna.

To make the dressing, fit the nylon blade and add all the ingredients to the work bowl. Process for 10 seconds. Pour over the macaroni and mix well. Chill for at least 1 hour before serving.

SERVES 10 TO 12

Tomato Aspic with Vegetables

Tomato Aspic with Vegetables

This also makes a light, crunchy starter or luncheon dish.

2 tablespoons powdered gelatine	1 small onion, quartered
300 ml/½ pint cold water	½ small green pepper, deseeded and cut into chunks
450 ml/¾ pint tomato juice	1 clove garlic
4 tablespoons lemon juice	½ cucumber, peeled and deseeded
1 tablespoon sugar	parsley and slices of lemon to garnish
1 teaspoon salt	
dash of Tabasco sauce	
1 stick celery, cut into small pieces	

Dissolve the gelatine in 3 tablespoons hot water over a basin of boiling water then add the cold water. Stir in the tomato juice, lemon juice, sugar, salt and Tabasco. Stir until the sugar dissolves, then chill until partially set. Using the metal blade, chop the celery, onion, green pepper and garlic all together and add to the gelatine mixture. Chop the cucumber, add to the mixture and combine well. Pour into a mould and chill until set. Turn out and garnish with parsley and lemon slices.

SERVES 8

Chick Pea Salad

450 g/1 lb chick peas	6 tablespoons oil
DRESSING	3 tablespoons vinegar
2 onions, quartered	GARNISH
3 sprigs parsley, stems removed	2 green peppers
1 bay leaf	a little oil
salt and black pepper	3 hard-boiled eggs
	10 black olives

Soak the chick peas in water overnight. Cook in boiling, salted water until tender – this takes approximately 2 hours in a saucepan or 25 minutes in a pressure cooker. Drain and cool. To make the dressing, use the metal blade to finely chop the onion and parsley. Add the remaining ingredients and pulse to combine. For the garnish, deseed the green peppers and cut into long strips. Brush with a little oil and grill for a few minutes. Quarter the eggs. Combine the chick peas and dressing and place in a salad bowl. Garnish with the green peppers, egg wedges and olives.

SERVES 6 TO 8

Peachy Rice Salad

julienne strips. Blanch in boiling water for 30 seconds, then refresh in cold water and drain well. Cook the peas for 4 minutes, drain and refresh. Coarsely flake the tuna. Combine all the ingredients in a large bowl and toss carefully. Cover and chill for at least 1 hour before serving. This salad may be kept overnight. To serve, turn into a salad bowl and allow to reach room temperature.

SERVES 6 TO 8

Hawaiian Salad

350 g/12 oz carrots	lemon juice to taste
1 (227-g/8-oz) can crushed pineapple, drained	salt and black pepper
	endive or lettuce to serve
225 g/8 oz cabbage	GARNISH
250 ml/8 fl oz water	slices of green pepper
1 packet lemon jelly	canned pineapple slices
2 teaspoons powdered gelatine	

Using the shredding plate, shred the carrots, add to the pineapple and set aside. Fit the slicing plate and slice the cabbage. Bring the pineapple juice and water to the boil. Pour onto the jelly and gelatine and stir until dissolved. Season to taste with lemon juice, salt and pepper. Chill until the mixture begins to thicken. Now stir in the carrot, cabbage and pineapple. Pour into a ring mould or loaf tin and chill for at least 4 hours. Turn out onto a bed of endive or shredded lettuce and garnish with slices of green pepper and pineapple. Fresh pineapple may be used, but it must first be cooked for a few minutes or the gelatine mixture will fail to set.

SERVES 6 TO 8

Peachy Rice Salad

225 g/8 oz rice	2 tablespoons chutney
450 ml/$\frac{3}{4}$ pint water	2 tablespoons mayonnaise (page 95)
1 teaspoon chicken stock powder	1 teaspoon curry paste
$\frac{1}{2}$ small onion, halved	1 tablespoon lemon juice
1 green pepper, deseeded and quartered	salt and black pepper
1 chilli, deseeded	GARNISH
1 (213-g/7$\frac{1}{2}$-oz) can peaches, drained	peach slices
	strips of green pepper

Cook the rice in the water with the chicken stock added, then cool. Using the metal blade, chop the onion, green pepper and chilli. Add the drained peaches and pulse twice. Combine all the salad ingredients in a bowl. Turn into a glass dish and garnish with peach slices and a few strips of green pepper.

SERVES 6

Asparagus Mayonnaise

Tender asparagus dipped in a well-seasoned fruity mayonnaise also makes a cool, appetising starter.

24–36 young asparagus spears, washed and trimmed	1 tablespoon dry sherry
250 ml/8 fl oz mayonnaise (page 95)	1 tablespoon finely grated orange rind
1 tablespoon fresh lemon juice	salt and pepper to taste
	lettuce leaves to serve
	parsley to garnish

Cook the asparagus in boiling, salted water until just tender (about 10 minutes). Plunge into cold water, drain well and chill. To make the sauce, fit the nylon blade to the processor and place all the ingredients, except the asparagus, in the work bowl. Process for about 10 seconds until well combined. Chill until ready to serve. Arrange the chilled asparagus on lettuce leaves, partially cover with sauce and garnish with parsley. Serve the remaining sauce separately.

SERVES 6

Pasta and Spinach Pesto ●

225 g/8 oz corkscrew-shaped noodles	450 g/1 lb frozen peas
salt to taste	1 (198-g/7-oz) can tuna, drained
a little oil	300 ml/$\frac{1}{2}$ pint Spinach Pesto sauce (page 97)
1 red pepper, deseeded and halved lengthwise	

Cook the noodles until just tender in boiling, salted water with a little oil added. Drain and rinse in cold water. Drain for 5 minutes. Using the slicing blade, slice the red pepper into

Dressings

Mayonnaise

1 egg
½ teaspoon mustard powder
½ teaspoon salt
pinch of white pepper
½ teaspoon castor sugar
1 tablespoon lemon juice
1 tablespoon vinegar
250 ml/8 fl oz oil

Fit the metal blade to the processor and add the egg, mustard, salt, pepper, sugar, lemon juice and vinegar to the work bowl. Process for 5 seconds to mix. With the machine running, slowly add the oil in a steady stream. Continue to process until the mayonnaise is thick. Transfer to a bowl, cover and refrigerate.

MAKES ABOUT 300 ML/½ PINT

Thousand Island Dressing

250 ml/8 fl oz mayonnaise
   (opposite)
5 tablespoons concentrated
   tomato purée
2 small gherkins, cut up
2 tablespoons chopped onion
1 hard-boiled egg, quartered
½ teaspoon castor sugar
1 teaspoon white wine vinegar

Fit the metal blade to the processor, add all the ingredients and process for 10 seconds or until well mixed. Store, covered in the refrigerator. Serve with a green salad, rice salad or fish salad.

MAKES ABOUT 350 ML/12 FL OZ

Top: Orange Mayonnaise (page 97), Cubed Blue Cheese Dressing (page 96). Centre: Thousand Island Dressing.
Bottom: Green Mayonnaise (page 97), Mayonnaise

Sesame Seed Dressing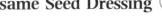

7 tablespoons oil	$\frac{1}{2}$ teaspoon mustard powder
4 tablespoons white wine vinegar	3 tablespoons sesame seeds
1 clove garlic, crushed	salt and black pepper

Using the metal blade, process the oil and vinegar for a few seconds. With the machine running, add all the remaining ingredients and process for 5 seconds. This dressing is excellent on lettuce or spinach salads.

MAKES 200 ML/7 FL OZ

Vinaigrette Dressing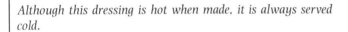

Although this dressing is hot when made, it is always served cold.

1 tablespoon parsley, stems removed	salt and black pepper
1 small dill pickle	1 teaspoon paprika
1 slice green pepper	1 tablespoon tarragon vinegar
4 chives, chopped	2 tablespoons cider vinegar
6 stuffed olives	5 tablespoons oil
1 hard-boiled egg	2 teaspoons olive oil

Using the metal blade, chop the parsley, dill pickle, green pepper, chives and stuffed olives. Add the egg and pulse until

chopped. Add the seasonings and vinegars. Heat the oils slightly, then pour in through the feed tube while the motor is running. Pour over fish, artichokes, asparagus or a salad and chill before serving.

MAKES 150 ML/$\frac{1}{4}$ PINT

Cubed Blue Cheese Dressing

Give a plain mixed salad the gourmet treatment by topping it with this frozen, tangy dressing.

250 ml/8 fl oz double cream	1 tablespoon lemon juice
4 stalks celery	100 g/4 oz blue cheese
100 g/4 oz cream cheese	1 teaspoon Worcestershire sauce
6 tablespoons mayonnaise (page 95)	salt and black pepper

Whisk the cream until thick. Pour into a bowl and set aside. Using the metal blade, chop the celery finely. Add the cream cheese, mayonnaise, lemon juice, blue cheese, Worcestershire sauce and seasonings. Blend until smooth. Add the cream and pulse to combine. Spread into an ice tray and freeze until firm. Cut into small cubes and add to the salad shortly before serving.

MAKES ABOUT 450 ML/$\frac{3}{4}$ PINT

Vinaigrette Dressing and Sesame Seed Dressing

Spinach Pesto

1 bunch spinach
75 g/3 oz Parmesan cheese
sprig of parsley, stems
   removed
50 g/2 oz walnuts
4 anchovy fillets

2 cloves garlic
1 teaspoon basil
salt and black pepper
200 ml/7 fl oz oil
3 tablespoons olive oil

Wash the spinach well, then place it in a saucepan without water and cook for a few minutes. The spinach should be still be firm. Drain very well. Using the shredding plate, shred the Parmesan cheese and set aside. Fit the metal blade and chop the parsley finely. With the machine running, add the walnuts, anchovy fillets, garlic, basil and seasoning. Process until smooth. Add the spinach and cheese and process again. With the machine running, pour both oils in a thin, steady stream through the feed tube and process until combined. This sauce will keep in the refrigerator for about 1 week or it may be frozen. Serve with various types of pasta, fish or chicken.

MAKES ABOUT 450 ML/$\frac{3}{4}$ PINT

French Dressing

300 ml/$\frac{1}{2}$ pint oil
150 ml/$\frac{1}{4}$ pint vinegar
2 teaspoons sugar
1 tablespoon mustard powder

2 teaspoons salt
pinch of cayenne
pinch of black pepper

Using the nylon blade, process all the ingredients until well mixed. French dressing will keep in the refrigerator for a week.
   For variation, add one or more of the following ingredients: crushed garlic, fresh or dried herbs of your choice, different flavours of vinegar, and lemon juice.

MAKES 450 ML/$\frac{3}{4}$ PINT

Orange Mayonnaise

300 ml/$\frac{1}{2}$ pint mayonnaise
   (page 95)
1 tablespoon grated orange
   rind

2 teaspoons caster sugar
1 tablespoon orange liqueur
2 tablespoons orange juice

Using the nylon blade, mix all the ingredients. Store in the refrigerator and serve with fruit salad, coleslaw or rice salad.

MAKES ABOUT 300 ML/$\frac{1}{2}$ PINT

Green Mayonnaise

2 parsley sprigs, stems
   removed
2 spring onions, including
   tops, cut into 1-cm/$\frac{1}{2}$-in
   pieces

450 ml/$\frac{3}{4}$ pint mayonnaise
   (page 95)
1 tablespoon cider vinegar
$\frac{1}{2}$ teaspoon tarragon

Using the metal blade, chop the parsley and spring onions. Add all the remaining ingredients and process until well mixed. Store, covered, in the refrigerator. Serve with salad greens, cold chicken or turkey, or hard-boiled eggs.

MAKES ABOUT 450 ML/$\frac{3}{4}$ PINT

Garlic Mayonnaise

300 ml/$\frac{1}{2}$ pint mayonnaise
   (page 95)
2 tablespoons chopped parsley
1 tablespoon white wine
   vinegar

2 tablespoons single cream
1 clove garlic, crushed
$\frac{1}{2}$ teaspoon caster sugar
pinch of salt
1 teaspoon chopped chives

Fit the metal blade to the processor, place all the ingredients in the work bowl and process for 10 seconds or until well mixed. Store, covered, in the refrigerator. Serve with cold meat or poultry, a green salad or as a dip for fresh vegetable pieces.

MAKES ABOUT 300 ML/$\frac{1}{2}$ PINT

Buttermilk Dressing

300 ml/$\frac{1}{2}$ pint mayonnaise
   (page 95)
$\frac{1}{4}$ small onion, cut up
1 clove garlic, crushed
sprig of parsley, stems
   removed

$\frac{1}{2}$ teaspoon salt
pinch of white pepper
$\frac{1}{4}$ small green pepper, cut
   up
300 ml/$\frac{1}{2}$ pint buttermilk

Fit the metal blade to the processor, add the mayonnaise, onion, garlic, parsley, salt, pepper and green pepper and process until the vegetables are finely chopped. Add the buttermilk and pulse three or four times to mix in. Turn into a bowl and stand for at least 2 hours before using. Serve with a green salad, hot vegetables or baked potatoes.

MAKES ABOUT 600 ML/1 PINT

Green Goddess Dressing

300 ml/$\frac{1}{2}$ pint mayonnaise
   (page 95)
6 tablespoons soured cream
2 anchovy fillets, drained
4 sprigs parsley
$\frac{1}{4}$ green pepper, cut into
   pieces

1 teaspoon lemon juice
1 tablespoon dry minced
   onion or chopped fresh
   onion
1 small clove garlic,
   crushed
pinch of white pepper

Fit the metal blade to the processor, add all the ingredients and process for 20 seconds or until the ingredients are chopped and well mixed. Store, covered, in the refrigerator.

MAKES ABOUT 450 ML/$\frac{3}{4}$ PINT

Sauces and Butters

Sauces have often been called the secret of gourmet cooking, and your food processor can make the secret yours. Not only does it chop, slice or shred ingredients for sophisticated sauces, but it also homogenises ingredients for light, flavourful ones. No longer will you have to stand over a hot stove, whisking large quantities of butter for sauces such as Béarnaise or hollandaise. These can be made in your processor at the last minute and served with vegetables such as broccoli and asparagus, or with fish.

The savoury and sweet butters included in this chapter are also made quickly and easily in the food processor. Use savoury butters to add distinctive flavours to meat or fish dishes, vegetables or sandwiches. Sweet or nut butters make delicious spreads for fruit breads and scones.

Espagnole Sauce

A well-seasoned brown sauce to serve with grilled or roast meats.

1 rasher bacon, rind removed	300 ml/½ pint beef stock
1 small onion, quartered	1 tomato, peeled
1 stick celery, cut into pieces	1 tablespoon concentrated tomato purée
6 mushrooms	1 bay leaf
1 small carrot, cut into pieces	2 tablespoons chopped parsley
3 tablespoons oil	3 peppercorns
50 g/2 oz flour	salt and pepper to taste

Cut the bacon into three or four pieces. Fit the metal blade to the processor and finely chop the bacon, onion, celery, mushrooms and carrot. Heat the oil in a saucepan, add the chopped mixture and sauté, covered, for 10 minutes. Remove the lid and sauté for a few minutes longer. Stir in the flour and cook over a low heat, stirring, until the mixture comes to the boil and thickens. Using the metal blade, chop the tomato and add to the sauce along with the tomato purée, bay leaf, chopped parsley and peppercorns. Cover and simmer for 50 to 60 minutes. Stir occasionally and skim off any fat that rises to the top. Strain the cooked sauce and season to taste with salt and pepper.

Espagnole sauce may be made in advance and kept for up to five days in the refrigerator. Reheat over boiling water.

MAKES ABOUT 300 ML/½ PINT

Freeze for two to three months.

Hollandaise Sauce

A sauce so easy to make, you'll wonder why you haven't tried it before.

3 egg yolks	dash of Tabasco sauce
1½ tablespoons lemon juice	100 g/4 oz butter, melted
½ teaspoon prepared mustard	

Fit the metal blade to the processor, add the egg yolks, lemon juice, mustard and Tabasco and process for 5 seconds to mix. Heat the butter to boiling and, with the machine running, slowly pour in a steady stream through the feed tube. Process for at least 60 seconds after adding the last of the butter. The sauce can be kept warm for a short time over hot water.

MAKES ABOUT 200 ML/7 FL OZ

Variations

Mustard Hollandaise: Add 2 teaspoons French mustard to the work bowl before adding the boiling butter to the ingredients in the basic recipe. Process for 5 seconds to mix. Proceed as for hollandaise sauce.

Steak with Espagnole Sauce

Dill Hollandaise: Add ½ teaspoon dill and a pinch of salt to the ingredients in the basic recipe, before adding the boiling butter. Process for 5 seconds to mix. Proceed as for hollandaise sauce.

Mousseline Sauce: Whip 4 tablespoons double cream into soft peaks and gently fold into the hollandaise sauce just before serving. Delicious with fish or vegetable dishes.

Bavaroise Sauce: Just before serving, stir 2 teaspoons prepared horseradish sauce into the hollandaise. Excellent with roast meats or fish.

Velouté Sauce

The type of stock used for this sauce depends upon the dish you wish to make.

25 g/1 oz butter	1 tablespoon lemon juice
25 g/1 oz plain flour	3 tablespoons cream
300 ml/½ pint lukewarm fish, chicken or veal stock	salt and white pepper to taste
6–8 button mushrooms	
pinch of freshly grated nutmeg	

Melt the butter in a medium saucepan, stir in the flour and cook, stirring, for 3 to 4 minutes. The roux should be a pale golden colour. Remove from the heat. Fit the metal blade to the processor and place the roux in the work bowl. With the machine running, slowly add the stock. Process until smooth, then return to the pan and place over a medium heat. Cook, stirring, until the sauce comes to the boil and thickens. Place the sauce in the top of a double boiler. Using the metal blade, chop the mushrooms and add to the sauce. Cook, covered, over simmering water for 30 minutes. Strain, stir in the remaining ingredients and use as desired.

MAKES ABOUT 300 ML/½ PINT

Broccoli with Hollandaise Sauce

Béarnaise Sauce

This tangy sauce is good with grilled meats. It also makes a marvellous fondue dip.

3 egg yolks	2 teaspoons tarragon vinegar
1 spring onion, cut up	$\frac{1}{2}$ teaspoon tarragon
$\frac{1}{2}$ teaspoon salt	3 tablespoons dry white wine
pinch of pepper	100 g/4 oz butter, melted

Fit the metal blade to the processor and place the egg yolks, spring onion, salt, pepper, tarragon vinegar, dried tarragon and wine in the work bowl. Process for 10 seconds to mix well. Heat the butter to boiling. With the machine running, slowly pour in the butter, then process for about 60 seconds. The sauce can be kept warm for a short time over hot water.

MAKES ABOUT 200 ML/7 FL OZ

Bordelaise Sauce

1 quantity of Espagnole	$\frac{1}{2}$ teaspoon tarragon
Sauce (page 99)	$\frac{1}{2}$ teaspoon thyme
1 small onion, quartered	$\frac{1}{2}$ teaspoon lemon juice
6 tablespoons dry red wine	2 teaspoon chopped parsley

Make the espagnole sauce and set aside. Using the metal blade, chop the onion. Place the wine in a saucepan, add the chopped onion and bring to the boil. Simmer until the liquid is reduced by half. Add the tarragon and thyme and stir in the espagnole sauce. Simmer for 10 to 12 minutes. Add the lemon juice and parsley just before serving. Serve with grilled meats.

MAKES ABOUT 450 ML/$\frac{3}{4}$ PINT

Chasseur Sauce

Try this sauce with roasted or grilled meats, or with roast duck or ham.

1 quantity of Espagnole	6 tablespoons dry white wine
Sauce (page 99)	1 tablespoon concentrated
1 small onion, quartered	tomato purée
100 g/4 oz mushrooms	1 tablespoon chopped parsley
25 g/1 oz butter	

Make the espagnole sauce and set aside. Using the metal blade, chop the onion and reserve. Change to the slicing plate and slice the mushrooms. Melt the butter, add the onion and fry until soft. Add the mushrooms and fry for 3 minutes. Stir in the wine, tomato purée and espagnole sauce. Simmer for 6 to 8 minutes. Season to taste and stir in the chopped parsley just before serving.

MAKES ABOUT 450 ML/$\frac{3}{4}$ PINT

Mushroom Sauce

1 onion, quartered	1 tablespoon oil
1 clove garlic	25 g/1 oz flour
2 parsley sprigs, stems	350 g/12 oz mushrooms
removed	150 ml/$\frac{1}{4}$ pint chicken stock
1 small stick celery, cut	(or part white wine, part
into pieces	chicken stock)
15 g/$\frac{1}{2}$ oz butter	salt and pepper to taste

Using the metal blade, chop the onion, garlic, parsley and celery together. Heat the butter and oil, add the chopped vegetables and sauté until the onion is tender. Stir in the flour. Using the slicing plate, slice the mushrooms and add to the onion mixture, together with the stock. Bring to the boil, stirring, then reduce and heat and simmer, covered, for 10 to 15 minutes. Season with salt and pepper. Serve with pasta, poultry or lamb.

MAKES ABOUT 450 ML/$\frac{3}{4}$ PINT

Mushroom Purée

225 g/8 oz mushrooms,	salt and black pepper
cleaned	BEURRE MANIÉ
25 g/1 oz butter	15 g/$\frac{1}{2}$ oz butter
7 tablespoons single cream	15 g/$\frac{1}{2}$ oz flour

Using the metal blade, process the mushrooms until finely chopped. Heat the butter and sauté the mushrooms for 2 to 3 minutes. Now add the cream, one third at a time, allowing it to come to the boil and reduce between each addition. To make the beurre manié, work the butter and flour together, then add it bit by bit to the simmering sauce. The sauce should be thick enough to spread. Season with salt and pepper, cover and set aside until required or refrigerate and use as desired.

MAKES ABOUT 250 ML/7 FL OZ

Onion Purée

100 g/4 oz rice	40 g/1$\frac{1}{2}$ oz butter
2 large onions, quartered	250 ml/8 fl oz veal stock
1 clove garlic	salt and black pepper

Blanch the rice in boiling water for 5 minutes, then drain. Using the metal blade, chop the onions and garlic finely and sauté in butter in an ovenproof casserole. Add the rice and stock and bring to the boil. Cover tightly and bake in a cool oven (150 c, 300 f, gas 2) for 1 hour. Return the mixture to the processor and process until smooth. Season to taste and use as desired.

MAKES ABOUT 600 ML/1 PINT

Mornay Sauce

600 ml/1 pint milk	10 peppercorns
1 carrot	15 g/½ oz Parmesan cheese
1 small onion	15 g/½ oz Gruyère cheese
2 cloves	25 g/1 oz butter
sprig of parsley	25 g/1 oz flour
piece of celery	2 egg yolks
blade of mace	7 tablespoons single cream
1 bay leaf	salt and pepper to taste

Scald the milk, add the carrot, the onion spiked with the cloves, parsley, celery, mace, bay leaf and peppercorns. Allow to infuse for 30 minutes, then strain. Using the shredding plate, shred both the cheeses. Melt the butter, add the flour and cook gently for a minute. Pour in half the milk, stirring constantly. Cook for 2 minutes. Remove from the heat, add the yolks and cream, beating well. Now add the cheeses. Season with salt and pepper beating well. Season with salt and pepper and cover until required or keep refrigerated and use as desired.

MAKES ABOUT 600 ML/1 PINT

Mint Sauce

3 tablespoons mint leaves	2 tablespoons boiling water
1 tablespoon sugar	7 tablespoons vinegar

Wash and pat dry the mint leaves. Fit the metal blade to the processor and place the mint leaves in the work bowl. Add the sugar and boiling water. Process for about 30 seconds or until the mint is finely chopped, scraping down the sides of the bowl when necessary. Add the vinegar and process for about 30 seconds. Pour into a bowl and allow to stand for at least 1 hour before using.

MAKES ABOUT 150 ML/¼ PINT

Tartare Sauce 🍂

300 ml/½ pint mayonnaise (page 95)	1 tablespoon chopped onion
1 tablespoon capers	2 teaspoons lemon juice
2 gherkins	1 teaspoon white wine vinegar
2 sprigs parsley, stems removed	2 tablespoons single cream

Fit the metal blade to the processor, place all the ingredients in the work bowl and process for about 20 seconds or until the ingredients are chopped and well mixed. Store in the refrigerator.

MAKES ABOUT 300 ML/½ PINT

Béchamel Sauce

450 ml/¾ pint milk	6 peppercorns
½ carrot	40 g/1½ oz butter
½ onion	25 g/1 oz flour
2 cloves	salt and pepper to taste
blade of mace	

Place the milk, carrot, onion spiked with cloves, mace and peppercorns in a saucepan. Heat, then allow to stand for about 20 minutes to draw out the flavour. Strain. Melt the butter, add the flour and cook, stirring, for a minute before adding the infused milk. Bring to the boil, stirring all the time, and cook for 3 minutes. Remove from the heat and season.

MAKES 450 ML/¾ PINT

101

Outdoor entertaining: Barbecue Sauce, Grenadine sparkler (page 153),
Best-ever Hamburgers (page 59), Spicy Cabbage Slaw (page 92)

Green Butter with Baked Potato

Barbecue Sauce ☯

A tasty favourite, its robust flavour goes well with meats and poultry.

1 onion, quartered	3 tablespoons concentrated
15 g/½ oz butter	tomato purée
1 tablespoon oil	1 large tomato, peeled and
25 g/1 oz plain flour	deseeded
175 ml/6 fl oz water	1 teaspoon prepared mustard
5 tablespoons white wine	50 g/2 oz soft brown sugar
vinegar	1 tablespoon dry sherry
2 teaspoons Worcestershire	2 sticks celery, cut into
sauce	pieces
½ teaspoon basil	salt and pepper to taste
2 tablespoons lemon juice	

Using the metal blade, chop the onion. Heat the butter and oil in a medium saucepan, add the onion and fry until pale golden. Stir in the flour and cook, stirring, for 1 minute. Slowly stir in the water followed by the vinegar, Worcestershire sauce, basil, lemon juice and tomato purée. Using the metal blade, chop the tomato and add to the sauce along with the mustard, brown sugar and sherry. Chop the celery in the processor, add to the sauce and bring to the boil. Reduce heat, cover and simmer for 30 minutes. If desired, strain the sauce before using. Season with salt and pepper.

MAKES ABOUT 350 ML/12 FL OZ

Butters

Caviar Butter

100 g/4 oz butter, softened   50 g/2 oz lumpfish caviar
1 tablespoon lemon juice

Fit the metal blade to the processor and place the butter and lemon juice in the work bowl. Process until the butter is creamy. With a spoon, mash the caviar until it is as smooth as possible. Add to the butter and process for 25 to 30 seconds, scraping the bowl when necessary. Chill and serve with seafood. Store, covered, in the refrigerator.

MAKES ABOUT 150 ML/$\frac{1}{4}$ PINT

Garlic Butter

Home-made garlic bread is always tempting

6–8 cloves garlic   1 piece lemon rind
3 sprigs parsley, stems   225 g/8 oz butter, softened
   removed   salt and black pepper
1 tablespoon fresh rosemary,   1 tablespoon lemon juice
   or 2 teaspoons dried
   rosemary

While the processor is running, drop the garlic onto the metal blade. Add the parsley, rosemary and lemon rind. Process until finely chopped. Add the butter, seasonings and lemon juice and process until well combined.

MAKES ABOUT 225 G/8 OZ

Smoked Oyster Butter

$\frac{1}{2}$ onion, cut into pieces   100 g/4 oz butter, softened
2 tablespoons parsley, stems   1 tablespoon lemon juice
   removed   2 tablespoons whisky
1 thick slice bread, cubed   salt and black pepper
2 (100-g/4-oz) cans smoked
   oysters, drained

Using the metal blade, chop the onion, parsley and bread until fine. Add the smoked oysters and butter and process until smooth. Lastly, add the lemon juice, whisky and seasonings and pulse to combine.

MAKES ABOUT 225 G/8 OZ

Mustard Butter

100 g/4 oz butter, softened   1 tablespoon French mustard
1 tablespoon lemon juice

Fit the metal blade to the processor and place the butter and lemon juice in the work bowl. Process until the butter is creamy. Add the mustard and process for 15 seconds. Chill and store, covered, in the refrigerator. Serve with lamb, shellfish or grilled steaks.

MAKES ABOUT 100 G/4 OZ

Green Butter

6 sprigs watercress, stems   2 large spinach leaves,
   removed   stems removed
2 teaspoons fresh tarragon $\frac{1}{2}$ small onion, cut into
   or 1 teaspoon dried   pieces
   tarragon   100 g/4 oz butter, softened
sprig of parsley, stem
   removed

Blanch the watercress, tarragon, parsley and spinach in boiling water for 3 minutes. Drain and add cold water to cover. Leave for 2 minutes, then drain well and pat dry. Fit the metal blade to the processor and place the herbs and spinach in the work bowl. Add the onion and process until finely chopped. Lastly, add the butter and process for 30 seconds, scraping the bowl when necessary. Chill and serve with fish or potatoes. Store, covered, in the refrigerator.

MAKES ABOUT 100 G/4 OZ

Parmesan Butter

50 g/2 oz Parmesan cheese, $\frac{1}{2}$ teaspoon onion salt
   cut into cubes   dash of Tabasco sauce
100 g/4 oz butter, softened
3 sprigs parsley, stems
   removed

Using the metal blade, process the Parmesan cheese a few cubes at a time until the cheese resembles fine crumbs. Add all the remaining ingredients and process for about 40 seconds, scraping the bowl when necessary. Store, covered, in the refrigerator.

MAKES ABOUT 150 G/5 OZ

Desserts

This section contains only desserts! Cakes, pastries and biscuits have a place of their own. We have selected an array of sweet, delicious concoctions that are a pleasure to make and delightful to eat.

When you begin making desserts in the food processor, you will be pleasantly surprised to find that your traditional recipes and old favourites take a fraction of the time to prepare, and desserts such as cheesecakes, sorbets, ice creams and crêpes are perfectly textured. Fruit salads and fruit desserts are created in seconds. Some dessert recipes can be whipped up at the last minute, while others may be made in advance and frozen or chilled until needed.

Desserts should be given careful consideration when you plan your menu and they should not be thought of as a sweet something hastily tacked onto the end of a meal. Rather, they should be considered as rounding off a balanced menu. When planning the dessert, consider the flavours and textures of the starter and main course. For example, if a fruit starter is served, do not follow with a fruit dessert, or if the main dish is rich and creamy, do not serve a creamy dessert. As a general rule, serve a light, fruit dessert with a heavy meal and a more substantial one with a less filling meal.

Sherbet Lemon Cups

8 lemons	5 tablespoons dry white wine
350 g/12 oz sugar	2 egg whites
600 ml/1 pint water	sprigs of mint to decorate
pared rind from 2 lemons	
1 tablespoon lime juice cordial	

Trim the bases from the lemons so they will stand upright. Slice off the tops and reserve for decoration. Carefully scoop out the flesh. Squeeze the flesh and retain the juice. Place the lemon cups in a plastic container, cover and store in the refrigerator for up to 24 hours.

Place the sugar, water and rind in a pan. Stir over a low heat until the sugar has dissolved, then bring to the boil and simmer for 5 minutes. Remove from the heat, add the lemon juice, lime juice and wine. Remove the pared rind before allowing the mixture to cool, then chill in the freezer until very firm but not solid. Whisk the egg whites until stiff. Cut the iced mixture into blocks and drop onto moving metal blades, using about a quarter of the ice at a time. As the ice becomes soft, add one quarter of the whisked egg white. Process until pale in colour and well aerated. Repeat until all the ice blocks and egg white have been used. Return to the freezer and freeze for up to two weeks.

To serve, place scoops of sherbet in the lemon cups. Place the lemon lid on top at an angle and decorate with a sprig of mint. The completed lemon cups (without the mint sprigs) may be kept in the freezer for 1 to 2 hours before serving.

SERVES 8

Minty Fruit Salad

Any combination of fresh fruits may be used for this fruit salad.

1 pawpaw	SAUCE
½ pineapple	50 g/2 caster sugar
½ melon	4 tablespoons water
3 peaches	6 sprigs mint
2 pears	6 tablespoons orange juice
2 apples	2 tablespoons lemon juice
4 bananas	pinch of salt
4 oranges	DECORATION
	mint sprigs
	maraschino cherries

First make the sauce. Place the sugar and water in a saucepan and bring to the boil, stirring constantly. Simmer for 5 minutes. Remove from the heat. With the metal blade, chop the mint roughly. Add to the hot syrup and allow to cool. Strain, then add the orange juice, lemon juice and salt.

Cut the pawpaw, pineapple and melon into slices, about 3 × 10 cm/1 × 4 in. Process with the chipper plate. In a split second the fruit will be perfectly diced. Peel the peaches, pears, and apples. Process them in the same way. Using the slicing plate, slice the bananas. Cut the oranges into segments. Combine all the fruits. Pour the sauce over the fruit and allow to stand for at least 2 hours before serving. Decorate the fruit salad with small sprigs of mint and maraschino cherries.

SERVES 8

Lemon Sherbet

The basic recipe uses about 6 lemons to make a tangy, refreshing ice. However, substitute fruit purée for the lemon juice to change the flavour according to the season.

450 g/1 lb caster sugar
1.15 litres/2 pints water
½ teaspoon salt
1 tablespoon grated lemon
   rind

300 ml/½ pint lemon juice
1 egg white, whisked
4 tablespoons double cream

Place the sugar, water and salt in a large saucepan and heat, stirring, until the sugar dissolves. Bring to the boil and simmer for 5 minutes. Now add the finely grated lemon rind and lemon juice. Bring back to the boil and simmer for a further 5 minutes. Allow to cool, then freeze.

Remove from the freezer and stand for 10 minutes. Break in pieces and place in the work bowl with the metal blade in position. Add the whisked egg white and the cream. Process until well mixed. Ice crystals should still be present in the mixture. Pour into a freezer tray and freeze for several hours or overnight. Allow to stand at room temperature for a few minutes before serving.

SERVES 8 TO 10

Minty Fruit Salad

Kiwi Sherbet

675 g/1½ lb kiwi fruits, peeled	4 tablespoons double cream
175 g/6 oz caster sugar	1 egg white, whisked
6 tablespoons water	DECORATION
3 tablespoons lemon juice	slices of kiwi fruit
	sprigs of mint

Using the metal blade, chop the kiwi fruit coarsely and set aside. To make the syrup, combine the sugar and water in a saucepan and bring to the boil, stirring to dissolve the sugar. Simmer for 5 minutes, then allow the mixture to cool. Purée the kiwi fruit, lemon juice and syrup in batches, then strain through a fine sieve. Pour the mixture into a freezer tray and freeze until firm but not solid. Break into pieces and process with the metal blade until fluffy. Refreeze until firm, but not solid. Return to the processor, add the cream and egg white and process until fluffy. Turn into an ice cream tray and refreeze. Remove from the freezer about 10 minutes before serving. Spoon into individual serving dishes and decorate with slices of kiwi fruit and sprigs of mint.

SERVES 6 TO 8

Rum Peachy Sherbet

1 (410-g/14½-oz) can peach slices	2 tablespoons rum
1 teaspoon lemon juice	2 teaspoons almond liqueur or ½ teaspoon almond extract
2 tablespoons honey	
2 teaspoons powdered gelatine	peach slices for decoration
3 tablespoons hot water	

Drain the peach slices, reserving the liquid. Fit the metal blade to the processor and purée the peaches. Measure the reserved peach liquid and make up to 350 ml/12 fl oz with water. Pour into a saucepan and add the lemon juice and honey. Dissolve the gelatine in the hot water over a basin of boiling water then add to the liquid. Now add the rum and almond liqueur. Stir in the peach purée, mix well and turn into a freezer tray. Freeze until firm, but not solid. Using the metal blade, purée the mixture in two batches until light and fluffy, then refreeze. Allow to stand at room temperature for a few minutes before serving. Decorate with peach slices.

SERVES 8

Old-Fashioned Vanilla Ice Cream

450 ml/¾ pint double cream	2 teaspoons vanilla essence or 1 vanilla pod
150 ml/¼ pint milk	
6 egg yolks	100 g/4 oz butter, cut into pieces
75 g/3 oz caster sugar	

Bring 150 ml/¼ pint cream and the milk to the boil. Cool and refrigerate overnight. Using the metal blade, cream the egg yolks and sugar for 1 minute. Now bring the remaining cream and the vanilla to the boil. Pour onto the creamed yolks and process for 45 seconds. While the machine is running, drop in

the butter a little at a time and continue to process until well blended and all the butter is used up. Turn into a mixing bowl and chill the yolk mixture over ice, stirring frequently. Return half this yolk mixture to the processor and add half the chilled milk and cream mixture. Process to combine, then pour into an ice tray. Repeat with the remaining mixtures. Freeze until firm, but not solid. Cut into blocks and drop a few blocks at a time onto the moving metal blades. Cream well. Repeat until all the ice cream blocks have been processed. Refreeze the mixture and use within two weeks.

SERVES 6

Variations

Rich Chocolate Ice Cream: Use 50 g/2 oz chopped plain chocolate in place of the vanilla when bringing the cream to the boil.

Double Coffee Ice Cream: Add an extra teaspoon vanilla essence and when processing the ice cream to make it light and creamy, add 2 tablespoons very finely ground coffee and freeze.

Rocky Road Ice Cream: Make the rich chocolate ice cream and when it has been finally processed, stir in 50 g/2 oz chopped milk chocolate, 50 g/2 oz chopped walnuts and 25 small marshmallows, then freeze.

Strawberry Banana Freeze

450 g/1 lb fresh strawberries	350 ml/12 fl oz buttermilk
2 ripe bananas, cut up	1 tablespoon orange liqueur
2 tablespoons strawberry jam	

Wash and hull the strawberries and reserve several of the best for decoration. Using the metal blade, purée the remaining strawberries with the bananas. Add the jam and buttermilk and process until well mixed. Lastly, add the orange liqueur and mix in. Freeze until nearly firm. Remove from the freezer and purée half the mixture with the metal blade. Repeat with the remaining mixture and refreeze. Before serving, stand at room temperature for a few minutes to take off the chill. Decorate with whole strawberries.

SERVES 6

Fresh Fruit Ice

350 g/12 oz fruit pulp (pineapple, apricot, plum, raspberries or mango)	450 ml/¾ pint water
	pared rind and juice of a small lemon
175 g/6 oz caster sugar	1 egg white, whisked

Peel and stone the fruit. Process with the metal blade, then weigh the purée. Place the sugar and water in a heavy-based saucepan and bring slowly to the boil, stirring constantly. Allow to boil only when the sugar has completely dissolved. Add the fruit purée, lemon rind and juice, bring back to the boil

Frozen desserts, from left to right: Rich Chocolate Ice Cream, Strawberry Banana Freeze, Rum Peachy Sherbet, Old-Fashioned Vanilla Ice Cream, Fresh Fruit Ice with Pineapple

and simmer for 5 minutes. Remove the rind and cool the mixture. Pour into ice cube trays and freeze until firm, but not solid. Cut the fruit ice into blocks and, using about a third at a time, drop them onto the rotating metal blades. As the mixture starts to break up, add about a third of the egg white and process until smooth and airy in texture and light in colour. Pour the mixture into a freezer container. Repeat until all the fruit ice has been processed. Cover and return to the freezer until very firm. The fruit ice should not be stored for longer than two weeks in the freezer.

SERVES 6

Variation

Fresh Fruit Ice Cream: When processing the semi-frozen fruit ice with the egg white, pour in 7 tablespoons double cream. Remember, the more cream you add, the richer the ice cream.

Fruit Dream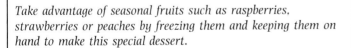

Take advantage of seasonal fruits such as raspberries, strawberries or peaches by freezing them and keeping them on hand to make this special dessert.

450 ml/¾ pint double cream	450 g/1 lb frozen,
75 g/3 oz caster sugar	unsweetened fruit

Using the metal blade, process the cream and sugar until the mixture begins to thicken. Take care not to over process. Add the frozen fruit a few pieces at a time and blend until smooth.

Serve immediately. This mixture may be frozen, but the texture will not be as smooth and creamy.

SERVES 6

Danish Apple Roll

1 quantity of Cream Cheese	generous pinch of mixed
Pastry (page 131)	spice
4 Granny Smith apples	2 teaspoons plain flour
150 g/5 oz raisins	25 g/1 oz butter
75 g/3 oz brown sugar	GLAZE
1 teaspoon ground cinnamon	50 g/2 oz icing sugar
2 teaspoons grated orange	a little lemon juice
rind	

Make the pastry and chill for 1 hour before using. To make the filling, peel, core and quarter the apples. Fit the chipper plate to the processor and chop the apples. Combine the remaining ingredients with the chopped apples. Roll the dough into a rectangle. The length should be the same as the length of a small loaf tin – 23 × 10 cm/9 × 4 in. Place the apple filling along the length of one edge of the pastry. Wet the opposite edge, then roll up. Carefully lift into the greased loaf tin. Using a knife or a pair of scissors, slash the pastry along the top. Bake in a hot oven (220c, 425 F, gas 7) for 20 to 25 minutes or until golden in colour. Cool before icing. Mix the sifted icing sugar with a little lemon juice, then drizzle the icing over the apple roll. Serve slightly warm or cold.

SERVES 6

This roll can be kept frozen for a week or two before cooking.

Strawberry Pigs' Ears

½ quantity of Soda Water
   Pastry (page 134)
sugar to dredge
1 punnet strawberries

2 teaspoons icing sugar
1 tablespoon Cointreau
300 ml/½ pint double cream

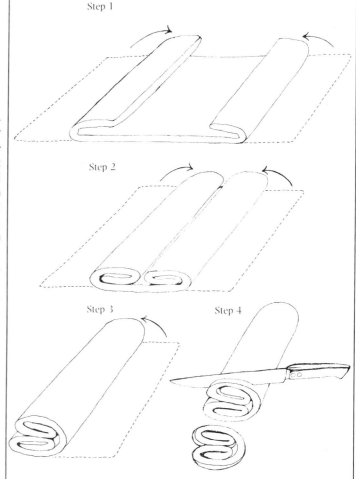

Step 1

Step 2

Step 3

Step 4

Divide the pastry in half and work with one piece at a time. Dredge a board with sugar instead of flour and roll the pastry into a rectangle 15 × 30 cm/6 × 12 in. Sprinkle with a little sugar. Fold each pastry end half-way to the middle (step 1); then over again to meet in the middle (step 2); lastly, fold completely in half (step 3); cut into 5 mm/¼ in slices (step 4) and place on a greased baking tray. Repeat the rolling and folding with the remaining pastry. Sprinkle the pastry with a little more sugar and reshape if necessary. Chill for at least 10 minutes, then bake in a hot oven, 220 c, 425 F, gas 7) for 8 minutes or until light caramel in colour. Turn over, sprinkle with a little sugar and bake for a further 4 minutes. Cool on a wire rack. Hull the strawberries, slice a few and reserve for decoration. Place the remaining strawberries in the work bowl and chop with the metal blade. Add the icing sugar and Cointreau to the chopped strawberries and set aside. Whisk the cream until stiff. Combine the cream and strawberries. Place one pig's ear flat on a surface, add a good scoop of strawberry cream, then place a second pig's ear at an angle on top of the cream. Decorate with a slice of strawberry. Depending on the size of the pig's ears, this dish may be served either as a dessert or a dainty tea-time treat.

SERVES 8

To freeze, place the uncooked pig's ear in the freezer for up to two weeks. Do not thaw before baking.

Honey Yogurt Freeze

7 tablespoons evaporated
   milk
2 tablespoons honey
1 teaspoon powdered gelatine
2 tablespoons hot water

250 ml/8 fl oz natural
   yogurt
½ teaspoon vanilla essence
pinch of nutmeg
few drops lemon juice

Combine half the evaporated milk with the honey, bring to the boil and simmer for 5 minutes. Dissolve the gelatine in the hot water over a basin of boiling water, add to the remaining evaporated milk then add to the hot milk and honey mixture. Fit the metal blade to the processor and combine the yogurt, vanilla, nutmeg and lemon juice in the work bowl. Process for about 15 seconds, then add the milk mixture and process for a further 15 seconds. Turn into a freezer tray and freeze until almost solid. Remove from the freezer, break into pieces and process with the metal blade until light and fluffy. Repeat the freezing and beating process once more, then freeze until solid. Before serving, remove from the freezer and stand for about 15 minutes. Break into pieces and process again to fluff up. Spoon into individual serving bowls and serve immediately.

SERVES 4

Peaches and Cream Tart

Make this dessert when fresh peaches are plentiful

600 ml/1 pint double cream
2 tablespoons buttermilk
6 ripe peaches, peeled and
   coarsely chopped
grated rind and juice of 1
   large orange
grated rind and juice of 1
   lemon
2 tablespoons lemon juice

½ teaspoon vanilla essence
a few drops of almond essence
2 teaspoons rum
100 g/4 oz caster sugar
1 × 23 cm/9 in Crumb Crust
   pie shell (page 132)
1 large peach, peeled and
   sliced, to decorate

Combine the cream and buttermilk, mix well and allow to stand at room temperature for an hour until thick. Fit the metal blade to the processor and add the peaches, orange rind and juice, lemon rind and juice, vanilla essence, almond essence, rum and sugar to the work bowl. Process until very well blended. Turn into a large bowl and carefully fold in the cream mixture. Partially freeze, then spoon into the crumb crust pie shell and return to the freezer. Before serving, allow to stand at room temperature for about 20 minutes. Cut into wedges and decorate each wedge with a fresh peach slice.

SERVES 6

Note: Cream soured with buttermilk has a better flavour than commercially-prepared soured cream which may, however, be used as a substitute.

Choux Puffs with Praline Filling

Choux Puffs with Praline Filling

1 quantity of Choux Pastry
  (page 135)
FILLING
50 g/2 oz unpeeled almonds
150 g/6 oz caster sugar

150 ml/$\frac{1}{4}$ pint water
pinch of cream of tartar
250 ml/8 fl oz double cream
1 tablespoon almond liqueur
icing sugar to dust

Make the choux pastry and, using a star nozzle, pipe into medium-sized rounds. Bake, cool and store until required. To make the praline, arrange the almonds over the base of a non-stick baking tray. Place the sugar and water in a saucepan and stir over a low heat until the sugar has dissolved. Add the cream of tartar and bring to the boil. Boil until the mixture becomes a good, deep caramel colour. Pour over the nuts and allow to harden. Break the praline into chunks. With the machine running, drop a few chunks of praline onto the rotating metal blade. Process until finely chopped. Remove from the bowl and repeat until all the praline has been ground. Whisk the cream until thick. Stir in the praline and the liqueur. Place the cream in a piping bag fitted with a plain nozzle. In the base of each puff, make a hole large enough for the end of the nozzle and fill with praline cream. Dust the top of the puffs with sifted icing sugar. Refrigerate until serving time. These puffs will keep for 3 hours.

SERVES 6 TO 8

Café au Lait

A light coffee and rum-flavoured dessert that isn't too heavy on the calories!

600 ml/1 pint strong coffee
100 g/4 oz caster sugar
2 tablespoons rum
150 ml/¼ pint evaporated milk

grated chocolate for decoration

Bring the coffee and sugar to the boil, stirring to dissolve the sugar. Simmer for 5 minutes, remove from the heat and cool for about 10 minutes. Now add the rum and evaporated milk and mix well. Allow to cool before pouring into freezer trays. Freeze until nearly firm, then turn the mixture into the work bowl and process until fluffy. Repeat the freezing and beating process once more. Just before serving, break the frozen mixture into pieces and process with the metal blade to fluff up. Spoon into individual serving bowls and decorate with grated chocolate.

SERVES 6

Layered Coffee Gâteau

2 (15-cm/6-in) trifle sponges
175 g/6 oz butter, softened
175 g/6 oz caster sugar
3 eggs
2 tablespoons instant coffee

2 tablespoons boiling water
2 tablespoons brandy
40 g/1½ oz pecan nuts or walnuts
300 ml/½ pint double cream

Slice each sponge into three layers. Place a disc of non-stick baking parchment on the base of a 20-cm/8-in round, deep cake tin. Fit the nylon blade to the processor and cream the butter well. With the motor running, pour the sugar through the feed tube and process for 1 minute, scraping down the sides of the work bowl when necessary. Add the eggs and process again for a few seconds. Dissolve the coffee in the boiling water. Cool, then add the brandy. Pour into the creamed mixture and process for 10 seconds. Arrange a layer of cake to fit the cake tin, cutting and joining where necessary. Pour half the creamed mixture on top. Add another layer of cake, then the remaining creamed mixture. Complete with the remaining layer of cake. Place a plate on top of the cake and weight it down. Refrigerate for at least 3 hours, or overnight.

For the final decoration, chop the nuts with the metal blade. Whisk the cream until stiff. Loosen the sides of the cake with a palette knife, then turn out onto a board. Thickly spread two-thirds of the whipped cream over the gâteau and decorate the sides with chopped nuts. If desired, use a palette knife to create a diamond pattern on top. Place the remaining cream in a piping bag fitted with a medium star nozzle, and pipe rosettes of cream around the edge of the gâteau. Return to the refrigerator until required.

SERVES 8

Cointreau Tart

100 g/4 oz Brazil or pecan nuts
50 g/2 oz margarine
100 g/4 oz caster sugar
75 g/3 oz coconut
FILLING
6 egg yolks
225 g/8 oz sugar

2 teaspoons powdered gelatine
4 tablespoons hot water
7 tablespoons Cointreau
450 ml/¾ pint double cream
DECORATION
150 ml/¼ pint whipped cream
Brazil or pecan nuts

To make the pastry shell, process the nuts with the metal blade until finely chopped. Add the margarine and, with the machine running, pour in the sugar. Cream well, then add the coconut. Press into the base and sides of a 24-cm/10-in pie plate. Prick the shell with a fork and bake in a moderate oven (160 c, 325 f, gas 3) for 12 to 15 minutes.

To make the filling, process the egg yolks well. With the machine running, pour the sugar in through the feed tube and process for 1 minute. Dissolve the gelatine in the hot water over a basin of boiling water. Now add the Cointreau and cool slightly. Whisk the cream until thick but not stiff. Carefully fold in the yolk mixture and quickly fold in the gelatine. Pour into the cooled shell and allow to set. Decorate with stars of whipped cream and pieces of Brazil nut or pecan nuts.

SERVES 8 TO 10

Chocolate Nut Pie

2 teaspoons powdered gelatine
4 tablespoons hot water
150 g/5 oz plain chocolate, broken up
7 tablespoons boiling water
2 eggs
50 g/2 oz caster sugar
pinch of salt

1 teaspoon vanilla essence
50 g/2 oz pecan nuts
250 ml/8 fl oz double cream, whipped
1 (23-cm/9-in) Nutty Crust Pie shell (page 132)
whipped cream and grated chocolate to decorate

Dissolve the gelatine in the hot water over a basin of boiling water. Melt the chocolate over hot water and, when melted, stir in the boiling water. Add the dissolved gelatine and stir until completely mixed. Fit the metal blade to the processor and place the eggs, sugar, salt and vanilla essence in the work bowl. Process until light and fluffy. Add the nuts and, with the machine running, pour in the chocolate mixture. Process until well mixed. Pour this mixture into a large bowl and gently fold in the whipped cream. Spoon into the nutty crust pie shell and chill until set. To serve, top with whipped cream and grated chocolate. Cut into wedges.

SERVES 8

Apple Streudel

The secret of making a good apple streudel lies in the long kneading required by the dough. Using a processor, you will find that this kneading is done quickly and perfectly for you. Homemade streudel is an impressive dish – serve it at a special tea or as a dessert.

150 g/5 oz plain flour	150 g/5 oz blanched almonds
generous pinch of salt	6–8 Granny Smith apples
1 egg	150 g/5 oz caster sugar
5 tablespoons tepid water	2 teaspoons ground
$\frac{1}{4}$ teaspoon vinegar	cinnamon
100 g/4 oz butter, melted	pinch of cloves
FILLING	150 g/5 oz sultanas
3 slices bread, cubed	1 tablespoon grated lemon rind

Apple Streudel

First make the dough. Fit the metal blade to the processor and place the flour and salt in the work bowl. Pulse three times to aerate. Combine the water, egg and vinegar. With the machine running, pour the liquid through the feed tube and process until a firm dough forms. Continue to process the dough for 45 seconds to knead it. With the machine running, add 2 teaspoons melted butter. Continue processing for a further 15 seconds. At this stage, the dough should be soft, smooth and elastic. Remove the dough from the bowl, brush it with melted butter, then cover and set aside for 30 minutes.

To make the filling, finely crumb the bread with the metal blade. Place the crumbs on a baking tray and toast lightly in a moderate oven (160 c, 325 f, gas 3). Cool before using. Process the blanched almonds with the metal blade until ground, then turn them into a large bowl. Peel, core and quarter the apples. Slice, using the slicing blade. Add to the ground almonds together with the caster sugar, cinnamon, cloves, sultanas and lemon rind. Mix well.

Flour a large clean work surface well. Brush the dough with a little more melted butter, and roll it out in a rectangle until 3 mm/$\frac{1}{8}$ in thick. Starting at the centre, stretch the dough outwards using the back and flat of your hands. Lift the dough up and continue to work it until it is paper thin. Trim the edges with a pair of scissors and use these scraps to patch any holes. The dough should be approximately 50 × 100 cm/20 × 40 in. in sizè. Brush the dough liberally with melted butter and sprinkle with breadcrumbs, reserving a few for the top of the pastry. Arrange the filling in a 7.5 cm/3 in wide strip along the long edge nearest you, leaving 5 cm/2 in clear at each end. Using the cloth as a lifter, roll the pastry up Swiss roll style. Do not roll too tightly as the dough will expand during cooking. Brush the top with butter and sprinkle with breadcrumbs. Curl into a horseshoe shape and lift onto a well greased baking tray. Bake in a hot oven (220 c, 425 f, gas 7) for 10 minutes, then reduce the heat to moderately hot (190 c, 375 f, gas 5) and continue to bake for about 20 minutes until crisp and brown. Serve warm or cool with whipped cream.

SERVES 10

Frozen Silk Cream

50 g/2 oz pecan nuts	2 eggs
100 g/4 oz plain flour	25 g/1 oz plain chocolate
50 g/2 oz soft brown sugar	COFFEE CREAM
225 g/8 oz butter, softened	250 ml/8 fl oz double cream
CHOCOLATE FILLING	2 tablespoons caster sugar
100 g/4 oz butter	1 tablespoon coffee liqueur
150 g/5 oz caster sugar	2 teaspoons strong black coffee

Using the metal blade, finely chop the pecan nuts. Add the flour, brown sugar and butter. Process for 45 seconds. Grease a 23-cm/9-in square baking tin and press the crumb mixture into the base. Smooth with the back of a spoon. Bake in a moderate oven (160 c, 325 f, gas 3) for 20 minutes. Allow the crust to cool in the pan.

To make the chocolate filling, cream the butter with the metal blade. Add the caster sugar and pulse until smooth. Drop in the eggs one at a time and process for about 15 seconds after each addition. Melt the chocolate and add to the mixture while the machine is running. Continue beating for 20 seconds. Spread this mixture over the cooled crust, cover and chill for 2 hours.

To make the coffee cream, whisk the cream and caster sugar until thick. Pour in the liqueur and coffee and stir to combine.

To assemble, use a knife to loosen the cake from the tin and cut in half to form two rectangles. Place one rectangle, crust side down, on a wire rack. Spread with half the coffee cream. Place the second layer on top of the cream, crust side down. Finally, pipe or spread the remainder of the cream all over the cake and freeze. Take out of the freezer and place in the refrigerator one hour before serving.

SERVES 10

This dessert will freeze well for a few weeks.

Crêpes Suzette

An air of mystery seems to surround their preparation; perhaps it is because they are almost always made by superior-looking waiters. Make the sauce at the table if you have a small gas unit or in the privacy of the kitchen. Fold the crêpes in advance, pour the sauce over them and ignite at the table for an impressive sight.

20 dessert crepes (see below)	150 ml/¼ pint water
SAUCE	2 tablespoons lemon juice
100 g/4 oz butter	2 teaspoons cornflour
225 g/8 oz caster sugar	zest of 2 oranges
5 tablespoons concentrated frozen orange juice	5 tablespoons orange liqueur
	5 tablespoons brandy

Melt the butter and allow to foam. Add the sugar and cook slowly until it begins to caramelise. Carefully pour in the orange juice, water and lemon juice. (The mixture may become stringy at this point.) Continue stirring over a low heat until the sauce becomes smooth, bring to the boil and simmer for 5 minutes. Mix the cornflour with a little water and stir into the orange sauce. Bring back to the boil, then add the orange zest. Combine the liqueur and brandy and add half to the sauce. Fold the crêpes in four and place in a chafing dish. Pour the sauce over. Warm the remaining liqueur and brandy in a ladle, ignite and flambé the crêpes with this at the table. Serve at once on warm plates.

SERVES 6

Dessert Crêpes 🌓 🔆

Prepare and cook these crêpes beforehand and freeze.

4 eggs	250 ml/8 fl oz milk
100 g/4 oz plain flour	4 tablespoons water
40 g/1½ oz sugar	1 tablespoon melted butter

Fit the nylon blade to the processor and place all the ingredients in the work bowl. Blend for 30 seconds. Scrape down the sides of the bowl and process for another 30 seconds. Refrigerate the batter for at least 1 hour before using. Cook the crêpes with an electric crêpe maker or in melted butter in a crêpe pan.

MAKES 20 TO 25 CREPES

To freeze, stack the cooled crêpes using a double thickness of waxed paper between each. Place in a plastic bag, seal well and freeze for up to six weeks. To use, separate the number of crêpes desired and thaw at room temperature for 10 minutes.

Romanoff Crêpes

2 punnets fresh, firm strawberries	2 tablespoons orange liqueur
50 g/2 oz caster sugar	250 ml/8 fl oz soft vanilla ice cream
8 cooked dessert crêpes	1 teaspoon finely chopped mint
250 ml/8 fl oz double cream	

Using the slicing plate, slice the strawberries and sprinkle with sugar. Arrange the strawberries on each of the crêpes. Whip the cream to soft peaks. Beat in the orange liqueur and ice cream. Spoon some of this mixture over the strawberries on each crêpe. Fold the crêpes over the filling and arrange in a serving dish. Spoon the remaining cream on top and sprinkle with chopped mint. Serve immediately.

SERVES 8

Fudge Walnut Pie ☯

This deliciously rich pie is definitely not for slimmers!

100 g/4 oz walnuts	vanilla ice cream
225 g/8 oz caster sugar	HOT FUDGE SAUCE
100 g/4 oz butter	75 g/3 oz butter
2 eggs	50 g/2 oz plain chocolate
2 tablespoons milk	225 g/8 oz caster sugar
1 teaspoon vanilla essence	250 ml/8 fl oz double cream
100 g/4 oz plain flour	pinch of salt
pinch of salt	2 teaspoons vanilla essence
50 g/2 oz plain chocolate, melted and slightly cooled	

Using the metal blade, chop the walnuts coarsely and set aside. Place the sugar, butter and eggs in a work bowl and process for about 45 seconds or until light and fluffy, scraping the bowl when necessary. Now add the milk, vanilla essence, flour and salt. Process until well mixed. Add the chocolate and process well. Lastly, add the nuts, pulsing two or three times to mix in. Spread the mixture in a greased 23-cm/9-in pie plate and bake in a moderate oven (180 c, 350 f, gas 4) for 30 to 35 minutes. Cool on a wire rack.

To make the sauce, melt the butter and chocolate over a low heat. Fit the metal blade to the processor and place the sugar, cream and salt in the work bowl. Pulse five times to mix well. Add the cream mixture to the chocolate and stir over a low heat until the sugar has melted and the mixture is well blended. Remove from the heat and stir in the vanilla essence. To serve, cut the pie into wedges and top with vanilla ice cream and hot fudge sauce.

SERVES 6

Crêpes Suzette

Mille Feuilles

Mille Feuilles

½ quantity of Quick Puff
  Pastry (page 132) or Soda
  Water Pastry (page 134)
1 beaten egg
2 punnets fresh strawberries
  or raspberries, or 2
  (410-g/14½-oz) cans
  apricots, drained and
  chilled

6 tablespoons double cream
FILLING
50 g/2 oz butter
75 g/3 oz plain flour
250 ml/8 fl oz milk
75 g/3 oz soft brown sugar
2 teaspoons vanilla essence
1 egg, separated
7 tablespoons double cream

Make the pastry and divide it into three. Roll out each piece to a rectangle 30 × 20 cm/12 × 8 in. The pastry should be about 5 mm/¼ in thick. With a sharp knife, trim the edges. Using the rolling pin, lift the pastry rectangles onto greased baking trays which have been splashed with cold water. Brush with a little beaten egg. Bake in a hot oven (220 c, 425 f, gas 7) for 10 to 15 minutes or until brown and crisp. Turn the pastry over and bake for about 5 minutes more. This will help to crispen the pastry. Cool on a wire rack.

If using strawberries or raspberries, clean the fruit, then chill. To make the filling, heat the butter in a medium saucepan, add the flour and cook for a few seconds. Remove from the heat, stir in the milk and add the sugar. Return to the heat and bring to the boil, stirring constantly. When cooked, the sauce should be very thick. Remove from the heat, cool slightly and stir in the vanilla and egg yolk. Cover with a piece of greaseproof paper to prevent a skin forming. Allow to cool completely. Using a mixer, beat the filling cream until stiff. Whisk the egg white. Stir one-third of the cream into the sauce, then fold in the remainder. Fold in the egg-white.

To assemble the dessert, use a sharp knife to trim the three sheets of pastry and save the crumbs. Select the best piece of pastry for the top and arrange the best strawberries, apricot halves or whole raspberries in rows across the pastry, leaving a space all the way around the edge. Whip the six tablespoons cream and place in a piping bag fitted with a star nozzle. Pipe stars of cream all the way around the edge of the pastry. Slice the remaining fruit and set aside. Divide three-quarters of the custard mixture between the two remaining layers of pastry, spread smooth and top with the sliced fruit. Arrange the three layers one on top of each other and spread the reserved custard around the edges. Crumble the scraps of pastry and use the crumbs to coat the sides (this neatens off the edges). Place on a serving platter and chill until required. This dessert should not be assembled more than 4 hours in advance.

As the preparation of this dessert is time consuming, the following work order can be followed with great success. Prepare and roll out the pastry some days in advance, cover and freeze on baking trays. The day the dessert is to be served, remove the pastry from the freezer. Brush with beaten egg and, without thawing, bake in a preheated oven. Prepare the fruit and make the custard early in the day. Cover and refrigerate. Assemble the dessert up to 4 hours in advance.

SERVES 10

Luscious Lemon Cheesecake

CRUST
1 packet Marie biscuits
50 g/2 oz caster sugar
100 g/4 oz butter, melted
FILLING
350 g/12 oz cream cheese

3 eggs, separated
7 tablespoons double cream
100 g/4 oz caster sugar
2 tablespoons plain flour
2 tablespoons lemon juice
½ teaspoon vanilla essence

For the crust, fit the metal blade to the processor and place the broken biscuits in the work bowl. Process until finely crumbed. Add the sugar and melted butter and process until well mixed. Press the mixture into the bottom and 5 cm/2 in up the sides of a 20-cm/8-in springform tin. Chill until required.

For the filling, use the metal blade to process the cream cheese and egg yolks until smooth. Add the cream, sugar, flour, lemon juice and vanilla essence. Process until well mixed, scraping down the bowl when necessary.

Whisk the egg whites until stiff peaks form. Fold the egg whites into the cream cheese mixture. Pour the cheese mixture into the prepared crust and bake in a moderate oven (180c, 350f, gas 4) for about 60 minutes, or until the cheesecake springs back when touched. Chill well before serving. Garnish with fruit, if desired.

SERVES 10

Frozen Plum Cassis Mousse

7 tablespoons plum juice
4 egg yolks
2 (410-g/14½-oz) cans
  plums, well drained
3 tablespoons crème de
  cassis liqueur
250 ml/8 fl oz double
  cream
2 egg whites

50 g/2 oz caster sugar
CASSIS SAUCE
250 ml/8 fl/oz plum syrup
  (drained from the plums)
3 tablespoons water
1 tablespoon cornflour
4 tablespoons crème de cassis
plum slices to decorate
  (optional)

Bring the plum juice to the boil. Meanwhile, whisk the egg yolks until thick and creamy. Transfer to the work bowl and use the nylon blade. With the machine running, pour in the boiling plum juice and process for 1 minute. Add the plums and liqueur, and pulse to combine. Small pieces of plum should still be visible. Chill the mixture well. Whisk the cream until thick. Fold into the chilled plum mixture. Whisk the egg whites until stiff and gradually fold in the caster sugar. Fold into the fruit mixture. Pour into a cake tin, lined with foil, or a mould and freeze overnight.

To make the sauce, bring the plum syrup to the boil. Combine the water and cornflour and add a little of the boiling liquid. Now add the cornflour mixture to the plum syrup and bring back to the boil, stirring until thickened. Remove from the heat and cool before adding the liqueur.

To serve, loosen the edge of the mousse with a palette knife. Turn onto a platter and, if desired, decorate with plum slices. Spoon a little of the cassis sauce around the base and serve immediately. The remaining sauce should be served separately.

This dish may be turned out well in advance. Return to the freezer then pour the sauce around just before serving.

SERVES 6 TO 8

Bitter Chocolate Truffles

100 g/4 oz plain dessert
  chocolate
4 tablespoons double cream
pinch of salt

few drops of almond or
  peppermint essence
cocoa powder to dust

Using the chipper plate, chop the chocolate. Bring the cream just up to the boil, remove from the heat and add the chopped chocolate. Stand for 5 minutes, then stir to combine. Add the salt and essence to taste. Spread the mixture out on a piece of heavy foil and chill for 30 minutes. Fit the metal blade and process the chocolate cream until firm and fluffy. Spoon into a piping bag with a plain nozzle. Pipe 1-cm/½-in mounds onto foil, then freeze. Toss in the truffles in cocoa powder, then return to the freezer until required.

MAKES 36 TRUFFLES

These keep well in an airtight container in the freezer.

Bittersweet Grapefruit Bites

Grapefruit bites are ideal for serving after dinner. They can be made well in advance and do not go tacky if the weather is wet. They make an unusual gift and will travel easily.

2 large grapefruit
225 g/8 oz caster sugar
4 tablespoons water
1 tablespoon golden syrup

2 tablespoons orange liqueur
sugar to dust
50 g/2 oz chocolate, melted

Cut the grapefruit in quarters and carefully remove the flesh. Pack the peel pieces, cut side down, into the base of the feed tube. Using a medium pressure, slice the peel with the slicing plate. Place the sliced peel in a large saucepan, cover with water and bring to the boil. Simmer for 5 minutes, then drain. Repeat this process twice more. Combine the sugar, water and syrup in a saucepan and bring to the boil over a low heat, stirring constantly. Add the liqueur and peel and simmer for 30 minutes or until the syrup is thick and the peel glossy. Drain well. Spread on a fine wire rack overnight. Toss in sugar, then dip the ends of some of the pieces into melted chocolate. Store in an airtight container or in the refrigerator for a few days.

Kiwi Cheesecake

Apple Tart with Cinnamon Crumble

PASTRY
50 g/2 oz nuts
225 g/8 oz plain flour
2 tablespoons cornflour
50 g/2 oz icing sugar
2 teaspoons baking powder
2 teaspoon ground cinnamon
175 g/6 oz butter
1 egg

1 teaspoon vanilla essence
a little icing sugar
FILLING
800 g/1¾ lb cooked apples
50 g/2 oz soft brown sugar
75 g/3 oz sultanas
rind and juice of 1 lemon
7 tablespoons soured cream

To make the pastry, chop the nuts with the metal blade, then add all the dry ingredients and pulse to combine. Cut the butter into pieces, add to the flour and pulse until the mixture resembles fine crumbs. Combine the egg and vanilla essence and pour through the feed tube while the machine is running. Stop processing as soon as the pastry forms a ball (about 5 seconds). Chill for 2 hours. Grease a 25-cm/10-in pie plate or springform tin. Divide the pastry in two and use the chipper plate to grate half the pastry. Press the grated pastry into the pie plate. Combine all the filling ingredients and place in the pastry shell. Now grate the remaining pastry and sprinkle lightly over the filling. Bake in a moderate oven (160c, 325 f, gas 3) for 45 minutes. Serve warm or cold, dusted with icing sugar.

SERVES 8 TO 10

Kiwi Cheesecake

CRUST
¾ packet digestive biscuits
3 tablespoons golden syrup
25 g/1 oz cocoa powder
75 g/3 oz butter
FILLING
250 ml/8 fl oz double cream

250 ml/8 fl oz condensed milk
225 g/8 oz cream cheese
7 tablespoons lemon juice
TOPPING
3–4 kiwi fruits, peeled

To make the crust, crumb the biscuits with the metal blade. Heat the syrup, cocoa powder and butter until the butter has melted. Pour this mixture through the feed tube and pulse until well combined with the biscuit crumbs. Grease a 23-cm/9-in pie plate or springform tin, press in the crumb mixture to form a crust, then chill. Whisk the cream until thick. Add the condensed milk and cream cheese and stir to combine. Pour in the lemon juice and mix thoroughly. Pour into the crumb crust and refrigerate for at least 2 hours. Using the slicing plate, slice the kiwi fruits. Arrange the slices on top of the filling so that they overlap. Refrigerate until required.

SERVES 8 TO 10

This cheesecake will freeze for up to three months. However, do not add the sliced kiwi fruit until a few hours before serving.

Melon Dessert Soup

The colour and flavour of this unusual soup will depend on the type of melon used.

2 medium or 1 large
  honeydew or ogen melon
250 ml/8 fl oz natural yogurt
2 tablespoons orange liqueur

6 tablespoons orange juice
few drops of almond essence
fresh mint sprigs to decorate

Fit the metal blade to the processor, cut the melon in half, remove the seeds and spoon the flesh into the work bowl. Purée the melon and add all the remaining ingredients except the mint. Process until well blended. Chill for several hours before serving. Decorate with fresh mint.

SERVES 6

Left to right: Golden Cherry Loaf (page 121)
Bee-Sting Cake (page 121), Nutty Cinnamon Rolls (page 123)

Quick and Yeast Breads

Breads are one of the most creative and satisfying kinds of food that anyone can prepare. A simple dough or batter magically rises and is transformed into a beautiful bread, soft rolls or deliciously light scones. Nothing beats the aroma and taste of a newly baked loaf, the crispness of the crust or of butter melting on a steaming muffin.

Making breads in the food processor allows you to be inventive and to prepare delicious results, even when time is short. Quick breads are really quick, being mixed and ready for the oven in seconds. Yeast breads are mixed and kneaded, ready to rise, in about 1 minute.

The secret of baking good bread is to start with fresh ingredients.

Yeast: This living organism, the active rising agent in batters and doughs, is available in two different forms. Fresh or compressed yeast, which comes in cake form, must be kept refrigerated. If it is purchased fresh, it will keep for about two weeks in the refrigerator or up to two months in the freezer. Dry yeast, available in granular form, will keep for several months if stored in a cool, dry place. It requires a warmer liquid to activate it than compressed yeast. A lukewarm, even temperature is needed to develop the yeast in bread doughs – too high a heat can destroy it and too low a temperature will slow it down.

Baking powder and bicarbonate of soda: These ingredients react to form bubbles of carbon dioxide when combined with a liquid. The carbon dioxide expands during baking to give a fine, delicate texture to quick breads. Baking powders and bicarbonate of soda must be kept dry as they will soon become stale if any moisture is present.

Flour: The major ingredient in breads, flour contains a substance called gluten. When mixed with liquid and kneaded, gluten develops to form the basic structure of bread while the rising action of yeast or baking powder provides the lightness in texture. A range of flour measurements is given in most yeast bread recipes, for changes in temperature and humidity affect the amount of flour necessary. On a humid day, more flour is needed to produce a dough that is easy to handle.

Sugar: Adds flavour, gives a golden crust and provides food for the yeast.

Salt: Used mainly for flavour, it also helps strengthen the structure of the bread.
Butter or margarine: Gives a tender, rich bread and improves the browning.
Liquid: An essential ingredient. Either water or milk, or a mixture of both, may be used. Water gives a hard, crisp crust and an open texture, while milk gives a tender, flavourful bread with a softer, browner crust.
Eggs: Add richness in flavour and colour, and give breads a fine texture.

Other ingredients such as spices, fruits or nuts, herbs, grated cheese or chopped onion can be added for their distinctive flavours.

Steps for successful bread making

Mixing: The food processor ensures that mixing is done quickly and efficiently. Be sure not to overmix quick breads.
Kneading: Although quick breads are never thoroughly kneaded, this is an important step in making yeast breads and is performed effortlessly in the processor. It takes about 1 minute to transform the dough from a sticky, unresponsive mass into an elastic, satin-smooth ball.
Rising: Quick breads do not need time to rise as the batter expands in the oven during baking. When yeast doughs rise, the yeast ferments and produces gas, making the bread light in texture. Cover yeast doughs and allow to rise in a warm place away from draughts, until doubled in bulk. To test that it has risen sufficiently, press two fingers about 1 cm/$\frac{1}{2}$ in into the dough. If the indentations remain, the dough is ready to be punched down.
Punching down: When the dough has doubled in volume, plunge your floured fist into the centre. Fold the edges of the dough to the middle and turn the ball onto a board. Knead lightly for a few seconds.
Shaping: Divide the dough into the required portions and shape each into a ball. The dough should rest a few minutes, then shape as desired. After shaping, cover the dough and allow to rise again in a warm place until nearly doubled in size before baking in a preheated oven.

Hints for perfect breads

• The recipes in this section were tested with the kind of yeast called for, so, for best results, follow the recipe.

• To test that a loaf is ready at the end of the baking time, tap the top lightly with the handle of a wooden spoon or the knuckle of one finger. If it sounds hollow, the loaf is done.

• Unless otherwise directed, remove the bread from the baking tin as soon as it comes out of the oven and cool it on a wire rack. Quick breads may need to cool in the tin for 10 minutes or so before turning out.

• Quick bread loaves slice best if completely cool and the flavour of many will improve after 24 hours. On the other hand, muffins and scones are best served warm and, as they take almost no time to mix and very little time to bake, they can be made just before serving.

A tasty array of quick and yeast breads, clockwise: French Braid, White Yeast Bread, Selection of rolls, Buttermilk Loaf, Honey Wholewheat Bread (page 120)

White Yeast Bread

Here is a basic white loaf that is so quick and easy you will make it often.

about 250 ml/8 fl oz warm water	2 tablespoons powdered milk
2 teaspoons dried yeast	25 g/1 oz butter, cut up
1 tablespoon caster sugar	1 teaspoon salt
350 g/12 oz strong plain flour	

Combine half the warm water with the yeast and sugar. Stir well and stand in a warm place for 5 to 10 minutes, until frothy. Fit the metal blade to the processor, add the flour, powdered milk, butter and salt to the work bowl and process for 3 to 4 seconds to combine. Add the yeast mixture and process until well mixed (about 10 seconds). With the machine running, slowly add the remaining warm water until the dough forms a ball. Allow the ball to turn around the bowl about 20 times, then turn the machine off and allow the dough to rest for 1 minute. Again process the dough until the ball has turned round the bowl another 20 times. Place the dough in a greased bowl, turning the dough to grease the top. Cover and stand in a warm place for about 1 hour, or until doubled in bulk. Punch the dough down, shape into a loaf and place in a greased 450-g/1-lb loaf tin. Stand in a warm place until doubled in size (about 45 minutes). Bake in a moderate oven (180 c, 350 f, gas 4) for about 30 to 35 minutes. Turn out and cool on a wire rack before slicing.

MAKES 1 LOAF

Buttermilk Loaf

Add dried or fresh herbs to this loaf for a special flavour.

4 tablespoons warm water	1 teaspoon dried mixed herbs or tablespoon fresh mixed herbs, e.g. parsley, dill, thyme, marjoram
2 teaspoons dried yeast	
2 tablespoons caster sugar	
350 g/12 oz plain flour	
25 g/1 oz butter or margarine, cut up	2 teaspoons salt
	about 250 ml/8 fl oz buttermilk

Combine the yeast and sugar with the warm water. Stir well and stand in a warm place for 5 to 10 minutes until frothy. Fit the metal blade to the processor and place the flour, butter, herbs and salt in the work bowl. Process for 3 to 4 seconds to combine. Add the yeast mixture and process for about 12 seconds, until well mixed. With the machine running, slowly add the buttermilk until the dough forms a ball which leaves the sides of the work bowl clean. Allow the ball to turn around the bowl about 20 times. Turn the machine off and allow the dough to rest for 1 minute. Again process so that the dough turns round the bowl 20 times. Turn the machine off and allow the dough to rest for 1 minute. Again process so that the dough turns round the bowl 20 times. If necessary, add a little more buttermilk. The dough should be soft but not sticky. Place the dough in a greased bowl, turning the dough to grease the top. Cover and stand in a warm place to rise for about 1 hour, or until doubled in size. Punch down the dough, shape into a loaf and place in a greased 450-g/1-lb loaf tin. Cover and stand in a

warm place for about 45 minutes, or until doubled in bulk. Bake in a moderately hot oven (190 c, 375 f, gas 5) for about 25 to 30 minutes. Turn out on a wire rack and cool before slicing.

MAKES 1 LOAF

French Braid

2 teaspoons dried yeast	1 teaspoon salt
2 teaspoons sugar	15 g/½ oz butter, melted
250 ml/8 fl oz warm water	1 egg white, lightly whisked
350 g/12 oz plain flour	1 tablespoon water

Dissolve the yeast with the sugar in half the warm water and leave for 5 to 10 minutes until frothy. Fit the metal blade to the processor and place half the flour and the salt in the work bowl. Add the yeast mixture, butter and warm water and process for 25 seconds. Scrape down the sides of the bowl and process for 10 seconds more. With the machine running, add enough flour to form a ball of dough that leaves the sides of the bowl clean. Allow the dough to turn around the bowl about 20 times. Turn the machine off and allow the dough to rest for 1 minute. Process the dough for about 15 more turns. The dough should be soft but not sticky. Place in a greased bowl, turning the dough to grease the top. Cover and allow it to rise in a warm place until doubled in size, about 1 hour. Punch down the dough and divide into three equal parts, forming each into a strip about 30 cm/12 in long. Braid the three lengths together and seal the ends. Place on a greased baking tray and brush with a mixture of egg white and water. Cover loosely and allow to rise in a warm place until doubled in bulk (about 45 minutes). Brush again with egg white mixture and bake in a moderately hot oven (190 c, 375 f, gas 5) for about 35 minutes, or until golden brown. Cool on a wire rack before slicing.

MAKES 1 LOAF

Dinner Rolls

Using the basic white yeast bread recipe, punch the dough down after the first raising and shape into smooth balls about 3 cm/½ in. in diameter. Place on a greased 20-cm/8-in round or square tin so that the sides just touch. For rolls that break apart easily, brush with melted butter. Cover and allow to rise in a warm place until doubled in size, about 45 to 60 minutes. Bake for 25 to 30 minutes in a moderate oven (180 c, 350 f, gas 4). Turn out onto a wire rack and serve warm or cool.

Finger Rolls

Using the basic white yeast bread recipe, punch the dough down after the first raising. Divide the dough into pieces, about the size of walnuts, and shape into rolls 7.5 cm/3 in long. Place in a greased 20-cm/8-in square baking tin so that the sides just touch, making two rows in the tin. Cover and allow to rise in a warm place until doubled in size, about 45 minutes, then bake in a moderate oven (180 c, 350 f, gas 4) for 25 to 30 minutes. Turn out on a wire rack and serve warm or cool.

Honey Wholewheat Bread

A slightly sweet bread full of goodness.

7 tablespoons warm water	½ teaspoon ground cinnamon
3 tablespoons honey	3 tablespoons powdered milk
2 teaspoons dried yeast	25 g/1 oz margarine, cut
225 g/8 oz strong plain	into pieces
flour	1 teaspoon salt
100 g/4 oz wholewheat flour	1 egg

Combine half the warm water with 1 tablespoon honey and the yeast. Stir well, allow to stand in a warm place for 5 to 10 minutes until frothy. Fit the metal blade to the processor and place the flour, wholewheat flour, cinnamon, powdered milk, margarine, salt and remaining honey in the work bowl. Process for about 10 seconds to combine. Add the yeast mixture and egg and process for 10 to 12 seconds to mix well. With the machine running, slowly add the remaining warm water until the dough forms a ball. Allow the ball of dough to turn around the bowl about 20 times. Turn the machine off and allow the dough to rest for 1 minute. Process the dough again until the ball has turned around the bowl about 20 times. Place the dough in a greased bowl, turning to grease the top. Cover and stand in a warm place for about an hour, or until doubled in size. Punch down the dough, shape into a loaf and place in a greased 450-g/1-lb loaf tin. Cover and stand in a warm place for about 45 minutes, or until doubled in size. Bake in a moderately hot oven (190 c, 375 f, gas 5) for 25 to 35 minutes. Remove from the tin and cool on a wire rack.

MAKES 1 LOAF

Country Garden Casserole Bread

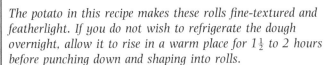

Country Garden Casserole Bread

The garden-fresh flavour makes this ideal to serve with soup or pâté.

1 tablespoon dried yeast	4 tablespoons molasses
300 ml/½ pint warm water	2 tablespoons oil
1 teaspoon caster sugar	1 egg
1 large carrot	100 g/4 oz wheat germ
350 g/12 oz plain flour	2 sprigs parsley, chopped
2 teaspoons salt	1 tablespoon chopped chives

Dissolve the yeast in half the warm water with the sugar and leave for 5 to 10 minutes, until frothy. Using the shredder plate, shred the carrot and set aside. Fit the metal blade and add 225 g/8 oz flour and the salt to the work bowl. Add the yeast mixture and pulse to combine. Now add the remaining water, molasses, oil and egg. Process for 15 seconds, scrape the bowl and process for 20 seconds more. Add the wheat germ, grated carrot, parsley and chives. Process to mix well. Add enough of the remaining flour to form a soft batter. Mix well then turn the mixture into a well-greased 1.75-litres/3-pints casserole. Cover and allow to rise in a warm place for 45 to 60 minutes, or until doubled in bulk. Bake in a moderately hot oven (190 c, 375 f, gas 5) for 50 to 55 minutes. Remove from the casserole and cool on a wire rack.

MAKES 1 LOAF

Refrigerator Rolls

The potato in this recipe makes these rolls fine-textured and featherlight. If you do not wish to refrigerate the dough overnight, allow it to rise in a warm place for 1½ to 2 hours before punching down and shaping into rolls.

100 g/4 oz potatoes	½ teaspoon salt
2 teaspoons dried yeast	25 g/1 oz margarine
1 teaspoon sugar	½ egg
150 ml/¼ pint milk and	1 beaten egg for glazing
water	poppy seeds
275 g/10 oz strong plain	
flour	

Cook the potatoes in their jackets, drain and peel. Using the metal blade, process until mashed. Dissolve the yeast and sugar in the milk and water mixture and leave for 5 to 10 minutes until frothy. Sift the flour and salt into the work bowl, add the margarine and pulse to combine, then add the egg. With the machine running, pour the yeast mixture through the feed tube. Process for about 1 minute until smooth. Place in a greased plastic bag and seal loosely. Leave to rise in the refrigerator overnight or longer (up to two days). Punch down the dough and shape into small rolls. Arrange on a greased baking tray, cover and allow to rise in warm place for 15 to 20 minutes. Lastly, brush with a little beaten egg and sprinkle with poppy seeds. Bake in a moderately hot oven (200 c, 400 f, gas 6) for 15 minutes.

MAKES ABOUT 12 ROLLS OR 1 LOAF

Hot Cross Buns

An Easter treat made in minutes in the food processor

1 tablespoon dried yeast	3 small eggs
75 g/3 oz caster sugar	50 g/2 oz dried currants
175 ml/6 fl oz warm milk	275 g/10 oz icing sugar
400 g/14 oz plain flour	1 egg white, lightly beaten
$\frac{1}{2}$ teaspoon salt	few drops of vanilla essence
1 teaspoon ground cinnamon	pinch of salt
6 tablespoons oil	a little milk

Dissolve the dried yeast with 1 teaspoon of the sugar in half the milk. Fit the metal blade to the processor and place 225 g/8 oz flour, the salt and the cinnamon in the work bowl. Heat the remaining milk, oil, sugar and salt until warm. Add to the dry ingredients along with the yeast mixture and eggs. Process for 20 seconds. Scrape down the sides of the bowl and process for 15 seconds more. Now add the currants. With the machine running, add enough of the remaining flour to make a soft dough. Allow the dough to turn around the bowl about 20 times. Turn the machine off and leave the dough to rest for 1 minute. Process until the dough has turned round the bowl 15 times more. Place in a greased bowl, turning the dough to grease the top. Cover and allow to stand in a warm place for about 1 hour, or until doubled in bulk. Punch down, divide evenly into 16 pieces and shape each into a smooth ball. Place on a greased baking tray about 3 cm/1 in apart. Cover loosely and allow to rise until doubled in size (about 30 to 40 minutes). Cut a shallow cross on the top of each bun, then brush with egg white. Bake in a moderately hot oven (190c, 375 F, gas 5) for 15 to 18 minutes. Remove from the oven and cool slightly before icing.

To make the icing, fit the nylon blade to the processor and combine the icing sugar, egg white, vanilla and salt. Process until well mixed, adding a little milk if necessary to make the icing of piping consistency. Using a piping bag, pipe icing crosses on each bun.

MAKES 16 BUNS

Golden Cherry Loaf

This cherry loaf is a wonderful example of the versatility of yeast breads. Make it when you next want to impress someone.

2 teaspoons dried yeast	5 tablespoons golden syrup
1 teaspoon sugar	50 g/2 oz hazelnuts, finely
175 ml/6 fl oz warm water	chopped
1 tablespoon oil	GLAZE
300 g/11 oz plain flour	3 tablespoons milk
$\frac{1}{2}$ teaspoon salt	3 tablespoons caster sugar
25–30 glace cherries	

Dissolve the yeast and sugar in the warm water, leave for 5 to 10 minutes until frothy then sprinkle 2 tablespoons of the measured flour on top. Cover with greased cling film and set aside in a warm place for 15 minutes. Now add the oil. Fit the metal blade to the processor, place the flour and salt in the work bowl and pulse a few times to aerate. With the machine running, pour the yeast mixture through the feed tube. Process until the mixture forms a stiff dough, then process for 1

minute more. Remove from the bowl and place in a greased plastic bag. Allow to rise in a warm place until doubled in size (about 45 minutes). Punch down the dough and break off enough to line the base of a greased 450-g/1-lb loaf tin. Divide the remaining dough into 25 to 30 pieces. Wrap each piece around a cherry and arrange in layers on top of the dough pressed into the base of the pan, leaving sufficient space for the dough round each cherry to rise. Drizzle each layer with a little golden syrup and sprinkle a few chopped nuts on top. Repeat these layers until all the dough-covered cherries have been used. Do not pour syrup over the top layer but reserve a few chopped nuts for decoration after cooking. Cover the tin and set aside in a warm place for approximately 20 to 30 minutes. Bake in a moderately hot oven (200c, 400 F, gas 6) for 30 to 35 minutes. For the glaze, bring the sugar and milk to the boil and brush over the loaf while hot. Cool the loaf slightly, then remove from the tin and cool on a wire rack. Sprinkle with reserved nuts.

MAKES 1 LOAF

Bee-Sting Cake

1 teaspoon dried yeast	TOPPING
2 tablespoons caster sugar	75 g/3 oz blanched almonds
4 tablespoons warm water	3 tablespoons caster sugar
2 tablespoons warm milk	$\frac{1}{2}$ teaspoon vanilla essence
225 g/8 oz strong plain	FILLING
flour	$\frac{1}{2}$ packet vanilla instant
generous pinch of salt	pudding
40 g/1$\frac{1}{2}$ oz margarine	150 ml/$\frac{1}{4}$ pint double cream
$\frac{1}{2}$ teaspoon lemon rind	5 tablespoons milk

Dissolve the yeast with 1 teaspoon of the sugar in the warm water and milk and stir well. Sprinkle with 2 tablespoons of the flour. Stand in a warm place for 10 to 15 minutes. Fit the metal blade to the processor, place the flour and salt in the work bowl and pulse a few times to aerate. Add the margarine and pulse to rub in. Now add the sugar and lemon rind and pulse to mix. With the processor running, pour the yeast mixture through the feed tube. If the dough is too stiff, add a little extra liquid. Process for 1 minute until smooth. Place the dough in a greased plastic bag, and set aside to rise in a warm place until doubled in size. Punch down and roll the dough into a circle about 1 cm/$\frac{1}{4}$ in thick. Place on a greased baking tray and shape into a perfect round. Cover with greased cling film and allow to rise in a warm place for about 15 minutes.

To make the topping, place the almonds in the processor and chop finely. Place all the topping ingredients in a saucepan and cook over a low heat until oily in appearance. Spread this mixture over the risen dough and bake in a moderately hot oven (200c, 400 F, gas 6) for 20 minutes. Remove from the oven and cool. Split the cake in half and fill. To make the filling, whisk all the ingredients together until thick. Stand for 5 minutes before using.

MAKES A 25-CM/10-IN ROUND CAKE

A yeast dough magically rises and is transformed into a beautiful bread or soft, warm rolls

Cinnamon Twist with Orange Glaze

25 g/1 oz caster sugar
2 teaspoon dried yeast
175 ml/6 fl oz warm milk
350 g/12 oz plain flour
1 teaspoon salt
5 tablespoons melted butter
1 egg
1 teaspoon vanilla essence
½ teaspoon ground cinnamon
FILLING
225 g/8 oz soft brown sugar

2 teaspoons ground cinnamon
½ teaspoon freshly grated
  nutmeg
GLAZE
275 g/10 oz icing sugar
1 tablespoon grated orange
  rind
1 tablespoon orange liqueur
2 tablespoons orange juice
4 tablespoons coarsely
  chopped nuts

Dissolve 1 teaspoon of the sugar and the yeast in the milk and leave for 5 to 10 minutes, until frothy. Fit the metal blade to the processor and place 225 g/8 oz flour and the salt in the work bowl. Pulse to combine. Add the yeast mixture, 3 tablespoons butter, the egg, remaining sugar, vanilla essence and cinnamon to the dry ingredients. Process for 20 seconds, scraping the bowl when necessary. With the machine running, add enough of the remaining flour to form a soft ball of dough that leaves the sides of the work bowl clean. The dough should be soft, not sticky. Allow the dough to turn around the bowl for about 20 times. Turn the machine off and rest the dough for 1 minute. Again process the dough until it has turned around the bowl 15 times. Place in a greased bowl, turning the dough to grease the top. Cover and allow to rise in a warm place for about 1 to 1½ hours or until doubled in size. Punch down the dough and divide into four parts. Roll each into a large rectangle and brush with the remaining melted butter.

For the filling, combine the cinnamon, nutmeg and brown sugar. Reserve 3 tablespoons of this mixture and sprinkle the remainder over the dough rectangles. Roll up the dough lengthwise and place the rolls side by side, 2.5 cm/1 in apart, in a well-greased 23 × 33-cm/9 × 13-in baking tin. Using scissors, make slashes almost through each roll at 2.5 cm/1 in intervals. Turn the cut pieces to the side, alternating the direction for each piece. Brush with melted butter and sprinkle with reserved filling mixture. Cover and allow to rise in a warm place until doubled in size (about 1 hour). Bake in a moderately hot oven (190 c, 375 f, gas 5) for 25 to 30 minutes or until golden brown.

Meanwhile prepare the orange glaze. Using the nylon blade, combine the icing sugar, orange rind, orange liqueur and orange juice. Process until well mixed. If necessary, add more orange juice to make a pouring consistency. Remove the tin from the oven, place on a wire rack and pour orange glaze over the cinnamon twist. Sprinkle with chopped nuts and allow to cool.

MAKES ONE CINNAMON TWIST

Nutty Cinnamon Rolls

40 g/1½ oz soft brown sugar
2 teaspoons dried yeast
7 tablespoons warm milk
225 g/8 oz plain flour
50 g/2 oz rolled oats
1 teaspoon salt
4 tablespoons melted butter
1 egg
FILLING
100 g/4 oz soft brown sugar
2 teaspoons grated orange
  rind

1 teaspoon grated cinnamon
TOPPING
5 tablespoons golden syrup
50 g/2 oz soft brown sugar
50 g/2 oz butter, softened
a few drops of caramel
  essence (optional)
50 g/2 oz coarsely chopped
  walnuts

Dissolve 1 teaspoon of the sugar and yeast in the warm milk and leave for 5 to 10 minutes, until frothy. Fit the metal blade to the processor and place half the flour, the oats, salt and the yeast mixture in the work bowl along with the remaining sugar. Pulse to combine. Add half the melted butter to the dry ingredients along with the egg and process for 20 seconds, scraping down the bowl when necessary. With the machine running, add enough flour to form a soft ball of dough that leaves the sides of the bowl clean. Allow the dough to turn around the bowl about 20 times. Turn the machine off and allow the dough to rest for 1 minute. Again process the dough until it has turned round the bowl 15 times. Place in a greased bowl, cover and allow to rise in a warm place for 1 hour or until doubled in size. Punch down the dough and roll into a large rectangle. Brush with the remaining melted butter.

For the filling, combine the brown sugar, orange peel and cinnamon and sprinkle over the dough. Roll up, Swiss roll fashion, and cut into 12 slices. For the topping, combine all the ingredients and spread over the base of a greased 23-cm/9-in baking tin. Place the slices of dough on top. Cover and allow to rise in a warm place until doubled in bulk (about 1 hour). Bake in a moderate oven (180c, 350f, gas 4) for about 35 minutes. Cool in the tin for 2 minutes, then invert over a wire rack and turn the rolls out.

MAKES 12 ROLLS

Poppy Seed Ring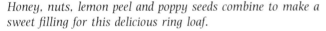

Honey, nuts, lemon peel and poppy seeds combine to make a sweet filling for this delicious ring loaf.

1 tablespoon dried yeast
50 g/2 oz caster sugar
200 ml/7 fl oz warm milk
350 g/12 oz plain flour
½ teaspoon salt
50 g/2 oz butter or
  margarine, melted
1 large egg

FILLING
50 g/2 oz poppy seeds
7 tablespoons boiling water
50 g/2 oz walnuts
4 tablespoons honey
1 teaspoon grated lemon rind
1 egg white

Dissolve the yeast and 1 teaspoon sugar in the milk and leave for 5 to 10 minutes, until frothy. Fit the metal blade to the processor, add half the flour and the salt to the work bowl and pulse once to combine. Add the yeast mixture to the flour and salt, add the remaining sugar then mix in the butter and egg. Process for 20 seconds, scrape the bowl and process for 15 seconds more. With the machine running, add enough of the remaining flour to make a moderately stiff ball of dough. Allow the dough to turn around the bowl about 20 times. Turn the machine off and allow the dough to rest for 1 minute. Process the dough until it has turned around the bowl 20 times more. Place in a greased bowl, turning the dough to grease the top. Cover and stand in a warm place until doubled in size (about 1 hour).

Meanwhile, make the filling. Place the poppy seeds in a small bowl, pour the boiling water over and stand for 30 minutes. Drain thoroughly. Fit the metal blade to the processor and place the poppy seeds, nuts, honey and grated lemon rind in the work bowl. Process until thoroughly mixed. Whisk the egg white until it forms soft peaks, then carefully fold into the poppy seed mixture.

Punch down the dough and roll into a 50 × 18-cm/20 × 7-in rectangle. Spread with poppy seed filling and roll up, Swiss roll fashion, pinching the seam to seal. Form into a ring and place seam down, in a greased 23-cm/9-in round tin. With a sharp knife, make shallow slashes across the top of the dough at 2.5 cm/1 in intervals. Cover and allow to rise in a warm place until doubled in bulk. Bake in a moderate oven (180c, 350f, gas 4) for 35 to 40 minutes. Remove from the tin and cool on a wire rack.

MAKES 1 RING

Basic Scones

Scones are the easiest of all tea-time treats to make.

225 g/8 oz plain flour
1 teaspoon salt
1 tablespoon baking powder
1 tablespoon caster sugar

100 g/4 oz butter, cut into
  pieces
1 egg, lightly beaten
about 200 ml/7 fl oz milk

Fit the metal blade to the processor and add the flour, salt, baking powder and sugar. Pulse to aerate, then add the butter. Process for 8 to 10 seconds or until the mixture resembles fine breadcrumbs. Combine the egg and the milk. With the machine running, add enough of the milk mixture so that the dough forms a ball. Be sure not to overmix. Turn out onto a lightly floured surface and knead very gently. Roll or pat to a 1.5 cm/¾ in thickness and cut into squares or rounds. Place on a greased baking tray and bake in a moderate oven (200c, 400f, gas 6) for 12 to 15 minutes until golden brown. Scones are best served warm from the oven.

MAKES 8 TO 12 SCONES

Variation

Drop Scones: Add enough liquid to the dry ingredients to make a 'sticky' batter, then drop large spoonfuls onto a lightly greased baking tray. Bake for 12 to 15 minutes in a moderate oven (200c, 400f, gas 6) until golden.

Scones with Oil

225 g/8 oz plain flour	1 egg
½ teaspoon salt	1 teaspoon vinegar
1 tablespoon baking powder	about 150 ml/¼ pint milk and
4 tablespoons oil	water combined

Fit the metal blade to the processor and add the flour, salt and baking powder. Pulse to aerate. Combine the oil, egg and vinegar and add sufficient water and milk to bring the liquid to 250 ml/8 fl oz. With the machine running, pour the liquid through the feed tube and process until just combined, about 5 seconds. Take care not to overmix. Turn out onto a floured surface and press or roll the dough to a 2.5 cm/1 in thickness. Cut into rounds and place on a greased and lightly floured baking tray. Brush the tops with a little milk before baking in a hot oven (220 c, 425 f, gas 7) for 10 to 15 minutes. Serve warm from the oven.

MAKES 12 SCONES

Variations

Cheese Scones: Add 100 g/4 oz grated Cheddar cheese, 1 teaspoon mustard and a pinch of cayenne to the flour.
Herbed Scones: Add 1 teaspoon dried mixed herbs, 1 teaspoon mustard powder and 1 teaspoon paprika to the flour.
Wholemeal Scones: Substitute one-third of the cake flour with wholemeal or nutty wheat flour.
Fruity Scones: Add 50 g/2 oz currants to the flour mixture.

Bran Muffins

50 g/2 oz bran cereal	½ teaspoon salt
200 ml/7 fl oz milk	100 g/4 oz rolled oats
100 g/4 oz plain flour	50 g/2 oz butter or
25 g/1 oz caster sugar	margarine, softened
1 teaspoon baking powder	4 tablespoons molasses
1 teaspoon bicarbonate of	1 egg
soda	

Combine the bran cereal and the milk and set aside to soften. Fit the metal blade to the processor and place the flour, sugar, baking powder, bicarbonate of soda, salt and oats in the work bowl. Process for 3 to 4 seconds to mix. In a mixing bowl beat the butter with the molasses, add the egg and then the bran mixture. Pour over the dry ingredients and process for a few seconds just to moisten. The batter should still be lumpy. Spoon the mixture into a greased muffin pan, filling each 'cup' about two-thirds full. Bake in a moderately hot oven (200 c, 400 f, gas 6) for 15 to 18 minutes. Remove from the muffin pan and serve hot.

MAKES ABOUT 12 MUFFINS

Lemon Nutty Muffins

100 g/4 oz pecan nuts	2 teaspoons finely grated
225 g/8 oz plain flour	lemon rind
25 g/1 oz caster sugar	1 egg, lightly beaten
2 teaspoons baking powder	200 ml/7 fl oz milk
½ teaspoon salt	5 tablespoons oil

Using the metal blade, chop the pecan nuts coarsely. Add the flour, sugar, baking powder and salt. Process for 3 to 4 seconds to mix. Now add the lemon rind. Mix the egg and milk with the oil and pour over the dry ingredients. Process for 8 to 10 seconds to just moisten. The batter should be lumpy and not overmixed. Spoon the mixture into a greased muffin pan, filling each 'cup' about three-quarters full. Bake in a moderately hot oven (200 c, 400 f, gas 6) for 20 to 25 minutes. Remove from the muffin pan and serve hot.

MAKES ABOUT 12 MUFFINS

Lemon Nutty Muffins

The versatile scone, clockwise: Drop Scones (page 123), Fruity Scones, Scones with Oil, Herbed Scones, Wholemeal Scones, Cheese Scones

Date Muffins

225 g/8 oz plain flour
75 g/3 oz caster sugar
2 teaspoons baking powder
1 teaspoon salt
50 g/2 oz butter or
   margarine, cut into pieces
100 g/4 oz chopped dates
50 g/2 oz chopped walnuts
7 tablespoons milk
1 egg, lightly beaten

Fit the metal blade to the processor and add the flour, sugar, baking powder and salt. Pulse two to three times to mix. Add the butter to the dry ingredients and pulse ten to twelve times until the mixture resembles coarse breadcrumbs. Add the dates and walnuts and pulse three or four times to mix. Combine the milk and egg and add to the dry ingredients. Process for a few seconds to moisten. Take care not to overmix.

Spoon the batter into a greased muffin pan, filling each 'cup' about three-quarters full. Bake in a moderately hot oven (200 c, 400 f, gas 6) for about 20 minutes or until golden brown. Remove the muffins from the pan and serve hot.

MAKES ABOUT 12 SMALL OR 8 LARGE MUFFINS

Orange Streusel Muffins

For a delicious cake, spread this batter in a large square tin, sprinkle with streusel topping and bake.

225 g/8 oz plain flour
75 g/3 oz caster sugar
1 tablespoon baking powder
1 teaspoon salt
50 g/2 oz pecan nuts or
   walnuts
1 egg
1 tablespoon grated orange
   rind
7 tablespoons orange juice
7 tablespoons orange
   marmalade
5 tablespoons milk
4 tablespoons oil
TOPPING
50 g/2 oz caster sugar
1 tablespoon plain flour
15 g/½ oz butter or margarine,
   softened
½ teaspoon ground cinnamon
pinch of nutmeg

First make the topping. Fit the metal blade and add all the ingredients to the work bowl. Process until crumbly and set aside.

For the muffins, place the flour, sugar, baking powder, salt and nuts in the work bowl. Process for 2 to 3 seconds to mix. Combine the egg, orange rind, juice, marmalade, milk and oil. Pour over the dry ingredients and process for a few seconds only, until the mixture is moistened. Do not overmix – the batter should still be lumpy. Spoon the mixture into a well-greased muffin pan, filling each 'cup' about two-thirds full. Sprinkle with the topping mixture and bake in a moderately hot oven (200 c, 400 f, gas 6) for 20 to 25 minutes until golden brown. Serve warm with butter and marmalade.

MAKES ABOUT 12 MUFFINS

Peachy Nut Bread

50 g/2 oz hazelnuts
50 g/2 oz maraschino
   cherries
1 (410-g/14¼-oz) can peach
   slices, well drained
225 g/8 oz plain flour
100 g/4 oz caster sugar
1 teaspoon baking powder
½ teaspoon bicarbonate of
   soda
½ teaspoon salt
pinch of allspice
1 tablespoon grated orange
   rind
75 g/3 oz butter or margarine,
   softened
2 eggs

Using the metal blade, chop the nuts and set aside. Coarsely chop the cherries and set aside. Purée the peach slices, then add all the remaining ingredients, except the nuts and cherries. Process until well mixed, scraping down the sides of the bowl when necessary. Add the nuts and cherries and process for a second or two to mix in. Spoon the mixture into a 450-g/1-lb greased loaf tin and bake in a moderate oven (180 c, 350 f, gas 4) for 50 to 60 minutes. Remove from the tin and cool on a wire rack. Cool thoroughly before slicing.

MAKES 1 LOAF

Pumpkin Loaf

Turn cooked pumpkin into a delicious tea-time treat.

100 g/4 oz pecan nuts or
   walnuts
225 g/8 oz plain flour
175 g/6 oz soft brown sugar
1 teaspoon salt
1 teaspoon bicarbonate of
   soda
1 teaspoon ground cinnamon
½ teaspoon nutmeg
pinch of ground ginger
100 g/4 oz butter or
   margarine, softened
2 eggs
250 ml/8 fl oz cooked,
   mashed pumpkin

Using the metal blade, chop the nuts coarsely and set aside. Place all the remaining ingredients in the work bowl and process for 15 seconds. Scrape down the sides of the bowl and process for 15 to 20 seconds more. Add the nuts and process for a few seconds to mix in. Turn the mixture into a 450-g/1-lb loaf tin which has been greased on the bottom only. Bake in moderate oven (180 c, 350 f, gas 4) for 60 minutes or until a skewer inserted in the centre comes out clean. Slide a sharp knife along the sides of the tin and turn out on a wire rack to cool.

MAKES 1 LOAF

Courgette Spice Bread

50 g/2 oz pecan nuts or walnuts	150 g/6 oz caster sugar
1 (2.5-cm/1-in) piece of lemon peel	1 teaspoon ground cinnamon
3 medium courgettes, unpeeled	½ teaspoon ground nutmeg
	pinch of ground cloves
1 egg	½ teaspoon salt
7 tablespoons oil	½ teaspoon baking powder
225 g/8 oz plain flour	½ teaspoon bicarbonate of soda

Using the metal blade, chop the nuts and lemon peel and set aside. Fit the shredding plate and shred the courgettes to make 250 ml/8 fl oz. Replace the metal blade and process the courgette, egg and oil until well mixed. Add the remaining ingredients, nuts and peel. Pulse about four to five times to combine. Do not overmix. Turn the mixture into a well-greased 20 × 10-cm/8 × 4-in loaf tin and bake in a moderate oven (160 c, 325 f, gas 3) for 60 to 65 minutes. Cool the loaf in the tin for about 10 minutes, then turn out and cool on a wire rack.

MAKES 1 LOAF

Banana Orange Loaf

Make this loaf the day before, so that the flavours of the banana, coconut and orange can mingle.

50 g/2 oz pecan nuts or walnuts	2 tablespoons orange juice
3 medium bananas	2 eggs
225 g/8 oz plain flour	3 tablespoons milk
175 g/6 oz caster sugar	1 tablespoon grated orange rind
1 teaspoon bicarbonate of soda	1 teaspoon vanilla essence
½ teaspoon salt	6 drops of almond essence
100 g/4 oz butter or margarine, softened	75 g/3 oz desiccated coconut

Using the metal blade, chop the nuts and set aside. Cut the banans in pieces and purée in the processor. Combine all the remaining ingredients except the nuts and coconut and process until well mixed, scraping down the sides of the bowl when necessary. Lastly, add the nuts and coconut and process for a few seconds to mix in. Pour into a greased 450-g/1-lb loaf tin and bake in a moderate oven (180 c, 350 f, gas 4) for about 60 minutes or until a skewer inserted in the centre comes out clean. Remove from the oven, turn out on a wire rack and cool thoroughly before slicing.

MAKES 1 LOAF

Cheese'n Apple Bread

50 g/2 oz pecan nuts or walnuts	½ teaspoon bicarbonate of soda
1 large cooking apple	½ teaspoon salt
50 g/2 oz mature Cheddar cheese	pinch of ground cinnamon
225 g/8 oz plain flour	100 g/4 oz butter or margarine, softened
100 g/4 oz caster sugar	2 eggs
1 teaspoon baking powder	

Using the metal blade, chop the nuts and set aside. Peel, core and quarter the apple. Using the shredding plate, first shred the apple, then the cheese. Add these to the nuts and set aside. Fit the metal blade and place the flour, sugar, baking powder, bicarbonate of soda, salt, cinnamon, butter and eggs in the work bowl. Process until well mixed. Now add the nuts, apple and cheese and process until well mixed. Turn into a well-greased 450-g/1-lb loaf tin and bake in a moderately hot oven (190 c, 375 f, gas 5) for 45 to 55 minutes. Remove from the tin, bread has a better flavour if made a day in advance.

MAKES 1 LOAF

From top to bottom: Cheese 'n Apple Bread, Pumpkin Loaf, Banana Orange Loaf, Baby Marrow Spice Bread, Peachy Nut Bread

Holiday Fruit Loaf

A rich, fruity bread to serve during the holiday season or anytime.

350 ml/12 fl oz canned apricot juice or nectar
225 g/8 oz raisins
6–8 dried apricots
1 tablespoon grated orange rind
350 g/12 oz plain flour
225 g/8 oz caster sugar

2 teaspoons bicarbonate of soda
1 teaspoon salt
15 g/½ oz butter or margarine
1 egg
5 tablespoons double cream
50 g/2 oz walnuts

Place the apricot juice, raisins, apricots and orange rind in a saucepan and bring to the boil. Reduce heat and simmer for 5 minutes. Set aside to cool. Fit the metal blade to the processor and add the apricot mixture and all the remaining ingredients to the work bowl. Process for about 60 seconds until well mixed, scraping down the sides of the bowl when necessary. Turn into a greased 450-g/1-lb loaf tin and bake in a moderate oven (180c, 350f, gas 4) for 55 to 60 minutes. Turn out on a wire rack and cool before slicing.

MAKES 1 LOAF

Soured Cream Herb Bread

100 g/4 oz wholewheat flour
100 g/4 oz plain flour
1 teaspoon bicarbonate of soda
½ teaspoon salt
1 teaspoon dried mixed herbs

1 tablespoon dried minced onion
100 g/4 oz cottage cheese
175 ml/6 fl oz soured cream
1 egg
2 tablespoons oil

Fit the metal blade to the processor and add the wholewheat flour, bicarbonate of soda, salt, dried herbs and dried onion. Pulse two to three times to mix. Combine the cottage cheese, soured cream, egg and oil and add to the dry ingredients. Process to mix well. Spoon the mixture into a greased 450-g/1-lb loaf tin and bake in a moderately hot oven (190c, 375f, gas 5) for 45 to 55 minutes until well risen and golden brown. Turn out on a wire rack to cool before slicing.

MAKES 1 LOAF

Wholemeal Yogurt Loaf

Serve this healthy, nutritious loaf with pâtés and spreads.

250 g/9 oz wholemeal flour
1 teaspoon bicarbonate of soda
1 tablespoon soft brown sugar
1 teaspoon salt

2 tablespoons wheat germ
1 egg
2 tablespoons oil
250 ml/8 fl oz natural yogurt
1 tablespoon sesame seeds

Fit the metal blade to the processor and add the flour, bicarbonate of soda, brown sugar, salt and wheat germ. Pulse to combine. Mix the egg, oil and yogurt together and pour over the dry ingredients. Process until well mixed, scraping the bowl if necessary. Turn the mixture into a greased 450-g/1-lb loaf tin and sprinkle with sesame seeds. Bake in a moderately hot oven (190c, 375f, gas 5) for about 50 minutes or until a skewer inserted in the centre comes out clean. Turn out on a wire rack to cool before slicing.

MAKES 1 LOAF

Savoury Cheese Bread

100 g/4 oz mature Cheddar cheese
4 slices bacon, crisply cooked
50 g/2 oz ripe olives, pitted
450 g/1 lb plain flour

1 tablespoon baking powder
1 teaspoon salt
½ teaspoon mustard powder
pinch of cayenne
350 ml/12 fl oz beer
1 egg

Using the shredding plate, shred the cheese and set aside. Fit the metal blade and chop the bacon, then the olives. Add both to the cheese and set aside. To the work bowl now add the flour, baking powder, salt, mustard powder and cayenne and pulse three to four times to mix. Lastly, add the cheese, bacon, olives, beer and egg. Process until well mixed, scraping down the sides of the bowl when necessary. Place the mixture in a greased 450-g/1-lb loaf tin and bake in a moderately hot oven (190c, 375f, gas 5) for about 50 to 55 minutes. Turn out on a wire rack and cool before slicing.

MAKES 1 LOAF

Streusel Cake

50 g/2 oz butter, softened
150 g/5 oz caster sugar
1 egg
7 tablespoons milk
175 g/6 oz plain flour
2 teaspoons baking powder
½ teaspoon salt

STREUSEL MIX
25 g/1 oz plain flour
2 teaspoons ground cinnamon
2 tablespoons melted butter
50 g/2 oz pecan nuts or walnuts

First make the streusel mix. Fit the metal blade to the processor and add all the ingredients to the work bowl. Process until crumbly and set aside.

For the cake, use the metal blade to cream the butter, sugar and egg until light and fluffy. Pour in the milk and pulse three to four times to mix. Add the sifted flour, baking powder and salt and process to mix well. Spread half the batter in a greased and floured 23-cm/9-in square baking tin. Sprinkle with half the streusel mix and spread the remaining batter on top. Lastly, sprinkle the remaining streusel mix over and bake in a moderately hot oven (190c, 375f, gas 5) for 30 to 35 minutes. Cut into squares and serve warm.

MAKES 9 SERVINGS

Soured Cream Herb Bread

Pastries

The earliest pastry was a simple flour and water paste used to coat meat and poultry so as to retain the juices during cooking, much as we would use aluminium foil today. Later, fat was added, making the pastry more tender. Today, however, pastry-making has advanced to the point where there are infinite varieties: some pastries are crumbly and crisp, such as shortcrust pastries, while others are very rich, such as *pâté brisée*; still others are light and flaky such as puff, rough puff and flaky pastries. In addition there are choux pastries, hot water pastries, sour cream pastries, wholemeal crusts – the list is nearly endless.

Perfect, feather-light pastries are one of the many miracles performed by the food processor. It short-circuits almost all the time-consuming stages of pastry making by quickly and efficiently rubbing butter into flour for shortcrust pastries and by effortlessly grating butter for puff, rough puff or soda water pastries.

Here are a few hints and tips for successful pastry making:

- Keep everything cool including the utensils and ingredients. The processor eliminates the problem of warm hands, as the ingredients are mixed in the bowl. Chill the metal blade before rubbing in, and chill the chipper plate before grating the butter. Use chilled water or liquid for mixing.

- Follow the recipe and measure the flour, butter or margarine accurately. Do not guess. Avoid too much flour as it tends to toughen pastry, and avoid too much fat as it makes the pastry greasy and crumbly.

- You may find that a little less liquid is required when making pastry in the processor. Pastry recipes are often vague about the amount of liquid required. This is due to the inaccurate measuring of flour or the age of the flour. Older flour will absorb more liquid.

- Avoid overprocessing the pastry by following the recipe directions carefully. Over-processed pastry will be difficult to roll out and will be tough when cooked.

- Chilling the pastry dough after mixing tenderises it, keeps it from shrinking during baking and makes it easier to handle when rolling out. Wrap the pastry in greaseproof paper or foil, then leave in the refrigerator for 30 minutes or more. Before rolling out, take the pastry out of the refrigerator and allow to stand until it can be easily handled.

- Roll out the pastry quickly and lightly, handling it as little as possible. Lightly flour the working surface beforehand so as to avoid working in more flour than necessary. When rolling out pastry, use a forward and backward motion and do not turn the pastry over.

- Use a rolling pin to lift the pastry before lining a pie plate or before shaping, then allow the pastry to settle gently into position. Do not stretch the pastry during shaping or it will shrink during baking.

- Start baking pastry in a hot oven to crispen and lighten the texture, then reduce the heat slightly to allow the filling to cook through and to prevent the pastry from over-browning.

- Many pastries can be frozen, though it is best to shape them before doing so.

Shortcrust Pastry

FOR A 20 TO 23-CM/8 TO 9-IN ONE-CRUST PIE:	FOR A 20 TO 23-CM/8 TO 9-IN TWO-CRUST PIE:
100 g/4 oz plain flour	225 g/8 oz plain flour
$\frac{1}{2}$ tablespoon salt	1 teaspoon salt
1 tablespoon caster sugar	2 tablespoons caster sugar
50 g/2 oz butter	100 g/4 oz butter
1 egg yolk	1 egg yolk
3 tablespoons cold water	5 tablespoons cold water

Fit the metal blade to the processor and place the flour, salt, sugar and butter in the work bowl. Process until the mixture resembles fine crumbs. Beat the egg yolk with the water and slowly pour through the feed tube while the machine is running. Process for a few seconds until the mixture forms a ball, then stop immediately. Turn the pastry onto a lightly floured surface, knead gently, then roll out and use as desired.

To freeze, seal well and label. Freezes for up to two months.

Variations

Sherry Pastry: Substitute sherry for water and use the pastry for fruit or chiffon pies.

Herbed Pastry: Leave out the sugar and add 1 teaspoon of either dill, dried mixed herbs or celery seeds and use for savoury pies, quiches and fish pies.

Lemon Pastry: Add 1–2 teaspoons finely grated lemon rind to the dry ingredients and replace 2 teaspoons of the water with 2 teaspoons lemon juice. Use for lemon meringue pies, apple pies or other fruit pies. Make orange pastry by using orange juice and rind instead of lemon juice and rind.

Cream Cheese Pastry

| 100 g/4 oz butter | 100 g/4 oz plain flour |
| 100 g/4 oz cream cheese | generous pinch of salt |

Fit the metal blade to the work bowl, add the butter and pulse to cream. Add the cream cheese and process for about 5 seconds. Sift in the flour and salt and pulse to combine. Refrigerate for at least 1 hour before using.

To freeze, roll the pastry to the required shape. Wrap, seal and label. Freezes for up to two months.

Cheese Pastry

100 g/4 oz mature Cheddar cheese	150 g/5 oz butter, cut into cubes
225 g/8 oz plain flour	1 egg
$\frac{1}{2}$ teaspoon salt	a little cold water
pinch of cayenne	

Using the shredding plate, shred the cheese and set aside. Fit the metal blade and add the flour, salt, cayenne and butter to the work bowl. Process until the mixture resembles fine crumbs. Now add the egg, cheese and enough water to blend. Process for a few seconds until the mixture forms a ball. Cover and chill for about 30 minutes before rolling out and using as desired. This pastry makes delicious cheese straws or fingers, or use it for apple pie or savoury quiches.

To freeze, roll out and line pie plates. Wrap and seal well. Freezes for up to two months.

Pastry shells: Lemon Shortcrust (page 131) and Cheese Pastry (page 131)

Quick Puff Pastry

275 g/10 oz plain flour	1 tablespoon lemon juice
generous pinch of salt	about 5 tablespoons iced
225 g/8 oz butter	water
1 egg	1 teaspoon cream of tartar

Place 225 g/8 oz flour and the salt in the freezer overnight. Using the chipper plate, grate the butter and freeze overnight. Sift the flour into a large bowl and add half the butter. Lightly beat the egg, lemon juice and water. Using a palette knife, stir the liquid into the flour mixture. Turn out onto a board and roll into a rectangle, approximately 30 × 18 cm/12 × 7 in. Place the remaining flour and cream of tartar in a sieve and sprinkle a little over the pastry. Scatter the remaining grated butter over half the pastry. Now fold the pastry in half to cover the butter. Roll into a rectangle and fold into three. Lightly sprinkle both the board and pastry with flour from the sieve. Turn the edge nearest you to the side and continue to roll and fold six times, making sure that all the flour is used. Wrap in foil and refrigerate for at least 1 hour before using. Use for Beef Wellington, Mille Feuilles or custard slices.

To freeze, roll the pastry to the required shape. Wrap, seal and label. Freezes for up to two months.

Coconut Crust

½ packet Marie biscuits	50 g/2 oz caster sugar
75 g/3 oz desiccated coconut	100 g/4 oz butter, melted

Using the metal blade, finely crumb the biscuits. Add the coconut and sugar and pulse three to four times to combine.

Now add the melted butter and process to mix well. Press the mixture into the base and sides of the pie plate and bake in a moderate oven (160 c, 225 f, gas 3) for 10 minutes. Cool and fill as desired.

MAKES A 20-cm/8-in crust

Nutty Crust

225 g/8 oz pecan nuts,	50 g/2 oz caster sugar
walnuts or hazelnuts	75 g/3 oz butter, softened
18 Marie biscuits	

Using the metal blade, chop the nuts and biscuits finely. Add the sugar and butter and process to mix well. Press the mixture into the base and sides of a pie plate and bake in a moderate oven (180 c, 350 f, gas 4) for 8 to 10 minutes. Cool. Use with ice cream fillings or for chiffon pies.

MAKES A 20-cm/8-in crust

Basic Crumb Crust

1 packet Marie biscuits	100 g/4 oz butter, melted
50 g/2 oz caster sugar	

Using the metal blade, finely crumb the biscuits. Add the sugar and melted butter and process until well mixed. Press into the base and sides of the pie plate and chill until needed.

MAKES A 23-cm/9-in crust

Variation

Crumb Crust de Luxe: Add 1 teaspoon ground cinnamon and 2 tablespoons double cream to the melted butter, pour over the biscuit crumbs and process until well mixed. Press into the base and sides of a pie plate and bake in a moderate oven (180c, 350f, gas 4) for 10 minutes. Chill until required.

Rough Puff Pastry

225 g/8 oz plain flour	175 g/6 oz chilled butter,
½ teaspoon cream of tartar	cut into small cubes
pinch of salt	150 ml/¼ pint iced water

Fit the nylon blade to the processor and place all the ingredients in the work bowl. Process for about 15 seconds, or until the mixture forms a ball. Turn the dough onto a well floured surface and lightly roll the pastry into a rectangle, about 1 cm/½ in thick. Fold the top third of the pastry down and the bottom third up. Seal the edges and chill for 30 minutes. Repeat the rolling, folding and chilling three more times. Finally, roll out and use as desired.

To freeze, roll the pastry to the required shape. seal well and label. Freezes for up to one month.

Crusty Pastry

275 g/10 oz plain flour	1 egg yolk
¼ teaspoon baking powder	1 teaspoon lemon juice
¼ teaspoon salt	a little iced water
175 g/6 oz margarine	

Fit the metal blade to the processor and add the dry ingredients. Pulse to aerate. Cut the margarine into pieces and add to the flour. Pulse two to three times until the mixture resembles breadcrumbs. Combine the egg yolk, lemon juice and a little water. With the machine running, add the liquid through the feed tube and process for a few seconds until the pastry forms a ball. Turn onto a lightly floured board and use as required.

To freeze, roll out the pastry and line pie plates. Seal well and label. Freezes for up to two months.

Hot Water Pastry

350 g/12 oz plain flour	250 ml/8 fl oz water
1 teaspoon salt	1 egg yolk
100 g/4 oz lard	

Fit the metal blade to the processor and place the flour and salt in the work bowl. Heat the lard and water to boiling point. With the machine running, pour the boiling mixture through the feed tube and process for 15 seconds. Add the egg yolk and process for 30 seconds or until the mixture leaves the side of the bowl clean and forms a smooth ball. Wrap the pastry in greaseproof paper and stand at room temperature for about 30 minutes before using. Use for raised pies.

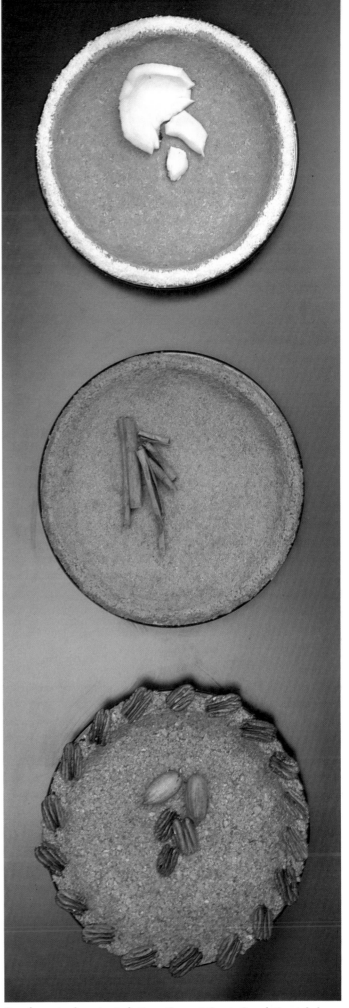

Crumb crusts, from top to bottom: Coconut Crust, Crumb Crust de luxe, Nutty Crust

133

Soda Water Pastry makes crispy Strawberry Pigs' Ears (page 108)

Soda Water Pastry

Use this pastry for sweet or savoury dishes. The results are similar to flaky or puff pastry, without all the hard work.

225 g/8 oz frozen margarine
225 g/8 oz plain flour
$\frac{1}{4}$ teaspoon cream of tartar
generous pinch of salt

1 tablespoon brandy
about 150 ml/$\frac{1}{4}$ pint cold soda water

Cut the block of margarine in half lengthwise. Fit the chipper plate to the processor and place a piece of margarine in the feed tube. With the food pusher in position, turn on the machine. Large slivers of margarine will form in the bowl. Repeat with the second block of margarine. Now sift the flour, cream of tartar and salt into a mixing bowl. Add the margarine and, using a palette knife, toss together. Combine the brandy and soda water and pour three quarters onto the flour. With the palette knife, mix to a stiff dough, adding more liquid if necessary. At this stage the mixture will be uneven in colour and texture.

Lightly flour a board and roll out the pastry to a rectangle, approximately 40 × 15 cm/16 × 6 in. Fold the rectangle into three and turn the edge nearest to you to the side. Repeat the rolling and folding once more. Now wrap the pastry in foil and allow to rest in the refrigerator for 20 minutes. Repeat the complete rolling and folding process twice more, resting in between, to give a total of six rollings. Finally, allow the pastry to rest for 10 minutes before rolling out and using as desired. Use for sweet and savoury pies, sausage rolls, cream horns and pig's ears.

To freeze, roll to the required shape. Wrap, seal and label. Freezes for up to two months.

Wholemeal Pastry

225 g/8 oz wholemeal flour
1 teaspoon salt

100 g/4 oz butter, cubed
cold water to mix

Fit the metal blade to the processor and place the wholemeal flour, salt and butter in the work bowl. Process until the mixture resembles fine crumbs. With the machine running, slowly pour in enough cold water for the mixture to form a ball, leaving the sides of the bowl clean. Turn out onto a lightly floured board and knead gently. Roll out and use as desired.

MAKES SUFFICIENT FOR A 20 TO 23-CM/8 TO 9-IN TWO-CRUST PIE

To freeze, roll out and line pie plates. Wrap and seal well. Freezes for up to two months.

Margarine Pastry

225 g/8 oz plain flour
½ teaspoon salt
1 teaspoon baking powder
175 g/6 oz margarine,
   chilled

1 egg yolk
4 tablespoons cold water
1 tablespoon vinegar

Fit the metal blade to the processor and add the flour, salt and baking powder to the work bowl. Pulse three times to aerate. Cut the margarine into pieces and add to the flour. Pulse until the mixture resembles breadcrumbs. Combine the egg yolk, water and vinegar. While the machine is running, quickly add the liquid through the feed tube and stop processing as soon as the dough forms a ball (about 5 seconds). Wrap the pastry in heavy foil and chill for at least 4 hours before using.

To freeze, roll out to the required shape. Wrap, seal and label. Freezes for up to two months.

Pâte Brisée

350 g/12 oz plain flour
100 g/4 oz butter, cut into
   pieces
½ teaspoon salt

1 egg
1 tablespoon oil
4 tablespoons iced water

Fit the metal blade to the processor and add the flour, butter and salt. Process for 20 seconds until the mixture resembles breadcrumbs. Combine the egg, oil and water. With the machine running, slowly pour the liquid through the feed tube and process for about 20 seconds until a ball of dough is formed, leaving the sides of the bowl clean. Cover and chill for at least an hour. Roll out and use as desired. Use for French flans and quiches.

To freeze, roll out to the required shape. Wrap, seal and label. Freezes for up to one month.

Soured Cream Pastry

225 g/8 oz plain flour
½ teaspoon salt
100 g/4 oz margarine,
   chilled

1 egg
about 6 tablespoons soured
   cream

Fit the metal blade to the processor and add the flour and salt. Pulse four times to aerate. Cut the margarine into six pieces and add to the dry ingredients. Pulse three to four times until the mixture resembles breadcrumbs. Now combine the egg and soured cream. While the machine is running, quickly pour the mixture through the feed tube and process for about 5 seconds or until a ball of dough is formed. Wrap the pastry in heavy foil and chill for at least 1 hour before rolling out and using as required.

To freeze, roll the pastry out to the required shape. Wrap, seal and label. Freezes for up to two months.

Choux Pastry

150 ml/¼ pint water
40 g/1½ oz margarine
generous pinch of salt
50 g/2 oz plain flour

2 eggs
½ teaspoon vanilla essence
   (sweet choux pastry only)

Bring the water, margarine and salt to the boil. Remove from the heat and add the sifted flour all at once. Stir well and return to the heat. Cook until the mixture forms a smooth ball and leaves the sides of the pan clean. Allow to cool. Fit the metal blade to the processor and place the pastry in the work bowl. Beat the eggs and vanilla lightly. While the processor is running, pour in half the egg mixture. Process until smooth. Pour in half the remaining egg and process again. Repeat until the mixture is soft but not runny. Process for a minute more. Pipe or place spoonfuls on a greased baking tray and bake in a moderately hot oven (200c, 400f, gas 6) for 30 minutes. Reduce the temperature to moderate (180c, 350f, gas 4) until the pastry is light brown and crisp. When done, remove from the oven and immediately make a small hole in the base of each pastry. Cool on a wire rack and store in an airtight container for one to two days.

Cooked choux pastry freezes extremely well. Freeze on a tray in one layer. When frozen, pack into containers or plastic bags and seal. To re-use, open the container and thaw on a wire rack. Should the pastry puffs be a little soft, arrange on a baking sheet and place in a moderate oven (150c, 325f, gas 3) for 5 minutes to crispen. Allow to cool before filling.

Choux pastry ready to be baked for Ham and Chicken Puffs (page 77)

Cakes, Cookies, Biscuits and Bars

The fact that most food processor cookbooks simply gloss over the section on baking presented an interesting challenge. Here are the best recipes for a wide variety of delicious cakes, cookies and biscuits.

Many ingredients such as chopped nuts, chopped rind, chopped dried or glacé fruit, mashed fruits and biscuit crumbs can be processed in seconds at the start of the baking session. Learn to process the dry ingredients first and save on washing up, as the same bowl can then be used to cream the butter and sugar and mix the remaining ingredients.

Cake has been called the aristocrat of foods and may be served warm from the oven with jam and cream or beautifully iced and decorated for an elegant tea. There is no magic attached to the art of baking cakes, but the following hints will help to ensure success.

●Always read the entire recipe carefully before you begin. Assemble all the ingredients and utensils and select bright and shiny cake tins of the correct size. Discoloured tins may cause uneven browning and warped tins will cause uneven baking. Prepare the tin by either greasing or lining, according to the directions given in the recipe. However, if you want the cake to turn out perfectly, it is worth taking the trouble to line the tin with either greaseproof paper or non-stick baking parchment. Preheat the oven before mixing the ingredients.

●Use fresh ingredients. Baking powder and bicarbonate of soda lose their strength the longer they are kept so you may wish to purchase small quantities if those items are seldom used. Measure correctly, do not guess. After you have used a recipe once or twice, you may wish to add different fruits or spices for variation.

●Unless you have a convection air oven, do not open the door to peek at cakes until they have been in the oven for at least 20 minutes. Test that the cakes are done before removing them from the oven. Some cakes will shrink away from the sides of the tin others will be springy to the touch. As a general rule, however, a fine skewer inserted in the centre of the cake will come out clean when the cake is done. Cool the cake in the tin for a few minutes before turning it out on a wire rack. If necessary, use a blunt knife to loosen the sides before turning out. The cake should be turned right-side up to cool.

●Be sure the cake has had sufficient time to cool before icing, unless otherwise directed in the recipe. Brush away all surface crumbs to ensure a smooth finish.

Cookies and biscuits may be a favourite of the younger set, but there are few of the older generation who can resist them. Many of the same rules for baking cakes apply to biscuits and cookies. You should always read the recipes carefully and measure accurately. Preheat the oven and use the correct temperature. Cookies and biscuits need careful watching as they tend to brown quickly towards the end of baking. It is always a good idea to use a timer set to the minimum baking time. If a single baking tray is used, place it in the centre of the oven. If two baking trays are used, they should be placed far enough apart to allow a good circulation of heat. Soft cookies and biscuits will spring back when touched. Crisp cookies and biscuits are done when they are fairly firm and lightly browned around the edges. Unless otherwise directed, remove the cookies and biscuits from the baking tray immediately after taking them out of the oven, and place them on a wire rack to cool.

Store cookies and biscuits in an airtight container. If crisp biscuits soften, place them in a cool oven (150c, 300f, gas 2) for about 5 minutes.

Butter Pecan Loaf

150 g/6 oz softened butter, cut into pieces	½ teaspoon vanilla essence
100 g/4 oz pecan nuts	½ teaspoon salt
225 g/8 oz sugar	175 g/6 oz plain flour
7 tablespoons milk	ICING
2 eggs	100 g/4 oz icing sugar
1 teaspoon baking powder	1 tablespoon milk

Melt 50 g/2 oz butter, add the pecan nuts and heat until golden brown. With a slotted spoon, remove the pecan nuts and set aside. Reserve the butter for the icing. Fit the metal blade to the processor and place the pecan nuts, sugar, butter, milk, eggs, baking powder, vanilla and salt in the work bowl. Process for 30 seconds. Scrape down the sides of the bowl and process for 5 seconds. Add the sifted flour and process for about 8 to 10 seconds to mix. Pour into a greased and floured 450-g/1-lb loaf tin and bake in a moderate oven (180c, 350f, gas 4) for about 55 minutes. Cool for 20 minutes in the tin before removing and placing on a wire rack. Ice the loaf when cold.

To make the icing, use the metal blade to combine the icing sugar, reserved butter and milk. Process until well mixed.

MAKES ABOUT 10 SLICES

Freezes well for up to six weeks.

(Opposite page) Chocolate Oil Cake (page 139)
(Above) Butter Pecan Loaf

137

Butterscotch Sherry Cake

This moist, rich cake is absolutely delicious!

100 g/4 oz hazelnuts or pecan nuts	7 tablespoons cream sherry
1 (225-g/8-oz) packet vanilla cake mix	4 eggs, beaten
	½ teaspoon ground cinnamon
1 (69-g/2.4-oz) packet butterscotch instant whip mix	pinch of nutmeg
	FOR THE GLAZE
	100 g/4 oz butter
7 tablespoons water	3 tablespoons water
7 tablespoons oil	150 g/5 oz caster sugar
	6 tablespoons cream sherry

Using the metal blade, coarsely chop the nuts and sprinkle over the base of a well greased and floured Balmoral tin. Place the dry cake mix and pudding mix in the work bowl and pulse two to three times to combine. Mix the water, oil and sherry with the beaten eggs and add to the dry ingredients, along with the cinnamon and nutmeg. Process for 10 seconds. Scrape down the bowl and process for a further 25 to 30 seconds. Pour the mixture into the prepared tin and bake in a moderate oven (180c, 350f, gas 4) for about 40 minutes, or until a skewer comes out clean. Turn out onto a wire rack and immediately spoon the hot glaze over.

For the glaze, melt the butter, then add the sugar and water. Heat, stirring, until the sugar has completely dissolved. Add the sherry and bring to the boil. Remove from the heat and pour over the cake. Allow the cake to cool before cutting.

SERVES ABOUT 16

Butterscotch Sherry Cake

Chocolate Marshmallow Cake

Rich and moist, this cake is more like a dessert.

225 g/8 oz plain flour
175 g/6 oz caster sugar
225 g/8 oz butter
3 tablespoons cocoa powder
250 ml/8 fl oz carbonated cola
7 tablespoons buttermilk
2 eggs
1 teaspoon vanilla essence
1 teaspoon bicarbonate of soda
350 ml/12 fl oz miniature marshmallows (or large marshmallows, cut up)
1 quantity of Chocolate Icing (page 147)

Fit the metal blade, place the flour and sugar in the work bowl and pulse to combine. Melt the butter and add the cocoa powder and cola. Bring to the boil, then cool slightly before adding to the flour and sugar. Process until well blended. Now add the buttermilk, eggs, vanilla essence and bicarbonate of soda. Process for 15 seconds, scrape down the bowl and process for a further 5 seconds. Drop in the marshmallows and pulse three or four times to combine. Pour the mixture into a greased and floured 23 × 33-cm/9 × 13-in baking tin and bake in a moderate oven (180 c, 350 f, gas 4) for 35 to 40 minutes, or until a skewer comes out clean. Remove the cake from the oven and ice with chocolate icing while still hot.

SERVES ABOUT 20

Chocolate Oil Cake

This is the lightest chocolate cake we have ever eaten. It is easy to make and keeps well.

4 tablespoons cocoa powder
6 tablespoons boiling water
150 g/5 oz plain flour
2 teaspoons baking powder
pinch of salt
4 eggs
175 g/6 oz caster sugar
4 tablespoons oil
1 teaspoon vanilla essence
1 teaspoon instant coffee
1 quantity of Continental Icing (page 146)

Blend the cooca powder and boiling water, then allow to cool. Sift the flour, baking powder and salt together. Using the metal blade, process 1 egg and 3 egg yolks for 30 seconds. With the machine running, add the caster sugar through the feed tube. Continue beating for 1 minute. Now add the oil, vanilla and coffee to the cocoa mixture. Add this liquid to the egg mixture in the processor bowl. Process to mix, then fold in the sifted flour. Whisk the egg whites until stiff and fold into the batter. Pour into two greased and floured sandwich tins 23 cm/9 in. in diameter, and bake in a moderately hot oven (100 c, 400 f, gas 6) for 25 minutes. Turn out onto a wire rack. When cold, sandwich together and decorate with icing.

Freeze either plain or iced.

Gingerbread with Marmalade

1 teaspoon bicarbonate of soda
2 tablespoons cold water
150 ml/¼ pint boiling water
100 g/4 oz margarine, softened
150 g/5 oz caster sugar
2 eggs
1 tablespoon syrup
2 tablespoons coarse-cut marmalade
225 g/8 oz plain flour
generous pinch of salt
1 teaspoon ground ginger
1 teaspoon ground cassia or cinnamon

Combine the bicarbonate of soda and cold water, add the boiling water and allow to cool. Fit the metal blade to the processor, place the softened margarine in the work bowl and pulse to cream slightly. Add half the sugar and pulse until well creamed. Remove from the bowl and set aside. Now add the eggs to the work bowl, pulse a few times, then add the remaining sugar. Process for 45 seconds until light and fluffy. Scrape down the sides of the bowl once or twice if necessary. Add the creamed margarine to the egg mixture and pulse three times to combine. Add the syrup and marmalade and pulse again. Sift together the flour, salt, ginger and cassia. Add a third to the bowl and pulse for a few seconds. Pour in a third of the cooled liquid, and pulse again. Repeat until all the ingredients are combined. Pour into a greased 450-g/1-lb loaf tin and bake in a moderately hot oven (190 c, 375 f, gas 5) for 45 minutes. Slice when cool.

SERVES 10 TO 12

Orange Peel Loaf

1 large orange
100 g/4 oz sultanas
50 g/2 oz pecan nuts or walnuts
175 g/6 oz plain flour
generous pinch of salt
1 teaspoon bicarbonate of soda
225 g/8 oz caster sugar
100 g/4 oz margarine, softened
3 eggs
250 ml/8 fl oz milk
TOPPING
3 tablespoons caster sugar
1 teaspoon ground cinnamon

Squeeze the orange, reserving the juice. Remove the membranes from the peel. Fit the metal blade to the processor, place the orange peel in the work bowl and pulse to chop finely. Add the sultanas and nuts, pulse four times and set aside. Place the sifted flour, salt and bicarbonate of soda in the work bowl and pulse twice to aerate. Add the sugar, softened margarine, eggs and milk. Process for 1 minutes. Now add the chopped fruit and peel and pulse to combine. Pour into a greased 1-kg/2-lb loaf tin and bake in a moderately hot oven (190 c, 375 f, gas 5) for 1 hour. Cool slightly in the tin, then turn out and carefully pour over the reserved orange juice. When cool, sprinkle liberally with a mixture of sugar and cinnamon.

MAKES 1 LOAF

This freezes very well. After thawing, sprinkle with a little more cinnamon sugar.

Carrot Cake

225 g/8 oz carrots
150 g/5 oz mixed dried fruit
7 tablespoons water
7 tablespoons oil
225 g/8 oz caster sugar
½ teaspoon ground cinnamon
½ teaspoon nutmeg
½ teaspoon ground ginger
pinch of salt

100 g/4 oz nuts
225 g/8 oz plain flour
1 teaspoon bicarbonate of soda
1 teaspoon baking powder
2 eggs, slightly beaten
1 quantity of Cottage Cheese Icing, page 147 (optional)

Fit the shredding plate and shred the carrots. Place the carrots, dried fruit, water, oil, sugar, spices and salt in a saucepan. Bring to the boil, cook for 5 minutes, then cool. Grate the nuts using the shredding plate and add to the fruit. Sift the dry ingredients and add to the fruit all at once. Now add the eggs and mix well. Pour into a lined 1-kg/2-lb loaf tin and bake in a moderate oven (180c, 350f, gas 4) for an hour. Cool slightly before removing from the tin. If desired, ice the cake with cottage cheese icing.

MAKES 1 LOAF

Peanut Crisps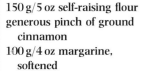

150 g/5 oz self-raising flour
generous pinch of ground cinnamon
100 g/4 oz margarine, softened

100 g/4 oz soft brown sugar
100 g/4 oz salted peanuts
2 teaspoons instant coffee
1 tablespoon hot water

Using the metal blade, process the flour and cinnamon to aerate. Add the margarine and pulse to rub in. Now add the sugar and peanuts and pulse twice. Dissolve the coffee in hot water. With the machine running, pour the coffee through the feed tube and process until the mixture binds together. Place small spoonfuls on a greased baking tray pressing down each one with a fork. Bake for 10 to 12 minutes in a moderate oven (160c, 325f, gas 3). Cool slightly before transferring to a wire rack.

MAKES ABOUT 36 BISCUITS

Freeze in airtight containers for up to six months. The biscuits will thaw in 20 minutes. Should they lose their crispness, place them on a baking sheet in a moderate oven (160c, 325f, gas 3) for 3 to 5 minutes.

Greek Cookies

100 g/4 oz unpeeled almonds
225 g/8 oz plain flour
225 g/8 oz butter, softened

75 g/3 oz caster sugar
icing sugar for dusting

Using the metal blade, process the almonds until finely ground. Add the flour and pulse twice. Cut the butter into pieces and add to the mixture while the machine is running. Pour in the sugar and process until the dough no longer turns easily. Take small quantities of dough and roll into half moons.

Place on a greased baking tray and bake in a moderate oven (160c, 325f, gas 3) for approximately 10 minutes until pale golden (do not brown). Roll in icing sugar while still warm and cool on a wire rack.

MAKES 24 TO 30 COOKIES

Old-Fashioned Banana Shortcake

The flavour may be old fashioned, but the method is thoroughly modern.

50 g/2 oz butter, melted
1 egg
200 ml/7 fl oz milk
pinch of salt
2 teaspoons baking powder
100 g/4 oz plain flour

FILLING
6 bananas
50 g/2 oz caster sugar
250 ml/8 fl oz double cream
few drops of vanilla essence

Fit the metal blade to the processor, add the butter, egg and milk to the work bowl and process until well mixed. Sift together the salt, baking powder and flour and add to the milk mixture. Process for a few seconds until just moistened. Spread the dough in a greased 20-cm/8-in round baking tin and bake in a hot oven (220c, 425f, gas 7) for about 15 minutes or until golden. Remove from the oven, allow to cool for 5 minutes, then cut into two layers.

For the filling, use the slicing plate to slice the bananas. Add the sugar to the cream and whisk to soft peaks. Stir in the bananas and vanilla essence. Spread the filling between the layers and cover the top of the shortcake. Cut into six wedges to serve.

SERVES 6

Snickerdoodles

175 g/6 oz butter, softened
150 g/5 oz caster sugar
1 egg
175 g/6 oz plain flour

1 teaspoon baking powder
pinch of salt
1 tablespoon ground cinnamon

Cream the butter and 100 g/4 oz of the sugar with the metal blade, then add the egg and process to mix well. Add the flour, baking powder and salt, and process to combine. Chill the dough for at least 30 minutes before using. Mix the remaining sugar with the cinnamon. Break the dough into small pieces, roll into balls, then roll in the mixture of cinnamon and sugar. Place about 5 cm/2 in apart on an ungreased baking tray and bake in a moderately hot oven (200c, 400f, gas 6) for about 10 minutes. Cool on a wire rack and store in an airtight container.

MAKES 36

Carrot Cake, Peanut Crisps, Greek Cookies, Chocolate Nut Bars (page 145)

Almond Fingers and Soured Cream Peach Cake

Almond Fingers

225 g/8 oz plain flour	TOPPING
½ teaspoon baking powder	150 g/5 oz blanched almonds
pinch of salt	100 g/4 oz caster sugar
150 g/5 oz butter, cubed	50 g/2 oz butter
50 g/2 oz caster sugar	1 tablespoon milk
½ egg	½ teaspoon vanilla essence

Fit the metal blade to the processor and place the flour, baking powder and salt in the work bowl. Pulse to aerate. Add the butter and process to rub in. Add the sugar and pulse to mix. Add the egg and process for a few seconds until the mixture has combined. Press the dough into a Swiss roll tin lined with foil. Prick the dough all over with a fork, then bake in a moderately hot oven (200 c, 400 f, gas 6) for 7 minutes.

Meanwhile, make the topping. Using the metal blade, chop the almonds. Place all the ingredients in a saucepan and bring to the boil. Reduce heat and simmer gently for 3 minutes. Spread this mixture over the half-cooked base. Return to the oven and bake for a further 15 minutes, until golden brown. Cool slightly before cutting into fingers. Leave in the tin until cold and store in an airtight container. Serve as a biscuit or with a scoop of ice cream for dessert.

MAKES ABOUT 24 FINGERS

Soured Cream Peach Cake

100 g/4 oz butter	250 ml/8 fl oz soured cream
175 g/6 oz caster sugar	2 fresh peaches, peeled and
2 eggs	sliced
pinch of salt	TOPPING
1 teaspoon vanilla essence	40 g/1½ oz plain flour
225 g/8 oz plain flour	pinch of ground cinnamon
1 teaspoon baking powder	50 g/2 oz soft brown sugar
1 teaspoon bicarbonate of	25 g/1 oz butter
soda	50 g/2 oz walnuts

First make the topping. Fit the metal blade to the processor and place all the topping ingredients in the work bowl. Process until crumbly, then set aside.

Using the metal blade, cream the butter and sugar. Break in the eggs and process until well combined. Add the salt and vanilla essence. Sift together the flour, baking powder and bicarbonate of soda and add to the egg mixture. Pulse to combine. Lastly, add the soured cream and process until well mixed.

Place half the batter in a greased 23 × 33-cm/9 × 13-in baking tin. Top with half the peach slices and half the topping mix. Repeat the layers, ending in a moderately hot oven (180 c, 350 f, gas 4) for about 35 to 40 minutes. Serve warm.

SERVES ABOUT 20

Chocolate Chip Cookies

100 g/4 oz plain chocolate	½ teaspoon vanilla essence
50 g/2 oz pecan nuts, or walnuts	1 egg
	150 g/5 oz plain flour
100 g/4 oz butter	½ teaspoon salt
75 g/3 oz soft brown sugar	1 teaspoon bicarbonate of soda
75 g/3 oz caster sugar	

Using the chipper plate, coarsely grate the chocolate and set aside. Fit the metal blade, coarsely chop the nuts and add to the chocolate chips. Continuing to use the metal blade, process the butter and sugars until light and fluffy. Add the vanilla essence and egg and beat until well mixed. Sift the flour, salt and bicarbonate of soda. Process to mix well. Now add the chocolate and nuts and pulse three to four times to mix in. If the dough is very soft, chill for 30 minutes. Drop spoonfuls of dough on a lightly greased baking tray and bake in a moderately hot oven (180 c, 350 f, gas 4) for 10 to 12 minutes or until pale golden. Cool on a wire rack.

MAKES ABOUT 30 COOKIES

To freeze, pack the cooled cookies into freezer containers and seal well. Freeze for up to two months if desired.

Surprise Brownies

225 g/8 oz butter	FILLING
350 g/12 oz caster sugar	225 g/8 oz low fat cream-style cottage cheese
4 eggs	
1 tablespoon brandy	75 g/3 oz soft brown sugar
pinch of salt	1 egg
100 g/4 oz cocoa powder	1 teaspoon vanilla essence
100 g/4 oz walnuts	
100 g/4 oz plain flour	

To make the filling, combine all the ingredients and process with the metal blade until well mixed. Turn out into a bowl and reserve. Without washing the work bowl, add the butter, sugar, eggs, brandy and salt and process until light and fluffy. Now add the cocoa powder and nuts and process until well mixed. Sift in the flour and process until well moistened. Spread half the batter in a greased and floured 23 × 33-cm/9 × 13-in baking tin. Top with the cottage cheese mixture, then smooth over the remaining chocolate batter. Lightly swirl the top layer with the filling to give a marbling effect. Bake in a moderate oven (180 c, 350 f, gas 4) for 35 to 45 minutes. Cool in the tin, resting on a wire rack. Cut into squares and serve.

MAKES 20 TO 24 BROWNIES

Freezes well for up to six weeks

Banana Oat Cookies

3 ripe bananas	½ teaspoon salt
2 eggs	1 teaspoon baking powder
225 g/8 oz butter, softened	½ teaspoon bicarbonate of soda
225 g/8 oz plain flour	
1 teaspoon ground cinnamon	150 g/5 oz quick cooking oats, uncooked
½ teaspoon nutmeg	
pinch of ground cloves	2 tablespoons cream sherry

Peel the bananas, cut into pieces and process with the metal blade until smooth. Add the eggs and butter and process until well combined. Sift together the flour, cinnamon, nutmeg, cloves, salt, baking powder and bicarbonate of soda. Add to the banana mixture and process until mixed. Now add the oats and sherry and pulse five to six times to mix in. Drop spoonfuls onto a greased baking sheet and bake in a moderately hot oven (190 c, 375 f, gas 5) for about 15 minutes.

MAKES ABOUT 36 COOKIES

Praline Thins

100 g/4 oz pecan nuts	1 egg
50 g/2 oz margarine, softened	2 teaspoons vanilla essence
	40 g/1½ oz plain flour
225 g/8 oz soft brown sugar	½ teaspoon baking powder

Using the metal blade, process the pecan nuts until very finely chopped. Remove from the bowl and set aside. Place the margarine in the bowl and pulse a few times to soften well. With the machine running, pour the sugar through the feed tube and process until well creamed. Add the egg and vanilla and process for 45 seconds. Now add the sifted flour and baking powder and process until well mixed. Lastly, add the chopped pecan nuts and pulse to combine. Line a baking tray with greaseproof paper and grease well. Drop spoonfuls of the mixture onto the baking tray leaving a good space between each one. Using a spatula, spread the batter out. Bake in a moderate oven (180 c, 350 f, gas 4) for 8 to 10 minutes, or until they are lightly coloured. Allow the thins to cool for 2 minutes before removing them from the sheet. Cool completely on a wire rack and pack in an airtight container.

MAKES ABOUT 36 CRISPY BISCUITS

Lemon Oil Cake

4 eggs
175 g/6 oz caster sugar
2 teaspoons lemon rind
1 tablespoon lemon juice
6 tablespoons hot water
4 tablespoons oil

150 g/5 oz plain flour
2 tablespoons cornflour
2 teaspoons baking powder
pinch of salt
1 quantity of Tangy Lemon
    Icing (page 146)

Line the bases of two 20-cm/8-in sandwich tins with non-stick baking parchment. Using the metal blade, process 3 egg yolks and 1 whole egg for 1 minute. With the machine running, gradually pour the caster sugar through the feed tube and process until light and fluffy. Now add the lemon rind and juice and process again until well mixed. Pour in the hot water and the oil, then process for 45 seconds. Sift the dry ingredients together and add all at once to the egg mixture. Pulse three to four times to combine. Using a mixer, whisk the egg whites until stiff and fold into the batter. Pour into the prepared tins and bake in a moderately hot oven (200c, 400f, gas 6) for 25 minutes. Remove from the oven and turn out into a wire rack. When cold, fill with lemon icing or lemon curd. Decorate the top with icing or dust with icing sugar.

Freezes well, plain or iced, for up to three months.

Christmas Mince Tart

3 tablespoons oil
225 g/8 oz caster sugar
3 eggs
100 g/4 oz plain flour
pinch of salt
1 teaspoon baking powder
800 g/1¾ lb quinces sliced

1 jar mincemeat
TOPPING
250 ml/8 fl oz double cream
100 g/4 oz caster sugar
1 teaspoon vanilla essence
1 tablespoon lemon juice

Using the metal blade, blend the oil, sugar and eggs for 1 minute. Sift the dry ingredients into the processor bowl one third at a time, processing for 15 seconds between each addition. Pour into a 33 × 18-cm/13 × 7-in greased oven proof dish. Carefully arrange the quince slices and mincemeat on top. Bake in a moderate oven (160c, 325f, gas 3) for 1 hour. To make the topping, bring all the ingredients to the boil. Reduce heat and simmer for 2 minutes. Remove the tart from the oven and cool for 5 minutes before pouring the hot topping mixture over. Serve warm or cold.

SERVES 8 TO 10

Spicy Raisin Bars

Quick to make, these bars freeze well. Make a double batch and always have some on hand in the freezer.

150 g/5 oz raisins
250 ml/8 fl oz hot water
7 tablespoons oil
225 g/8 oz caster sugar
1 egg
50 g/2 oz walnuts
275 g/10 oz plain flour

1 teaspoon bicarbonate of
    soda
pinch of salt
1 teaspoon ground cinnamon
½ teaspoon nutmeg
½ teaspoon allspice
pinch of ground cloves
icing sugar to dust

Fit the metal blade to the processor and place the raisins in the work bowl. Pour in the hot water and leave to cool. Now add the oil, sugar, egg and nuts. Blend just until the nuts are chopped. Sift together the flour, bicarbonate of soda, salt and spices. Pour the raisin mixture over and mix well. Spoon into a greased 23 × 33-cm/9 × 12-in baking tin and bake in a moderately hot oven (190c, 375f, gas 5) for about 18 minutes. Cool slightly before cutting into squares and dusting with icing sugar. Serve as a tea-time treat or with custard or ice cream as a dessert.

MAKES ABOUT 20 BARS

To freeze, place in a freezer container and seal well. Freeze for up to two months. Thaw at room temperature.

Chocolate Kisses

100 g/4 oz margarine,
    softened
50 g/2 oz caster sugar
5 tablespoons condensed milk
1 teaspoon vanilla essence
150 g/5 oz plain flour
50 g/2 oz cocoa powder

pinch of salt
100 g/4 oz chocolate, melted
ICING
50 g/2 oz butter, softened
100 g/4 oz icing sugar
25 g/1 oz cocoa powder
a little strong, black coffee

Using the metal blade, cream the margarine and caster sugar, scraping down the sides of the bowl at least once. Add the condensed milk and vanilla essence and process for 15 seconds. Sift the dry ingredients and add a third at a time, processing for only a few seconds between each addition. Place the mixture in a piping bag fitted with a large star nozzle. Pipe flat stars on a greased baking tray. Chill for 10 minutes. Bake in a cool oven (150c, 300f, gas 2) for 12 to 15 minutes. Cool slightly before removing from the baking tray and placing on a wire rack. Sandwich together with icing, then drizzle melted chocolate over the top.

To make the icing, cream the butter with the nylon blade. Add the sifted icing sugar and cocoa powder and moisten with a little coffee. Process until well mixed.

MAKES 30

A selection of biscuits and bars, from left to right: Lemon Bars (page 146), Apricot Bars, Chocolate Kisses, Cream Wafers (page 146), Bachelor Buttons (page 146), Apricot Bars, Tulips (page 146)

Chocolate Nut Bars

150 g/5 oz plain chocolate	1 packet (69-g/2.4-oz)
50 g/2 oz pecan nuts or	instant chocolate whip mix
walnuts	2 eggs
1 packet (225-g/8-oz)	100 g/4 oz butter, softened
chocolate cake mix	6–7 tablespoons milk

Using the chipper plate, coarsely grate the chocolate and set aside. Now fit the metal blade and chop the nuts. Set aside with the grated chocolate.

Place half the cake mix and half the pudding mix in the work bowl. Pulse two to three times to combine. Add the eggs and butter and process until smooth. Now add the remaining cake and pudding mixes as well as the milk. Process for 30 seconds, scraping down the bowl when necessary. Lastly, add the chocolate and nuts and pulse three to four times to mix in. Spread the batter in a greased 23 × 33-cm/9 × 13-in baking tin and bake in a moderate oven (180 c, 350 f, gas 4) for 25 to 30 minutes. Remove the tin from the oven and place on a wire rack. Cool the mixture in the tin before cutting into squares.

MAKES ABOUT 20 BARS

The bars freeze well for up to one month.

Apricot Bars

75 g/3 oz dried apricots	½ teaspoon baking powder
100 g/4 oz butter, softened	pinch of salt
50 g/2 oz caster sugar	½ teaspoon vanilla essence
150 g/5 oz plain flour	50 g/2 oz nuts
2 eggs	icing sugar
225 g/8 oz soft brown sugar	

Cover the apricots with water, bring to the boil and simmer for 10 minutes. Cool in the water, then drain and set aside. Using the metal blade, process the butter, sugar and 100 g/4 oz of the flour until crumbly. Press into a greased 20-cm/8-in square baking tin and bake in a moderate oven (180 c, 350 f, gas 4) for about 25 minutes.

To make the topping, process the eggs and brown sugar until light and fluffy. Add the remaining flour, baking powder, salt, vanilla, nuts and drained apricots. Process until well mixed. Spread over the baked shortcrust layer. Return to the oven and continue to bake for a further 30 minutes. Place on a wire rack and cool in the tin. Cut into squares and sprinkle with icing sugar.

MAKES 16 SMALL SQUARES

Tulips

50 g/2 oz plain flour	2 egg whites
50 g/2 oz caster sugar	40 g/1½ oz butter

Fit the metal blade to the processor and place the flour and caster sugar in the work bowl. Pulse to aerate. Add the unbeaten egg whites and process for 45 seconds. Melt the butter and allow to cool slightly before pouring in through the feed tube. Process for 15 seconds. Grease the baking tray very well. Drop 5–10 ml/1–2 teaspoons of the mixture onto the baking tray and spread out thinly with a spatula. Baking only four at a time, place in a moderately hot oven (200 c, 400 f, gas 6) for 5 minutes. Remove from the oven and lift off the baking tray immediately. Shape quickly by either curling around the handle of a wooden spoon, forming into a horn inside a small glass, or draping over the curve of a rolling pin. These biscuits crispen after a few seconds and should be stored in an airtight container. Serve plain or with ice cream as a wafer. For a special effect, dip the ends in melted chocolate.

MAKES 24

Lemon Bars

Tangy lemon icing tops these golden bars.

100 g/4 oz butter	2 eggs
150 g/5 oz plain flour	225 g/8 oz caster sugar
50 g/2 oz icing sugar	½ teaspoon baking powder
2 tablespoons lemon juice	1 quantity of Tangy Lemon
grated rind of 1 lemon	Icing (below)

Fit the metal blade to the processor and place the butter, 100 g/4 oz flour and icing sugar in the work bowl. Process until well mixed, then press into a greased 23-cm/9-in square baking tin. Bake in a moderate oven (160 c, 325 f, gas 3) for 15 minutes. Now blend the lemon juice, rind and eggs in the processor for 5 seconds. Add the remaining flour, sugar and baking powder and process to mix well. Spread this mixture over the baked crust and bake in a moderate oven (180 c, 350 f, gas 4) for about 25 minutes. Remove from the oven, place on a wire rack and cool in the tin. Ice with tangy lemon icing when cool.

MAKES 24 BARS

Bachelor Buttons

100 g/4 oz butter	75 g/3 oz maraschino
150 g/5 oz soft brown sugar	cherries, cut in half
1 egg	275 g/10 oz plain flour
75 g/3 oz desiccated coconut	1 teaspoon bicarbonate of soda
½ teaspoon ground cinnamon	pinch of salt
50 g/2 oz walnuts	a little milk

Process the butter and brown sugar with the metal blade until light and fluffy. Add the egg and process until well combined. Now add the coconut, cinnamon, walnuts and cherries and process until well mixed. Sift together the flour, bicarbonate of soda and salt. With the machine running, add the dry ingredients through the feed tube and process until well combined. If the mixture is very dry, add a little milk. Drop spoonfuls onto a greased baking tray and bake in a moderate oven (180 c, 350 f, gas 4) for about 15 minutes.

MAKES ABOUT 36 CHERRY-FLAVOURED BISCUITS

Cream Wafers

Delicious double biscuits with a flavoured filling.

225 g/8 oz margarine,	100 g/4 oz icing sugar
softened	1 egg yolk
7 tablespoons single cream	1 teaspoon flavouring
225 g/8 oz plain flour	(vanilla, coffee, almond,
granulated sugar to coat	orange, lemon, etc)
FILLING	
50 g/2 oz butter, softened	

For the wafers, fit the metal blade to the processor and add the margarine, cream and flour to the work bowl. Process until well mixed. Chill the dough for about 30 minutes. Take a third of the dough and roll out thinly on a lightly floured board. Cut into 2.5 cm/1 in diameter circles. Repeat the rolling and cutting until all the dough has been used up. Place the wafers on wax paper or greaseproof paper generously covered with sugar. Turn over so both sides are well coated. Place the sugared wafers on an ungreased baking tray and bake in a moderately hot oven (190 c, 375 f, gas 5) for 6 to 8 minutes. Cool, then sandwich with filling.

For the filling, combine all the ingredients and process with the metal blade until well mixed.

MAKES ABOUT 36 DOUBLE WAFERS

Icings

Continental Icing

100 g/4 oz butter, softened	2 teaspoons dissolved
6 tablespoons golden syrup	instant coffee
50 g/2 oz cocoa powder	¼ teaspoon almonds essence

Using the nylon blade, cream the butter. Add the syrup, sifted cocoa powder and coffee and process to mix well. Lastly, add the almond essence and pulse to combine.

Tangy Lemon Icing

225 g/8 oz icing sugar	1 teaspoon grated lemon rind
1 tablespoon lemon juice	a little cream

Using the metal blade, process the icing sugar, lemon juice, rind and enough cream to make the icing of spreading consistency.

Chocolate Icing ☯

40 g/2 oz butter
2 tablespoons cocoa powder
7 tablespoons carbonated cola

100 g/4 oz pecan nuts or
  walnuts
450 g/1 lb icing sugar

Combine the butter, cocoa powder and cola and bring to the boil. Meanwhile, use the metal blade to chop the nuts, then add the icing sugar. Pour in the boiling mixture and blend well. Use this icing while still hot as it thickens when it cools.

Creamy Chocolate Icing ☯

300 g/12 oz icing sugar
1 egg
3 tablespoons water
50 g/2 oz granulated sugar

pinch of salt
100 g/4 oz butter, softened
1 teaspoon vanilla essence
50 g/2 oz chocolate, melted

Fit the metal blade to the processor and combine the icing sugar and egg in the work bowl. Place the water, granulated sugar and salt in a saucepan and bring to the boil over a medium heat, stirring until the sugar has dissolved. Boil for 1 minute. While the machine is running, slowly add the boiling liquid and process until well mixed. Finally, add the butter, vanilla and chocolate and beat until creamy. Use as desired.

Caramel Icing ☯

100 g/4 oz butter
175 g/6 oz soft brown sugar

3 tablespoons milk
350 g/12 oz icing sugar

To make the caramel, melt the butter in a heavy saucepan. Add the brown sugar and bring to the boil over a low heat, stirring all the time. Boil for 2 minutes, stirring constantly. Now add the milk and heat, stirring continuously, until the mixture boils. Remove from the heat and allow to cool. Fit the metal blade to the processor and place the icing sugar in the work bowl. Add the caramel mixture and process until well mixed and of a spreading consistency.

Cottage Cheese Icing ☯

100 g/4 oz butter, softened
225 g/8 oz cottage cheese
450 g/1 lb icing sugar

100 g/4 oz pecan nuts or
  walnuts (optional)
1 teaspoon vanilla essence
a little cream if needed

Combine the butter and cheese and process with the metal blade until smooth. Add the icing sugar and nuts and process until well mixed. Now add the vanilla and, if necessary, a little cream to make the icing of spreading consistency. Process until well mixed.

Note: This icing can be flavoured with orange juice or lemon juice. Use the juice in place of the vanilla essence and cream.

Lemon Oil Cake (page 144) with Cottage Cheese Icing

Beverages

Within this section you will find our selection of delicious and unusual drinks – a welcome change from gin and tonic, or brandy and coke. We have included drinks made with fruit juices and milk shakes too, and several of these make superb desserts.

Use the food processor to crush the ice, purée the fruit and blend the ingredients. The next time you have people for drinks, use the processor to mix a tall jug of one or two of these special beverages and a simple get-together may turn into a party.

Grapefruit Stinger

8 ice cubes
150 ml/¼ pint vodka
3 tablespoons lemon juice
5 tablespoons Mandarine
   Napoleon
600 ml/1 pint fresh
   grapefruit juice
600 ml/1 pint soda

Fit the metal blade to the processor. With the machine running, drop the ice cubes through the feed tube onto the moving blade. When crushed, add the vodka, lemon juice and Mandarine Napoleon. Process for 5 seconds. Combine the grapefruit juice and soda in a tall jug. Pour in the vodka mixture and stir well. Add a few extra ice cubes and serve.

SERVES 6

Peach Shake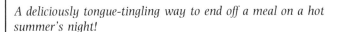

1 (410-g/14½-oz) can sliced
   peaches
600 ml/1 pint cold milk
6 tablespoons peach yogurt
4 scoops ice cream
3 drops of almond essence

Make this drink in two batches, using half the ingredients for each batch. Drain the peaches and place them in the work bowl fitted with the metal blade. Pulse three or four times to purée. Add the remaining ingredients and process for about 5 seconds. Pour into glasses and serve at once.

SERVES 4

Don Pedro

A deliciously tongue-tingling way to end off a meal on a hot summer's night!

16 scoops vanilla ice cream
150 ml/¼ pint Scotch whisky

Fit the metal blade to the processor and place six scoops of ice cream and all the whisky in the work bowl. Turn the machine on and, as the ice cream becomes liquid, drop more ice cream through the feed tube. Continue until all the ice cream is liquid. Pour into four stemmed glasses and serve with short straws.

SERVES 4

Mexican-Style Coffee

25 g/1 oz plain chocolate
2 tablespoons coffee liqueur
2 teaspoons granulated sugar
1 litre/2 pints strong filter
   coffee
150 ml/¼ pint single cream
a little ground cinnamon

Fit the shredding plate to the processor, shred the chocolate and set aside. Take four Irish coffee glasses and add one measure of liqueur and sugar to each glass. Fill almost to the top with hot coffee and stir well. Whisk the cream until thick. Float the cream on top of the coffee by pouring it over the back of a teaspoon. Sprinkle generously with the shredded chocolate and a little cinnamon.

SERVES 4

Café Brûlot

3 tablespoons caster sugar
thinly pared rind of an
   orange
thinly pared rind of a lemon
pinch of ground cloves
7 tablespoons brandy
4 tablespoons Curaçao
1 litre/2 pints strong black
   coffee
250 ml/8 fl oz double cream
a little ground cinnamon to
   sprinkle

Fit the metal blade to the processor. With the machine running, add the sugar and rinds through the feed tube onto the moving blades. Process until well combined. Add a pinch of cloves, the brandy and Curaçao. Divide between six glasses. Pour in the black coffee, stirring well. Whisk the cream until thick. This will take only a few seconds. Float the cream on the coffee by pouring it over the back of a teaspoon. Sprinkle with cinnamon. Serve immediately.

SERVES 6

(Opposite page) Grapefruit Stinger
(Below) Left: Mexican-Style Coffee, Right: Café Brûlot

Iced Kir

A typically French aperitif

6–8 ice cubes
250 ml/8 fl oz crème de
  cassis
750 ml/1¼ pints dry white
  wine, chilled

1 litre/2 pints soda water,
  chilled
a few strawberries
1 small lemon

Fit the metal blade to the processor and, with the machine running, drop the ice cubes onto the rotating blade. Add the crème de cassis and pulse to mix. Pour the liquid into a large jug or punch bowl. Add the wine and soda water, stirring well. Using the slicing plate to slice a few strawberries and the lemon. Add to the chilled drink and serve.

SERVES 10

Brown Cow

350 ml/12 fl oz milk
1 scoop ice cream
2 tablespoons cola
  concentrate

2 tablespoons chocolate
  syrup
whipped cream to top
a little shredded chocolate

Fit the nylon blade to the processor. Pour in the milk, ice cream, cream, cola concentrate and chocolate syrup. Process for a few seconds. Pour into two glasses, top with whipped cream and shredded chocolate.

SERVES 2

Iced Kir

Irish Cream Liqueur

2 eggs
250 ml/8 fl oz cream
7 tablespoons evaporated
  milk
200 ml/7 fl oz sweetened
  condensed milk

1 teaspoon vanilla essence
1 teaspoon caramel
  flavouring
3 tablespoons coffee
  liqueur
7 tablespoons Irish whiskey

Using the nylon blade, process the eggs and cream for about 15 seconds until well mixed. Mix the evaporated milk with the condensed milk, vanilla, caramel and coffee liqueur. With the processor running, pour this milk mixture through the feed tube. Process for 15 seconds. With the machine still running, pour the whiskey through the feed tube. Process for 15 seconds. Taste and add more whiskey if desired. Store in the refrigerator. This liqueur will keep for several weeks.

MAKES ABOUT 600 ml/1 PINT

Spiced Egg Nog

6 eggs, separated
½ teaspooon ground
  cinnamon
½ teaspoon nutmeg
175 g/6 oz caster sugar
450 ml/¾ pint whisky

450 ml/¾ pint single cream
450 ml/¾ pint milk
7 tablespoons brandy
grated rind of 1 orange
grated rind of 1 lemon
grated nutmeg to garnish

Process the egg yolks with the metal blade until a light lemon colour. With the machine running, add the cinnamon and nutmeg, then gradually add the sugar and process until it has dissolved. With the machine still running, add the whisky and process to mix well. Transfer this mixture to a punch bowl, cover and allow to stand for about 1 hour. Stir in the cream and milk, then the brandy. Chill for at least 2 hours.

With an electric mixer, whisk the egg whites until stiff peaks form. Fold into the egg nog along with the orange and lemon rind. Lastly, sprinkle with nutmeg and serve.

SERVES ABOUT 30

Tropical Fruit Cooler

350 ml/12 fl oz pineapple
  juice
1 banana, peeled and cut
  into pieces

1 ice cube
6 tablespoons light rum

Using the metal blade, process the pineapple juice and banana until smooth. Add the ice cubes and rum and process for 20 seconds. Pour into cocktail glasses and serve immediately.

SERVES 4

Irish Cream Liqueur

Summer Sundowners, from left to right: Frozen Fruit Daiquiri, Pina Colada de Luxe, Strawberry Cooler, Spicy Cucumber Cocktail, Frozen Alexander

Pina Colada de Luxe

4 tablespoons coconut cream
  (page 153)
7 tablespoons pineapple
  juice
2 tablespoons white rum

4 tablespoons Malibu
6 ice cubes
DECORATION
slices of pineapple
maraschino cherries

Place all the ingredients in the processor, except the ice cubes.
Process for a few seconds. Drop the ice cubes through the feed
tube and process until the cubes disappear. Serve in glasses
with pineapple slices and cherries.

SERVES 3

Strawberry Cooler

½ punnet strawberries,
  hulled
8 ice cubes
2 tablespoons Southern
  Comfort

2 tablespoons Grand
  Marnier
1 tablespoon caster sugar
1 tablespoon lemon juice
orange slice to decorate

Fit the metal blade to the processor, add the strawberries and
pulse to chop. Remove and set aside. Drop the ice cubes onto
the moving blade, then pour in the remaining ingredients.
Process until 'slushy' and then add the strawberries. Process
for about 5 seconds. Decorate with a slice of orange.

MAKES ONE TALL DRINK

Grenadine Sparkler ❷

8 ice cubes
3 tablespoons Grenadine
  syrup
250 ml/8 fl oz fresh orange
  juice

600 ml/1 pint white wine
600 ml/1 pint soda water
orange slices to decorate

Fit the metal blade to the processor. With the machine running, drop the ice cubes through the feed tube. Process for about 15 to 20 seconds until crushed. Add the Grenadine syrup and orange juice and process for 5 seconds. Pour into a large jug or a punch bowl. Add the white wine and soda water. Decorate with thinly sliced orange.

SERVES 6 TO 8

Frozen Alexander ❷

5 ice cubes
2 tablespoons single cream
2 tablespoons brandy
2 tablespoons crème de
  cacao

1 tablespoon Irish Cream
  (page 151)
a little cocoa powder

Fit the metal blade to the processor. With the machine running, drop the ice cubes through the feed tube. When well crushed, add all the ingredients except the cocoa powder. Process for 15 seconds. Pour into a long stemmed glass and sprinkle with a little sieved cocoa.

MAKES 1 DRINK

Spicy Cucumber Cocktail ❷

1 small cucumber, peeled
600 ml/1 pint tomato juice
1 teaspoon lemon juice
1 teaspoon Worcestershire
  sauce

salt and pepper to taste
6 ice cubes
7 tablespoons vodka

Cut the cucumber in half, remove the seeds and cut each half in pieces. Using the metal blade, process the cucumber with the tomato juice for about 15 seconds. Add the remaining ingredients and process until the ice is finely chopped. Pour into tall glasses and serve immediately.

SERVES 4

Frozen Fruit Daiquiri ❷

150 ml/¼ pint fruit pulp
  (mango, peach, apricot,
  plum, strawberry)
15 ice cubes

1 tablespoon caster sugar
4 tablespoons light rum
4 tablespoons lemon juice
1 tablespoon Cointreau

Fit the metal blade to the processor. Add the fruit and pulse until smooth. Remove from the bowl. Working in two batches, drop the ice cubes onto the moving blade and process until well crushed. Add all the ingredients and pulse a few times to combine well. Pour into two stemmed glasses and serve with short straws.

MAKES 2 DRINKS

Gold Cadillac ❷

5 ice cubes
3 tablespoons single cream

3 tablespoons crème de cacao
3 tablespoons Galliano

Fit the metal blade to the processor. Turn the machine on and drop the ice cubes through the feed tube. Pour in the cream, then the liqueurs. Blend until smooth. Pour into a well chilled glass.

MAKES 1 DRINK

Coconut Cream ❷

Coconut milk is sometimes called for in recipes. Here is how to make a good substitute.

225 g/8 oz desiccated
  coconut, or fresh coconut,
  cut into small pieces

350 ml/12 fl oz water
150 ml/¼ pint double cream

Fit the metal blade to the processor and place the coconut in the work bowl. If fresh coconut is used, chop finely. Now mix the water and cream together and bring to the boil. With the machine running, slowly add the boiling liquid to the coconut. Process for 1 minute, then allow the mixture to cool for at least 5 minutes. Strain through a sieve lined with a double thickness of damp cheesecloth. Press the coconut with a wooden spoon to extract the liquid, then bring the corners of the cloth together and squeeze out any remaining liquid. Keep the liquid tightly covered in the refrigerator and use as desired.

MAKES ABOUT 450 ml/¾ PINT

Index

154